The ANTECHAMBER *of*
HEAVEN

Bill Lowry

"As in the years to come the forces of Southern Methodism gather here for recuperation and preparation, may we not hope that Junaluska shall indeed prove to be for them an antechamber of heaven, where they shall see such visions and gather such inspiration as shall send them forth to achievements that shall mightily count for the Kingdom of God?"

From the historical forward of *The Junaluska Conference,* written by Dr. C. F. Reid

Antechamber: *A chamber or room that serves as a waiting room and entrance to a larger room.*

—*The Random House Dictionary of the English Language*

BILL LOWRY

FOREWORD BY JIMMY L. CARR

The ANTECHAMBER *of* HEAVEN

A HISTORY OF
LAKE JUNALUSKA ASSEMBLY

Providence House Publishers

WWW.PROVIDENCEHOUSE.COM

FRANKLIN, TENNESSEE

Printed in the United States of America

First Edition

14   13   12   11   10   1   2   3   4   5

Library of Congress Control Number: 2010925805

ISBN: 978-1-57736-439-9

Cover illustration courtesy of Lake Junaluska Assembly

Cover and page design by LeAnna Massingille

PROVIDENCE HOUSE PUBLISHERS
238 Seaboard Lane • Franklin, Tennessee 37067
www.providencehouse.com
800-321-5692

For Barbara

"LOVE OF MY LIFE"

CONTENTS

$\bullet \quad \bullet \quad \bullet \quad \bullet \quad \bullet \quad \bullet \quad \bullet \quad \bullet \quad \bullet \quad \bullet \quad \bullet \quad \bullet \quad \bullet \quad \bullet$

FOREWORD

• • • • • • • • • • • • • • •

Lake Junaluska Assembly is unique in The United Methodist Church. It is the largest conference and retreat center in the church, serving thousands every year. Within the center is a ministry area that has offered life changing opportunities for worship, discipleship training, mission education, and evangelism. It boasts a community of residents nestled around the two hundred-acre lake. It is a place of respite for thousands who desire to use its resources for recreation, relaxation, and reflection. Those who have come to the lake have come to know and desire the Junaluska Experience.

From its beginning as a dream of leaders of the Methodist Episcopal Church, South, Lake Junaluska's "beginnings as the Southern Assembly was spartan" with only land, a lake, and an auditorium—a steel umbrella built to shield participants from the rain and sun. One could hardly have imagined that in the years that followed it would become a fully developed campus with hotels, lodges, apartments, and a campground all of which can serve more than two thousand people at a time. It also includes a golf course and public works that would rival a small town. Though it was a rocky road, its existence bears out the truth that nothing is impossible for persons who have a passion, a vision, a plan, and the audacity to make it a reality.

Change was no stranger to Junaluska. In 1909, the Southern Assembly was owned and operated as an incorporated business under a Board of Commissioners. It was given to the Methodist Episcopal Church, South in 1938 and was under a Board of Trustees. When the Methodist Episcopal Church, South, the Methodist Episcopal Church, and the Methodist Protestant Churches merged in 1939, it was owned by the Methodist Church and a Board of Trustees. In 1948, it was given to the Southeastern Jurisdiction and a new Board of Trustees was established. In 1988, the Southeastern Jurisdiction organized its ministries and institutions under the Southeastern Jurisdictional Administrative Council and provided governance to Junaluska. In 2008, the Southeastern Jurisdiction reorganized and established Lake Junaluska as an agency governed by a new board of directors.

Lake Junaluska has had a significant influence across the spectrum of Methodism. It has provided a sense of identity, place, and connection for laity and clergy of the Southeastern Jurisdiction. It has served as a place for the church to gather, worship, study, and interact. Many say that it has contributed to the strength of the jurisdiction. It has significantly contributed to the Sunday school movement, the ministry with youth, missions, evangelism, and worship in the Church.

The process that called Lake Junaluska into being was a passion, a vision of an Assembly, a challenge to church leaders, and a request for the Methodist Church to provide financial support. Most of the organizations and ministries in the Southeastern Jurisdiction used the Southern Assembly model for organization and support. Many emerged through Lake Junaluska. It could be argued that there may never have been a Commission on Archives and History in the Jurisdiction and the United Methodist Church, a Hinton Rural Life Center, The Intentional Growth Center, or Native American Ministry had it not been for Lake Junaluska.

As we prepared to celebrate the Centennial of Lake Junaluska in 2013, it was appropriate that an extended history be written. It was obvious that the best person to write such a history was Rev. William T. Lowry, or "Bill," as he is affectionately known. Lowry is a United Methodist elder and a member of the Mississippi Conference. Besides having a love of the Lord and his church and serving as a pastor, he is a historian at heart. He has always had an innate love of history. While pastoring in Vicksburg, Mississippi, he served as a guide in the Vicksburg National Military Park. When he retired, he began working for The Heritage Center doing major research on Lake Junaluska. He was given the Chief Junaluska Award by the Junaluska Associates in 2008, an action that recognized his enormous contributions to Lake Junaluska. We appreciate Bill's willingness to tackle writing this book. We also thank the Junaluskans for supporting this project with a writing stipend and leading the first selling phase.

As the church changed, so did Lake Junaluska. During every era, Lake Junaluska has held strongly to its mission and adjusted the way it served. Adversities and change have strengthened Lake Junaluska, even though there have always been those during every era that wanted it to remain the same. History allows us the opportunity to consider the past in order to have a brighter future. *Antechamber of Heaven: A History of Lake Junaluska* provides us an understanding of our history to lead us into the next one hundred years.

Jimmy L. Carr, *Executive Director*

PREFACE

• • • • • • • • • • • • • • •

Early in 1994, I came to the Heritage Center at Lake Junaluska Assembly to work as part-time staff, organizing what was called "The Junaluska Collection." It consisted of more than one hundred twenty archival storage boxes containing all of the collected material that was related to the history of the Assembly. These boxes were on shelves which covered the entire back wall of the repository area of the Center. With a wave of her hand, Gerry Reiff, then director of the Center, stated "These contain all the material we have collected and we don't really know what is in them." My task would be to go through the boxes, read the material, and catalogue it. The task would wind up taking the next ten years.

On several occasions, after giving a talk or a presentation, someone would come to me and suggest that I write a book. Each time I would answer them by shaking my head and, at times, suggesting that perhaps they might like to do it. After all, I had organized the material to make it easier for them to do the research! There were no takers. The last histories were written by Dr. Mason Crum in 1950 and by Dr. Elmer Clark in 1963. There was a lot of history that had yet to be written.

One day while seated at my desk reading the historical forward to the proceedings of the 1913 Missionary Conference as recorded in the book *The Junaluska Conference,* I came across a fascinating statement. Reverend C. F. Reid, the secretary of the Laymen's Missionary Movement, had written in reference to the new Assembly which this conference inaugurated. He wrote:

> *As in the years to come as the forces of Southern Methodism gather here . . . may we not hope that Junaluska shall indeed prove to be for them an antechamber of heaven, where they shall see such visions and gather such inspiration as shall send them forth to achievements that shall mightily count for the Kingdom of God? (emphasis mine)*

This reminded me of other times when people had said to me such things as "If a person doesn't believe in heaven, just send them to Junaluska." or "To me Junaluska is the closest thing to heaven that I know of." I wrote on a card a note that this term "antechamber of heaven" would make a good title for a book about the Assembly, thinking that I would pass it along to some future author. Then I tucked the note away and forgot it.

Still later, after writing and presenting a multi-media production on the origins of the Assembly, my long-time friend Jimmy Carr approached me again and insisted that it was time for me to write the history, suggesting that I was not getting any younger! I finally agreed. I had become convinced that this was a story that had to be told.

The journey from that moment to the present has been an exciting walk back through history. I have felt a part of so many experiences. I have met so many persons now long gone. I have come to appreciate their dedication and their efforts. I have come to share in their vision and celebrate what they accomplished. Lake Junaluska Assembly is a very special institution. Having spent what amounts to fifteen years delving into every area of its history that I could find, I am more convinced than ever that this institution is of God. Not that the Assembly has been perfect, or even always right. God works through human beings and we are far from perfect. Thus, there have been times when imperfect persons made poor decisions. There have been other times when imperfect persons responded to the siren calls of pride, selfishness, prejudice, and other weaknesses which plague us all. But I have never felt that they had other than the best interest of the Assembly at heart, however misdirected their decisions might have been. On the other hand, I have come to appreciate the multitude of dedicated, courageous, even heroic at times, persons who gave far more than could ever be expected because they experienced what God was doing in this place. I sense that God has moved through it all to continue to use the Assembly to change and enhance the lives of all of his children.

And so here is the history that begged to be written. It is certainly not perfect, but no history ever is. It is not exhaustive, for there is more that could be said about almost any portion of the book. It is a compromise, albeit imperfect, between "all that could be said," and "enough to be comfortably readable."

I invite you to join with me in the exciting story of the first century of the antechamber of heaven, Lake Junaluska Assembly.

B.L.

ACKNOWLEDGMENTS

. . . .

I cannot begin to list, individually, all of those who have come to me with words of encouragement and admonitions to persevere. The Junaluska family is a caring, loving fellowship that I wish all the world could embrace. To every person who has cheered me on, lifted me up, and challenged me to continue, I can only say a most sincere "thank you."

There are some who have meant so much to me that I simply must single them out to especially say thanks.

My special thanks go to The Junaluskans organization that made the writing of this book possible by giving me the chance to lay everything else aside while working on this project.

Thanks to Gerry Reiff. It was Gerry who really got me into this. It was she who encouraged me to become a part of the Heritage Center staff. It was Gerry who taught me the "nuts and bolts" of archival preservation and in so doing reawakened a long dormant love of history in me. She was one of the ones who continued to say those words, "You need to write a book!" Likewise, she was one of those whom I chose to read the manuscript, knowing she would be kind but also unyielding in her insistence on the high standard of historical integrity in writing such a book.

Another reader was her husband, Dr. Lee Reiff. Lee is one of those detail persons, insisting that every thing had to be just right. The kind of nit picker that every author should have. He is a person who tends to find any overlooked error. I needed that.

To write such a book, I also needed a person to whom I could turn who would be an encourager while at the same time would keep my perspective on history correct. Just such a person was Dr. Wright Spears. As a former trustee and chairman of the Board of Trustees, he was the person I turned to for historical accuracy many times. Mix that with a tender loving spirit and you have a perfect encourager. By managing to live well into his nineties and keep a mind that is far sharper than mine, he has been so helpful.

Of course, the other person I must thank is Jimmy Carr. Where others had failed to convince me to write the book, Jimmy succeeded. Then he proceeded to open every door and every file drawer I could ever need. He has continued to encourage me along the way. No one could have been blessed with more cooperation and encouragement than he gave to me.

CHAPTER ONE

The Early Years

• • • • • • • • • • • • • • • • •

On a lovely summer day in July of 1899, on the eve of a new century, a father and daughter were riding in a carriage at Chautauqua Lake in New York. The father turned to his daughter and told her that he would like to see a facility such as New York's great Chautauqua Lake Assembly built in the South.[1] The man was Dr. James Atkins, a clergyman of the Methodist Episcopal Church, South, and his daughter was Love Branner Atkins. Upon his return to Nashville, he wrote several articles promoting the idea of a "Southern Chautauqua," which were published in church magazines. This account is the earliest known reference to the establishment of an Assembly for the church, and thus the earliest reference to what would become Lake Junaluska Assembly. In September of 1901, he brought the General Sunday School Board of the Methodist Episcopal Church, South to his home in Waynesville, North Carolina in an effort to convince them of the need for such an Assembly ground. In an editorial entitled "A Great Southern Assembly," which was printed in the *Sunday School Magazine* in August of 1903, Atkins wrote of a proposed Assembly in the South: "The times are ripe for such an enterprise. . . . If such an Assembly as we have in mind were established . . . it would be attended by multiplied thousands of our best people every summer. . . . Our Sunday School Board already has this under serious consideration. . . ."[2] In 1906, Atkins was elected a bishop in the Methodist Episcopal Church, South.

Atkins's dream of a great southern Assembly was shared by another well-known clergyman. They had met when they shared a small house much earlier in their lives. It was located in Morristown, Tennessee and had only two rooms. Nevertheless, the two young men found it adequate for their needs. Atkins was then a young Methodist preacher in his twenties just starting his career. The other was George Rutledge Stuart, a teenager who had come to Morristown, TN in the mid-1870s for the purpose of attending high school. He needed a place to live and the preacher offered him one of the rooms. He would work his way through high school by working as janitor of the school and by chopping wood at nights. It gets cold in East Tennessee in the winter and there was precious little heat in the house. Most of it was in the room used by the preacher and on many evenings, he would invite young George into his room. It was said of George that ". . . he never forgot the kindness, and through all the years a warm personal friendship existed between them, by which the younger man profited in guidance and inspiration."[3] These two men would become lifelong friends and co-workers in the ministry. The young high school student, George R. Stuart, would become a great evangelistic preacher and pastor of several large churches. The young preacher, James Atkins, would become a well-known leader in Christian education and later be elected a bishop. The two would become the prime movers in the development of a great institution unique in American Methodism. But in the early days in Morristown, they little dreamed of the impact they would have in years to come.

Their paths would soon part, but over the years they stayed in touch and on several occasions they worked together. In 1884, while Stuart was a pastor in Cleveland, Tennessee, they worked together promoting a centennial fund to commemorate the first century of American Methodism.[4]

George Stuart was a forceful and an animated pulpiteer. He was noted for his humor and homespun anecdotes. He was both impressed and influenced by the famous evangelist Sam Jones. He was equally impressed by another famous evangelist, Billy Sunday. He had built a cottage at Winona Lake, Indiana where Sunday, Homer Rodeheaver, and others had homes and held services. In the summer, he and his family would spend time there. He had a dream that someday there might be such a facility in the South.[5]

Atkins found his ministry path leading into fields of Christian education. At one time, he was president of Emory and Henry College, a Methodist college in Virginia. In 1896, he became editor of *Sunday School Publications* for the Methodist Episcopal Church, South. This position resulted in his attending several events at Chautauqua Lake in New York. He was greatly impressed by the facility. His election to the episcopacy gave him even more widespread influence in the region. About the same time, George R. Stuart was continuing to promote the idea of an Assembly or "camp meeting ground" somewhere in Tennessee. Whether these two old friends shared their feelings in those early days we do not know. Feeling as strongly as they did, it would certainly be a natural thing for them to share their visions.

In 1900, there was an upsurge of interest in foreign missions. It was given new emphasis by the first Ecumenical Missionary Conference held in New York in April of that year. At the conclusion of the conference, the delegates from the Methodist Episcopal Church, South met in the lobby of their hotel to seek ways to conserve the energy of that meeting. Following a time of prayer, Atkins proposed that there be a General Missionary Conference for the Methodist Episcopal Church, South. His proposal was presented to the Board of Missions and accepted a few days later. As a result, the New York conference was followed in 1901 by a General Missionary Conference of the MEC,S that was held in New Orleans.[6] The conference was a great success. Building on the impetus of this meeting, the Laymen's Missionary Movement was organized in 1907. The first general meeting of this movement was an event that became known as the Laymen's Missionary Conference of 1908 and was held in Chattanooga, Tennessee. Though the conferees could hardly have known it at the time, the conference became the incubator out of which hatched the Assembly that Atkins, Stuart, and others had dreamed of for so long.

On the evening of Tuesday, April 21, 1908, the opening session of the Conference began. President Dr. John R. Pepper called the conference to order. He then recognized the Hon. W. R. Crabtree, mayor of Chattanooga, who welcomed the one thousand men who had gathered there. They came from all over the Southeast. For three days, these dedicated men listened to challenging messages concerning missions. They passed resolutions related to a variety of issues regarding missions. They also passed a resolution that would set in motion plans to build a new Assembly ground in the Southeast. The result of this action would be the birth of Lake Junaluska Assembly.

That resolution read:

> **Resolved:** *That it is the sense of this Conference that it would be well for the Methodist Episcopal Church, South, to have a great Assembly ground on the order of Northfield, Mass., for the gathering together of our forces at stated times, and that such grounds should be located and so improved as to make*

them suitable for the various conferences of our Church when desirable to hold
them there and for Bible institutes and such other organizations for the help of the
preachers and laymen and the general upbuilding of the church and her forces as
may be decided upon in our outward movement for the evangelization of the world.

Resolved: *That a committee be appointed consisting of John R. Pepper, John*
P. Pettijohn, Gen. Julian S. Carr, B. M. Burger, R. S. Schoolfield, R. B.
Davenport, A. D. Reynolds, with the request to take this matter in hand and
take such steps as they may think best, with the approval and under the direc-
tion of the Executive Committee.[7]

How did this resolution come about? In her booklet on the birth of the
Assembly, Atkins's daughter writes, "I was in my father's home while the
Chattanooga Conference was in session, and I distinctly remember
hearing my father say at that time to my mother: 'Ella, I am going to send
a telegram to George Stuart suggesting that we get together on our plans
for a Southern Assembly.'"[8] During the conference Stuart who, at that
time, was pastor of Centenary Methodist Church in Chattanooga, entertained a group of the leaders at a luncheon. Among these was Dr. W. W.
Pinson, who would later write of the luncheon, "During the lunch he
urged upon our attention the need for provision for our young people in
the South similar to that at Winona Lake. The result of that was a resolution which he presented to the body at the succeeding session. This
resolution provided for such an Assembly as we had discussed."[9]

THE RICHLAND VALLEY WAS CHOSEN FOR THE LOCATION OF LAKE JUNALUSKA AND THE
SOUTHERN ASSEMBLY

Another significant personality related to the origin of the Southern Assembly was John R. Pepper. Pepper was a businessman from Memphis, Tennessee. His business ventures were highly successful and he became quite wealthy. Early on he joined First Methodist Church in Memphis and soon became superintendent of the Sunday school, a position he held for more than fifty years. He was extremely active in lay activities and was elected president of the Laymen's Missionary Movement. After the resolution calling for the establishment of a southern Assembly was passed at the Laymen's Missionary Conference in 1908, Pepper chaired the study committee named by the conference. Later, he became a member of the Board of Commissioners of the Southern Assembly. He built one of the initial thirteen summer homes on the campus. He was a well-known summer resident at the Assembly and his afternoon story hours were legendary. He served the Assembly in many leadership roles over his lifetime.[10]

Whatever the case, the passing of the resolution set in motion the planning, and ultimately the establishment of, what was originally called The Southern Assembly. As called for in the resolution, the committee came into being and began to formulate plans for such an endeavor. On June 13, they met in Tate Springs, Tennessee. At that time, they wrote a prospectus that outlined the concept for the Assembly and some of the means that would be used to bring about its construction. In this document, they indicated that they envisioned its use to include not only religious conferences, but also for it to be a place for family gatherings for the purpose of recreation and amusement. They saw it as the ". . . great Methodist Chautauqua of the South."[11] They also saw the Assembly as a health resort with outstanding mineral waters, mountain scenery with facilities for fishing, boating, and "other aquatic recreations."[12] The prospectus observed that the project would involve a large investment. They were quick to point out that they were interested in investments, rather than donations. They closed by reporting that the question of location was currently under advisement.

The location of the new Assembly was critical. Whether this became a great gathering place for the people called Methodist or not depended on ease of travel and comfort for those attending the conferences and other events held there. There were several considerations. Since activities would be limited to the summer months and the South was noted for its summer heat, the feeling of the commission was that it should be located at an elevation that would promise mild days and cool nights. Likewise, since the vast majority of visitors would arrive by train, there had to be rail service nearby. (In the early 1900s, more than 90 percent of travel was still by rail.)

On July 18, the executive committee of the Laymen's Missionary Movement met in Monteagle, Tennessee. Present that day were Chairman J. R. Pepper, F. M. Daniel, E. D. Newman, and W. F. Lambuth. Also in attendance were a group of lay leaders: A. E. Barnett, Alabama; R. F. Burden, South Georgia; Dr. S. C. Tatum, North Alabama; Major A. D. Reynolds, Holston; and W. F. Webb, Tennessee. At this meeting there were two presentations in regard to the location of the Assembly. One was presented by Bishop James Atkins, who proposed Waynesville, North Carolina and the other by Rev. R. A. Child, who proposed Hendersonville, North Carolina. No decision was made at this meeting and, apparently, no decision was made until early in 1910. It would appear that several factors caused the group to consider the Waynesville location over other proposals.[13] Two of these were the natural beauty of the Richland Valley east of the town along with the availability of the railroad. In addition, there was a proposal on the part of Waynesville businessmen to raise $100,000 for the construction of the Assembly.[14] There can be little doubt that the zeal and influence of Bishop Atkins played a large part in the decision. He had a home in Waynesville and had many contacts there. Undoubtedly, he had been indirectly responsible for the financial incentive from that community.[15] The combination of the availability of the railroad and the economic support seemed to have won the day and the committee agreed on Haywood County as the location.[16] Finally, the community in which the Assembly would be located was settled. There was still the matter of the exact location. It had to be on Richland Creek so that a lake could be constructed; but where on Richland Creek? The first choice was an area along the creek where Howell Mill was located. The advantage of this location was that the valley was very narrow right at the mill site and, thus, a smaller dam would need to be built. The lake created by the dam would reach right to the edge of Waynesville.[17] There was a major problem related to this site, however. In order to build the dam, the Southern Railway would have to move their tracks. They were not so inclined. In fact, Atkins and Stuart were about to make a trip to Washington to argue this issue with the Southern Railway officials when a new development occurred.[18] Three of the members of the committee were traveling from Asheville to Waynesville on the train. Just as they rounded "Horseshoe Curve," about three miles east of Waynesville, they looked out the window into a beautiful valley framed on all sides by the mountains. They were struck by the natural beauty of the area.[19]

Upon arrival in Waynesville, the trio contacted Atkins. It seemed that the commissioners already had options on three farms in that valley. They urged him to rethink the location of the Assembly and to buy the three farms. They further urged buying as much of the surrounding land as possible. The farms belonged to A. Eugene Ward, James Rufus Long, and Philette Howell. The bottomland covered approximately two hundred fifty acres and was in corn. Richland Creek ran right through it. The two hundred fifty acres would become the area covered later by Lake Junaluska.[20] Following the decision, it was reported that one of the commissioners observed that it was a good choice since the Richland Valley was "above the mosquito line."

If the decision to locate the new Assembly in Haywood County was well received by the committee, it was received with even more excitement by the people of Haywood County and Waynesville. An article on the front page of the *Western Enterprise* dated June 23rd 1910 proclaimed in bold headlines, "Southern Assembly Grounds to Be at Waynesville!"[21] The business community rightly sensed that the economic impact from the Assembly would be huge. As construction continued over the next several years, anticipation grew. One article proclaimed, "The opening of the Assembly will be the greatest event in the history of Western North Carolina and the greatest possible benefit to Waynesville."[22] Another headline proclaimed, "Junaluska Presents Many Great Opportunities,"[23] while still another article informed its readers of the "Advantages of the Chautauqua to the Farmers of Haywood."[24] The article pointed out that the Assembly would provide a much larger market for their produce.

Nevertheless, acquiring the land for the Assembly was no easy task. For the most part, the land was in farms that had been handed down through generations of the same family. In what borders on the miraculous, the commissioners were able to convince the landholders to sell their ancestral lands. In her book, *Think on These Things*, Glenine T. Miller, a descendent of the Ward family, writes: "Land was the family heritage and after grandfather's death in 1898, grandmother was not willing to dispose of one acre. In the early 1900s Bishop Atkins, representing the Methodist

Conference, came to her proposing that the Conference buy some of her property on which would be built a Methodist Assembly Center. Grandmother would not sell. When warned that the Bishop was coming down the road to discuss the proposal, she would hide and refuse to see him. Her land was not for sale."[25]

Following Mrs. Long's death, the property was inherited by her daughter, Mary Caroline Long Ward. She and her husband, Eugene, were of the same mind as had been her mother. Eugene Ward said that the bottom land adjacent to Richland Creek was the best corn-growing land in the area. Thus, when approached by Atkins, he refused to sell. Tiring of the continuous attempts to persuade him to sell, he finally decided that he would agree and set such an outrageous price so that they would leave him alone. And thus one hot summer day when, once again, the preachers came to call, he offered to sell at what he thought was an impossible price. To his surprise, they agreed. Being a man of integrity and living by the high mountain values which demanded that a man's word was his bond, Ward felt compelled to live up to his word. And thus a key piece of property in the Richland Valley was acquired by the commission.[26]

During 1909, an act of incorporation was passed by the North Carolina General Assembly. This act created a corporation under the

AN EARLY PICTURE OF THE ASSEMBLY IN 1920. FROM LEFT TO RIGHT: VIRGINIA LODGE, TERRACE HOTEL, STUART AUDITORIUM, AND THE PUBLIC SERVICE BUILDING

name of the Southern Assembly. It had certain features of a private corporation. It was owned and controlled by the stockholders. These stockholders, in turn, elected a Board of Commissioners that would govern the corporation.[27]

The act of incorporation also gave the corporation powers and rights usually found in a municipality. The commissioners had the right to levy taxes. Nevertheless, it granted the corporation tax exemption. It also gave them the right to enact ordinances for governing the municipality, including the right to establish a cemetery. The act that passed the General Assembly was a strange piece of legislation that ultimately proved to be unconstitutional in some of its provisions. In 1914, after many challenges by Haywood County and the state, the North Carolina Supreme Court ruled that, in effect, the Assembly could not "have it both ways." They could not be both a religious community and a stock corporation. It went on to rule that the Assembly was not exempt from taxation.[28]

Following the passage of the act of incorporation by the North Carolina Assembly the road was now open for the legal organization of the Southern Assembly. The commissioners then set out to bring the Assembly into existence. We are fortunate to have the original minute book of the early meetings of the Board of Commissioners. This book contains the handwritten minutes by S. C. Satterthwait, the first secretary. The first entry in the book records the proceedings of a meeting held at the Waynesville residence of Bishop Atkins on June 10, 1910. It states: "for the purpose of organizing and proceeding with the business pertaining to said Southern Assembly under and by virtue of authority given said original in the public laws of NC for the year 1909, chap. 419."[29] With the passage of the act of incorporation and the organizational meeting, the name "Southern Assembly" became official.

At this meeting, a board of commissioners comprised of Bishop James Atkins, S. C. Satterthwait, B. J. Sloan, Alden Howell, and George R. Stuart was named. All were present with the exception of Stuart. Atkins was elected chairman, Satterthwait, secretary, and Sloan, treasurer. The group discussed fundraising and authorized Atkins to secure agents to sell Southern Assembly stock. They likewise authorized C. H. Welch to close on options for the land that had been chosen for the Assembly grounds.[30]

Further business included discussion of a road connecting Waynesville with the Assembly grounds and dialog and a document of agreement between the incorporation committee and the committee formed by the

Laymen's Missionary Conference. In addition, the design for the corporate seal was approved.[31]

The end of this meeting marked the birth of the Southern Assembly. Although at this point there was nothing physical that could bear this name, the project was underway and would gain momentum rapidly.

The next meeting of the Board of Commissioners of the Southern Assembly took place on July 24. By this time, the sale of stock was well underway. Reverend R. A. Childs was engaged at a salary of two hundred dollars a month to sell stock. He was instructed to sell the stock in blocks of no less than five thousand dollars.

One of the most important items of business at the meeting was to hire engineer James W. Seaver to do preliminary work on the design, to estimate the cost of a dam, and to determine the level of the lake that would be produced by the dam. Seaver would go on to become the engineer for the entire project and would be highly influential in the total design of the project including location of roads, buildings, and other important decisions.

By the time the Board met on August 1st, Seaver had completed his initial survey and had drawn the first map of the area. He also reported correspondence with a landscape design company located in Brookline, Massachusetts called Olmstead Brothers Landscape Designers. This company was formed by the sons of the famed landscape architect, Fredrick Law Olmstead, the designer of Central Park in New York City and the grounds for George Washington Vanderbilt's Biltmore Estate in Asheville, North Carolina. Fredrick Law Olmstead died in 1903 and his sons continued the business. The Board authorized Seaver to employ Olmstead Brothers to design the grounds of the new Assembly.

Seaver was also given permission to continue with preliminary work on the site for the dam and to proceed with tests for the foundation. There was discussion of a road from the end of the existing road to the site of a proposed hotel.

As the frequent meetings of the Board of Commissioners continued and decisions regarding construction moved forward, the excitement and anticipation of what was to follow grew quickly.

J. O. Olmstead, son of Fredrick Law Olmstead, arrived in Waynesville on September 1st and immediately met with the Board of Commissioners. Along with Seaver, the Board members sat down with Olmstead to discuss the purpose and scope of the proposed Southern Assembly. They pored over maps, which Seaver had prepared along with

AN EARLY VIEW FROM INSPIRATION POINT INCLUDED THE TERRACE HOTEL, THE BOAT HOUSE, AND VIRGINIA LODGE

other data. Eagerly the Board shared their dreams and visions. When the meeting concluded, the group adjourned with plans to meet at 9:00 AM the following morning, at the site for the new Assembly.

A group of very excited men gathered in a farm valley three miles north of Waynesville, North Carolina on September 2, 1910 to use their imagination and expertise to visualize what would become one of the premier institutions of Methodism over the next century.

The group examined the site and showed Mr. Olmstead over the grounds. Details of the proposed Assembly grounds were discussed. Seaver was instructed to provide Olmstead with whatever plans and data he required. At the end of the day, Olmstead indicated that he would make his report as soon as possible after his return to Brookline.

At some point in the planning, the group decided on a name for the lake. The following headline and article appeared in one of the local newspapers: "They Have Named It Lake Junaluska." "At the meeting last week of the principal officers of the Southern Assembly it was decided to call the body of water to be filled by the sparkling Richland 'Lake Junaluska.'"[32] Many other names were suggested, but this was voted the most beautiful, as well as the most appropriate. "Junaluska" is a name which has been associated with Waynesville and Eagles Nest and has been extensively advertised by the latter.

The name "Junaluska" is that of the celebrated Cherokee Indian chief, the friend of Andrew Jackson and one of the heroes of the battle of Horseshoe Bend where the Creek Indians were destroyed. The Plott Balsams have been known as the Junaluska mountains, though the name as thus was never generally adopted. ". . . That the lake which is to shimmer in the sunshine at the foot of these eminences should bear the name of the noble warrior and leader of the Red Men is eminently fitting."[33]

The most dramatic view of the valley came from an elevated ridge overlooking the valley. It would later come to be known as Inspiration Point. Over the years, many photographs have been taken from this spot. It was also on this spot that the Junaluska Cross was erected some fifteen years later. At the far end of the valley is the eastern end of the Plott Balsam range. The highest mountain to be seen was, at that time, called Junaluska Mountain.[34] The mountain was named for a famous Cherokee Indian. Junaluska had saved the life of General Andrew Jackson at the battle of Horseshoe Bend during the War of 1812. He later walked to Oklahoma with his people during the infamous Trail of Tears only to return to North Carolina later. He was honored by the State Assembly of North Carolina and given citizenship late in life. It was obvious that once the lake was constructed, Mount Junaluska would reign over the lake like a benevolent overseer. Thus it was decided that the lake should be named for the mountain. The new lake would be Lake Junaluska.

Meetings of the commissioners continued on a regular basis. The wisdom of appointing local businessmen to the Board became obvious when the necessity for frequent meetings and the difficulty and expense of travel was considered.

Having settled on the location and design of the new Assembly, the Board turned its attention to the necessity of fundraising. An endeavor such as this was extremely expensive. Big dreams and great visions come at a high price if they are to become reality. Adjusted for inflation over the century, this was a multi-million dollar project.

The meetings of the commissioners were held as the need demanded. These meetings were held at Atkins's home in Waynesville, in the mayor's office, in the office of the Bank of Waynesville, and other locations determined by the kind of business that would be transacted. Alden Howell was elected chairman of the Board to act in the absence of Bishop Atkins at times when Atkins's episcopal responsibilities precluded his presence at a meeting.[35]

It is at this point that the concept of selling lots for the purpose of raising additional funds appears in the minutes. A reoccurring subject in these meetings related to the borrowing of money for the purpose of purchasing additional land, expenses related to design and construction, and other needs.

On December 30, a meeting was held for the purpose of securing a loan of ten thousand dollars. Other loans of lesser amounts were also discussed. At this meeting, the first reference is made to the possibility of a Southern Railway depot for the Assembly, along with the kind of passenger service they would provide. It was reported that this matter was well in-hand and that the depot would be built with no cost to the Southern Assembly. A later meeting the next year produced a verbal agreement between the commissioners and representatives of the railroad that included a promise of lower fares for attendees and a commitment to build a depot at the Assembly.[36]

A brochure to be used for attracting more investors was produced. This booklet included the following statement:

The Southern Assembly is the result of an organized movement on the part of the laity and ministry of the Methodist Episcopal Church, South, to establish at the most suitable place a great permanent Assembly which will meet the growing need of the Church for rest, recreation, conference, training, and inspiration.

It is planned to make the Southern Assembly the great recognized summer rallying place of all the official arms of service of the Methodist Episcopal Church, South.[37]

The year 1911 began with plans for the new Assembly continuing. At a meeting held on January 2, the commission saw a set of nine color drawings that were to be used for the purpose of selling stock. Plans were made for a series of dinners to be held across the Southeast, at which the plans for the Assembly would be presented to key persons in the church. At these dinners, opportunity for stock subscription would be offered.

In the promotional brochure, reference is made to these dinners. [The promotion committee]:

has visited nearly forty towns and cities from North Carolina to Louisiana, and have presented the plans of the Laymen's Movement and the methods adopted to put those plans into execution . . . already about three hundred of the leading laymen and preachers of the Methodist Episcopal Church, South, have subscribed to stock in the company. In no case was any donation asked for or any collection taken.

The money received [from stock sales] will be used in payment for the land, for building the great dam necessary for the formation of the lake, and for the erection of the auditorium, hotel, Assembly buildings, the grading of roads, and the development of the property for the sale of lots for cottages.[38]

The new year also brought the necessity for the election of officers. On January 11, the Incorporators of the Assembly met at the office of Atkins & Atkins. An election was held and the following officers were elected:

Bishop James Atkins, *President*
John R. Pepper, *Vice President*
S. C. Satterthwait, *Secretary*
B. J. Sloan, *Treasurer*
James Cannon, *General Superintendent*
W. F. Tillett, *Superintendent of Bible Conferences*
George R. Stuart, *Superintendent of Programs and Evangelistic Work*
J. E. McCullough, *Superintendent of Missionary Training School*

Interestingly enough at this meeting, James Cannon and John R. Pepper, who had not previously been members of the commission, were elected "Associates to the Incorporators." It is also significant that with the election of these officers, Cannon became the first superintendent of the Assembly.

The choice of James Cannon was a fortuitous one indeed. Cannon was uniquely equipped for the role. A graduate of Randolph-Macon College and Princeton Theological Seminary, he was a member of the Virginia Annual Conference of the Methodist Episcopal Church, South. He had served three appointments before being named as principal of the Blackstone Female Institute. While in this position, he became editor of the *Baltimore and Richmond Christian Advocate*. In 1911, he resigned his position at Blackstone to give full time to his role as the first superintendent of the

HOUSE BUILT IN 1922 BY BISHOP JAMES ATKINS AFTER HIS SECOND MARRIAGE

Assembly. His abilities of organization and fundraising were exactly what were needed at this point. He not only was able to lead in the fundraising efforts, but also invested large amounts of his own resources. A few years after being named superintendent, he built a hotel as one of the earliest accommodations for attendees at the Assembly. He was elected a bishop in 1918 and shortly thereafter resigned his position at the Assembly.[39]

At this point, there was not one building, nor any other structure related to the Assembly. Thus, two weeks later in a meeting the law firm of Atkins & Atkins offered to add another story to their building on Main Street in Waynesville. This would be for the purpose of providing office space for the new Assembly. A sketch of the new addition was shown to the group. The commission voted to accept the proposal and agreed to pay rent in the amount of $12.50 per month. This became the first head-quarters for the Southern Assembly.

At this meeting, the Board called for the work on the proposed dam to commence as soon as possible. It further reported that James Seaver should be hired as general engineer, along with the assistance of an additional consulting engineer. Work was to begin within twenty days. This marks the beginning of actual construction on the site of the Assembly.

Subsequent meetings primarily involved continued fundraising and land acquisition. Some swapping of land is noted in the minutes. Streets and avenues were laid out and were under construction. Locations for hotels and other buildings were chosen. A committee was appointed to set prices for various lots as quickly as they were completed. The terms of sale would be 25 percent cash with the balance paid in six, twelve, and eighteen months as 6 percent interest. One action by the Board called for land to be donated to the general bodies of the church as might be desired to erect houses for their purposes.

As 1911 drew to a close, the Assembly moved from preparation to active construction. What had been the beautiful placid farm valley now buzzed with activity. A dummy railroad line was built from the Southern Railway tracks on the south ridge of the valley to facilitate moving material to the site of the new dam. Soon the dam itself began to rise above Richland Creek. Over two hundred workmen, primarily from Haywood County, formed the construction force. Shortly thereafter, the foundation for the new auditorium was completed and the structure began to rise on the north side of the valley. The building, patterned after similar structures at other assemblies including Chautauqua Lake and

AN EARLY SCENE ON NORTH LAKESHORE DRIVE. THE LARGE HOUSE ON THE LEFT WAS BUILT BY GEORGE R. STUART AND NAMED WINONA

Winona Lake, was built using a steel umbrella design. Simply put, there is a center shaft with steel ribs running out from it. These two structures would be the first to be completed.

Not far from the site of the new dam, a large hotel was under construction. It was so massive that it would take years to complete. Likewise, not far from the auditorium another structure (not as large, but impressive nevertheless) was being built. Both of these would be hotels of the future but they would not be completed by the time the Assembly opened.

Also under construction were several houses. A catalogue of homes was distributed. A two story, four-bedroom house was offered for the construction cost of sixteen hundred dollars while a small bunkhouse cottage, which would sleep six, would cost six hundred twenty-five dollars. By the end of 1913, there would be thirteen private houses completed.[40] Some of these would be ready for occupancy in time for the opening conference. Stuart, Atkins, and Pepper were among those whose summer cottages were under construction. Likewise, "Private" John Allen was having a house built.

Allen, a politician from Mississippi, was said to have been the most quoted man in the nation during his eight terms in the U.S. House of Representatives from 1884–1901. He acquired the nick-name "Private" as a result of an incident early in his political career. While running for office his opponent, retired General W. S. Tucker, remarked that he had spent the night in a nearby grove of trees after a battle and urged voters to vote for him. Allen, not one to pass up an opportunity so thrust upon him, replied that on that night he was a private guarding the general. He then asked all who had been generals to vote for Tucker and all who had been privates to vote for him. He won the election. Now an old man and a dedicated Methodist, he was building a home at the new Southern Assembly.[41]

On October 9, 1912 the Board of Commissioners entered into a contract with the Southern Railway, whereby they granted the railroad a right of way for an industrial spur. This opened the way for the construction of the Junaluska Depot.

Fundraising continued. The sale of lots and stock took on new urgency as the financial needs grew. Dinners continued to be held throughout the Southeast in an effort to raise funds. George R. Stuart was the most popular speaker for these affairs. His popularity and status as a great preacher meant that the mere mention of his name would guarantee a large crowd. As the activity related to the establishment of the new

THE HART HOUSE ON OXFORD ROAD IS ONE OF THE ORIGINAL THIRTEEN HOUSES BUILT AT THE ASSEMBLY

HANDSOME COTTAGE
SOUTHERN ASSEMBLY GROUNDS
(NEAR WAYNESVILLE, N.C.)
BUILT FOR $1600.00

A PAGE FROM AN EARLY BROCHURE, CIRCA 1912, ADVERTISING HOUSES WHICH THE ASSEMBLY WOULD BUILD ON ORDER

A CROWD GATHERS AT THE SOUTHERN ASSEMBLY AUDITORIUM, CIRCA 1913

Assembly continued, the interest and fervor for missions continued in the Methodist Episcopal Church, South.

Following the close of the Laymen's Missionary Conference in 1908, there was a series of meetings and conferences. A second general missionary conference of laymen was held in Dallas, Texas on February 22, 1910. The attendance was double that of the conference in Chattanooga. At the conclusion of this conference, it was decided that the next such conference would be held in 1913. In May of 1910, the General Conference of the MEC,S met in Asheville, North Carolina. At this conference, the Laymen's Missionary Movement was officially recognized as a work of the denomination. Later, as preparations began for the conference of 1913, the secretary of the Laymen's Missionary Movement realized that this conference should involve more than just this organization. Thus, he set up a meeting of missionary board secretaries and suggested this. As a result, further meetings were held and it was decided that the 1913 conference would be enlarged to include all missionary activities of the church. At a later meeting on July 25, 1912 that included the executive officers of the Board of Missions, it was decided that this conference would be called "The Missionary Conference of the Methodist Episcopal Church, South." At this meeting, John R. Pepper was named as chair of the general committee to oversee the planning. The date for the opening of the conference was set for June 25, 1913. On October 29, at a committee meeting in Nashville, Dr. James Cannon invited the committee to select the Southern Assembly Grounds as the meeting place

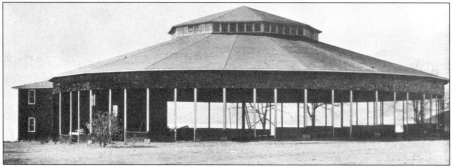

TOP: THE SOUTHERN ASSEMBLY AUDITORIUM DURING CONSTRUCTION, CIRCA 1912
BOTTOM: THE RECENTLY COMPLETED SOUTHERN ASSEMBLY AUDITORIUM, CIRCA 1913

for the conference. He proposed to furnish an auditorium with lighting, to entertain the officers and invited speakers, and to furnish literature for advertising purposes. This was indeed an act of faith, since none of the facilities were completed at this time. Indeed, construction of some of the promised facilities had not even begun! On October 31, the College of Bishops met in Greenwood, South Carolina. During this meeting, the bishops passed a resolution stating approval of the upcoming conference. The final details of the conference were approved by the full Board of Missions at its regular session in Dallas in May of 1913. It would thus become the "Second General Missionary Conference of the Methodist Episcopal Church, South."[42]

Now there was truly a sense of urgency at the construction site. Would they be ready to accommodate this conference? Would the facilities be ready? As the date grew ever closer and the work progressed it became apparent that the dam would, indeed, be completed though there would be little water in the lake. Likewise, the auditorium was nearing completion but it would be very close. The primary concern was the hotels. They would not be ready. How would they accommodate the crowds they hoped would attend? Who would provide transportation to and from the Assembly site? Where would the meals come from? Could they really pull off this ambitious and exciting gathering? Most important, would God bless their efforts?

CHAPTER TWO

An Auspicious Beginning

• • • • • • • • • • • • • • •

The J. A. Baylors were excited. It was Monday, June 23, 1913 and they were about to see their new summer cottage at the Southern Assembly for the first time. They had boarded a train early that morning to travel from their home in Bristol, Tennessee to the mountains of Western North Carolina. They arrived at the little Tuscola flag stop late that afternoon. They planned to get settled in their house just in time for the opening of the Second General Missionary Conference of the Methodist Episcopal Church, South on Wednesday night. They spent a while at the general store that also served as the post office for the community of Tuscola. Dr. John R. Long, who operated the store, welcomed them. Later they set out to walk to their new house. They walked down the tracks a way and then turned to walk across the top of the new dam that would create the lake.[1] As they did so, they noticed that the workman were still putting the finishing touches on the large structure. They continued on a pathway which skirted the soon-to-be edge of the lake and then climbed over an elevated point overlooking the valley. They were surprised to note that there was very little water in the lake. Only a small area just below the dam was under water. They knew the gates on the dam had been closed but, so far, there was very little of the scenic lake that was to come.

The Baylors finally reached their new cottage only to discover it was not finished. The shell and the roof were there, but no windows or doors. Piles of lumber were everywhere. Upon seeing this, Mrs. Baylor sat down on a rock and burst into tears. Just at this moment, Mrs. George Stuart arrived to welcome them. Upon seeing her distress, Mrs. Stuart reassured her saying, "Cheer up, Sister Baylor, we are in the same fix."[2] During that first year of the Assembly, thirteen private summer homes would be built, including the Stuart's (which they named "Winona") and one belonging to Bishop Atkins.

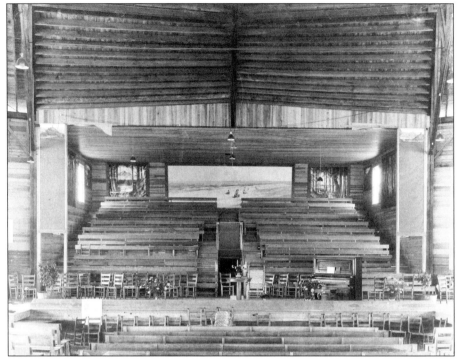

THE ORIGINAL CHOIR LOFT AND SPEAKERS PLATFORM IN THE AUDITORIUM. NOTE THE
BEACH PAINTING BEHIND THE CHOIR.

Such was the state of things as the time for the first conference at the new Southern Assembly grew near. Everything was progressing, but nothing was quite ready. To add to the sense of urgency, all signs indicated that the attendance would be quite large. No one seemed sure just how many would attend but, for several days now, persons had arrived on the daily passenger trains and settled into accommodations primarily in Waynesville's hotels, boarding houses, and even some private homes. *The Waynesville Courier* reported in its June 6 edition that "a dozen hotels providing for 50 to 200 each and fifty boarding houses with a capacity from 20 to 40 each together with private homes thrown open . . . will accommodate the crowd."[3]

At the new auditorium, William Quillian was a worried man. As president of the Methodist Training School in Nashville, he had been given the responsibility of making the arrangements and having the auditorium ready for the opening service on Wednesday evening. Things were going fairly well. The platform and pulpit area were in place. A good layer of sawdust covered the dirt floor and on it were the rough wooden pews. He felt like there would be ample room to the attendees. His major concern was the lighting. A generator operated by a turbine had been installed at the dam. They had strung wires from it to the auditorium where there were electric lights. But there were problems with the connections and no one was sure they would work. The first ever public electric lighting had been installed in New York a mere thirty years earlier. As the week progressed, there was no time to test the system.[4]

Wednesday arrived and so did the people. The Southern Railway had agreed to run shuttle trains from Waynesville to the new Assembly site. For most of the day, the trains ran back and forth the three miles. The fare for a round-trip ticket from Waynesville to the Assembly and back was ten cents. People began to arrive early to join the Baylors and the others of the fortunate few who had accommodations at the Assembly site. Some brought picnic lunches for their evening meal. For most of the day there was a steady stream of persons making the walk from the Tuscola Station across the dam, around the point, and down the hill to the auditorium. At one time, the line of persons walking from Tuscola to the auditorium stretched over a mile in length.[5] To arrive at the point where they could see the auditorium for the first time was thrilling. There were even a few adventurous persons who walked across the dry lakebed until they found a place where they could step over the creek.

The crowd, slowly at first, increasingly began to gather until the auditorium was full and then continued until there were many standing along the edge of the building. Those who entered discovered that around the edge of the auditorium were posters displaying long lists of needed building enterprises on seven different mission fields. These lists included such needs as chapels, schools, houses, hospitals, and lots. These lists were to capture the attention of the delegates. Through the entire conference they would be studied over and over. They would form the basis for the great collection that would follow.[6]

By late in the afternoon, there were well more than two thousand persons gathered in what had been a cornfield only a few years before. Anticipation grew as the afternoon wore on and the time for the opening service drew near. Daylight was beginning to fade. The service was about to begin.

Bishop E. R. Hendrix rose and called the conference to order. He then called on the song leader, J. Dale Stentz, for the opening hymn. The congregation stood and sang "Take the Name of Jesus With You." Following this, Bishop Atkins offered words of welcome. Atkins recounted the events that led to the calling of the Second General Missionary Conference of the Methodist Episcopal Church, South. He also welcomed the conferees to, "Western North Carolina and to the crown of it, Waynesville."[7] He then introduced the preacher of the evening, Dr. Robert E. Speer, one of the secretaries of the Presbyterian (U.S.A.) Board of Missions. In the gathering darkness, Speer rose to speak on the subject, "Prayer and Missions." As he approached the pulpit, the auditorium was suddenly bathed in light. At the dam the switch had been thrown and the electrical system worked! It was an auspicious beginning for the Missionary Conference and for the new Southern Assembly!

It was also an auspicious day for the Atkins family. After his election as a Bishop in 1906, James Atkins passed his office as editor of *Sunday School Publications* to others. Later, in 1915, Dr. John W. Shackford became superintendent of the General Sunday School Board of the Methodist Episcopal Church, South. Shackford and Love Branner Atkins had fallen in love and married. As the Missionary Conference began in the new auditorium below, a new life began in Bishop Atkins's summer home a block away. His daughter, Love, gave birth to a grandson. They named him Joe T. Shackford and, like his father and grandfather before him, he became a Methodist minister.

Thursday was designated as Home Missions Day. There were twelve addresses that day in the morning, afternoon, and evening. Continuing the ecumenical note that was struck by having a Presbyterian give the opening address, the speakers of the evening session were a secretary of the International YMCA Committee from New York, Dr. Peter Roberts, and a representative of the Southern Baptist Convention, Dr. B. D. Gray. It is significant also that two of the speakers were women and that Professor G. W. Dyer spoke on the subject "The Negro in His Relationship to Our Church."

Friday was Foreign Missions Day. On this day, representatives of mission efforts from all over the world addressed the group. Reports were given on mission work in many lands including Mexico, Brazil, Cuba, China, India, and Malaysia. There were speakers representing mission work through the Methodist Episcopal Church and the Presbyterian Church. There was a discussion on "Women of the East," led by a Miss Claiborne from China.

AN EARLY PHOTO OF GEORGE R. STUART'S SUMMER HOME WINONA

Saturday was Laymen's Day. These sessions were presided over by John R. Pepper of Memphis, one of the original commissioners named by the 1908 Laymen's Missionary Conference. On this day, fraternal greetings were received from the Episcopal Church along with input from the Southern Presbyterian Church. There was no afternoon session. Saturday evening was given to messages from various missionaries. Represented in these presentations were works in Japan, Mexico, Korea, along with several home missionaries.

It was on Saturday that the great collection began. It started as a spontaneous response to what the attendees had been hearing since Wednesday evening. It was fed by the needs that were on display and it was inspired by the atmosphere created by all that had taken place. G. B. Winton, who edited the report of the conference, put it this way: "The collection trickled along in a most charming manner. Like a mountain stream, it would at times seem to eddy and even stop at a barrier. Then it would suddenly pour over it and flow on again. It rose to fifty-seven thousand dollars."[8]

By lunch time on Saturday, the train that shuttled the people back and forth to Waynesville arrived but there was no waiting crowd. They were still at the auditorium caught up in the excitement of the moment. After waiting as long as they felt they could, the shuttle returned to Waynesville empty while those in auditorium fasted!

The collection paused then continued to rise until it reached eighty-nine thousand dollars. At this point, Bishop Hendrix began to insist that they could reach the hundred-thousand-dollar mark. As the train signaled its departure for Waynesville, the coveted hundred-thousand was reached and still it rose. By the time the train had reached Waynesville, it had reached one hundred and six thousand; the congregation sang the doxology and declared a time of rest.

That afternoon the women in attendance had a meeting of their own and raised enough to push the total to one hundred and fifteen thousand dollars. Following the services on Saturday, telegrams were sent to persons who were absent from the conference. These were to result in a continued rise in the collection and were reported the next day.[9]

The climax of the conference was on Sunday. The day began with a prayer meeting, which was followed by a sermon preached by Bishop J. H. McCoy. Following his message, the collection began to swell again and rose to one hundred and twenty-six thousand dollars.

After a break for lunch, the afternoon session was given over to the work in Africa. Dr. W. M. Morrison of the Presbyterian Mission on the Congo came to the pulpit. The rapidly building climax of the conference was further heightened when a thunderstorm broke out punctuating Morrison's sermon with its rumbling thunder.

Following the message by Morrison, Bishop Walter Russell Lambuth spoke and then consecrated, by the laying on of hands, six young people who had committed their lives to service as missionaries. The moving service touched a responsive chord in many who were present.

Sunday evening was slated to be the closing service and had been carefully planned. However, the plans for the evening were changed at the last minute. The speakers for the closing service were unable to be present. The decision was made to allow several missionaries who had not spoken earlier to share their experiences with the congregation. This was to be followed by a closing address by Dr. W. W. Pinson, secretary of the Board of Missions. Before he could begin, the collection resumed and began to creep up to the much-anticipated goal of one hundred-fifty thousand dollars.[10] When this was reached, the attendees passed a resolution addressed to the church, sang the doxology, and adjourned sine die.

The Second General Missionary Conference of the Methodist Episcopal Church, South had come to a glorious end. In days to come, it would come to be known as simply "The Junaluska Conference." Out of this conference came the founding of Soochow University in China, now located in Taipei, Taiwan.[11]

It would be difficult to over emphasize the significance of the opening event at the Southern Assembly. Although the living arrangements were less than what would be desired and the site only partially completed, the attendance and the success of the conference established the Assembly as a place were God came and touched lives and the results would literally be felt all over the world. Its reputation as a place of spiritual renewal and as a destination to be desired was established. Dr. Mason Crum expressed it well when he said:

> *I think enthusiasm for spreading the gospel never reached loftier heights among Methodists than it did in 1913 at Lake Junaluska. The most prominent laymen and ministers in the South were there, as well as a host of visitors, many of them distinguished in missionary and other religious activities. The generosity of the people was exceptional; they vied one with another in giving to the cause of missions.*[12]

The Missionary Conference ended on Sunday night. The second conference to be held at the new Southern Assembly began the next day and unlike the Missionary Conference that had lasted five days, this conference lasted two weeks. It was titled "The Bible and Evangelistic Conference." There were ten speakers for this conference, including at least four who had spoken at the previous event. The first week of this conference was devoted to messages related to the Bible, while the second week had evangelism as its theme.

As had been the case the week before, the leadership was made up of outstanding personalities who were recognized as leaders of their day. Included were Dr. Charles L. Goddell, who was billed as "the most successful pastor-evangelist in American Methodism."[13] Dr. Camden M. Cobern, professor of the English Bible in Allegheny College in Allegheny College, Pennsylvania; Dr. Lincoln Hulley, president of Stetson University; Professor George M. Sleeth of Western Theological Seminary; Reverend J. A. Rice, pastor, Fort Worth, Texas; and Dean Wilbur F. Tillet of Vanderbilt University in Nashville, Tennessee.

Those who participated in the Missionary Conference the week before and were also speakers in The Bible and Evangelistic Conference included Bishop James Atkins, Dr. George R. Stuart, Bishop Walter Russell Lambuth, and Mr. John R. Pepper.

The music was led by three singers: Revs. Charles Tillman, Luther B. Bridges, and Oliver W. Stapleton.

An interesting feature of this conference was that there was no registration fee for attendance. Likewise, the brochure observes that accommodations were available at hotels in Waynesville.[14]

The Bible and Evangelistic Conference was followed by the third and last conference of the initial year of the Assembly. This conference was titled "The Epworth League and Sunday School Conference." This was to be the first conference held at the Assembly where the conferees stayed on the grounds. Tents were provided. One of the featured speakers for the conference was Dr. Henry Snyder, president of Wofford College.[15] As in the case of the other two conferences that summer, Bishop Atkins welcomed the attendees and, in this case, preached the first sermon.

With the conclusion of the Epworth League Conference, the first season of the Southern Assembly ended. But the work at the site continued. Most of the thirteen homes were still under construction, although some had been used during the conferences by owners. The Public Service Building, which would be the first Assembly-owned hotel, was still under construction and though it had been used in a limited way during the Epworth Conference, it would not be completed until the next season.

At the west end of the lake, George R. Stuart had completed what perhaps was the earliest lodge at the Assembly. He gave it a good Methodist name, Epworth Lodge, using the name of the English village which had been the boyhood home of John Wesley, the founder of the Methodist movement. The program book for 1915 called it "a very unusual building . . ." with "nice small rooms, nice dining and living rooms at one end."[16] It was a rustic building located along the North Lakeshore road just across the Stuart Spring from Stuart's home, "Winona." A few years later, it was demolished and a larger lodge, using the same name, was constructed. The new Epworth Lodge was located at the upper end of Stuart Circle and had openings on the Circle and also on Oxford Road.

Also under construction was an extremely large hotel located on the north side of the lake above the dam and between the dam and the auditorium. It would be named Junaluska Inn and would become known as the "pride of Junaluska." Its design followed the architecture common to the grand hotels built in many locations at the turn of the century. It was so large and so elegant that it would be several more years before it was completed. A notation in the 1914 program book informs its readers, "It has been impossible to get the Junaluska Inn open for this season."[17] The hotel would not be ready for guests until the spring of 1917. Likewise under construction was a hotel that, at that point, was slated to be named the College Inn.

One could not have imagined a more auspicious beginning for the Southern Assembly. The Assembly now consisted of a 250-acre lake created by a magnificent dam, a very impressive auditorium capable of seating thousands, two hotels under construction, thirteen summer homes in various stages of completion, many additional property owners with plans for still more homes, and miles of roadways. Crowds exceeding expectations had attended three conferences. The largest collection for missions ever received by the Methodist Episcopal Church, South had taken place during one of the conferences. The dreams and visions of Atkins, Stuart, and others had become reality. God had indeed blessed this special place. The future looked bright indeed.

CHAPTER THREE

The Teens

• • • • • • • • • • • • • •

W hen the summer of 1914 arrived, the new Southern Assembly was poised for another grand experience. The three conferences of 1913 had surpassed all expectations in terms of participation, excitement, and results. The time had come to continue what had started so well. There was much to be done. Living conditions had been primitive and the conference events limited. The time had come to complete the facility and to build a program that would fulfill the expectations of both the visionaries and the public.

Those persons who had attended the opening conferences of the Southern Assembly in 1913 were no doubt very impressed by the changes they noted upon arrival the next summer. By 1914, the massive Junaluska Inn on the ridge overlooking the lake was beginning to rise and it was already obvious that this would be an impressive structure. As indicated in the program book for 1914, the inn was far from completed. Indeed, it would be three years before it would be used as the premier lodging for persons attending events. In the program books for each of those years the same statement would read, "It has been impossible for us to complete the Junaluska Inn in time for this summer."[1] A similar statement was made concerning College Inn, a privately owned hotel, which was off and on under construction. It was being built by Dr. J. M. Rhodes who was president of Louisburg College in North Carolina.

Across the street from the new auditorium, a hotel was nearing completion. Since it would house just about everything related to the Assembly it would be initially named "The Public Service Building."

An interesting comment is made in the 1914 program book: "Bishop Atkins's home has been rented and is run as a first-class boarding house. . . . Twenty minutes walk from the station."[2] In years to come, the Atkins house would be used both as a summer home for the Atkins family and as an inn.

In the summer of 1914 there were only two lodging facilities available on the Assembly grounds. For most persons attending conferences in the summer of 1914 it was still necessary to find accommodations in Waynesville. Such was the case for the Herbert family. Earlier in 1912, an illness suffered by Mrs. Herbert caused them to visit in Waynesville.[3] While there, Dr. Cannon had given them a tour of the area that would become the Assembly. In 1914, they returned and spent the entire summer in Waynesville. They attended several of the events and determined that they would, some day, have a cottage there. It was not until 1920 that they were able to fulfill their plans.

As promised, the Southern Railway completed the Junaluska Depot in time for the 1915 summer season. A typical depot of its day, it had the usual waiting rooms, ticket windows, baggage area, and station master's office. Also located in the building was the telegraph office. Young boys spending summers at the Assembly would be hired to deliver telegrams received at the station. There was a freight building and covered loading platforms. Cleon Williams, agent-operator of the station from 1943 to 1966 described the waiting room of the Junaluska station as larger than the waiting room at the station in Asheville.[4] Herbert Gibson Jr., son of the first station agent-operator estimated that the waiting room was sixty feet long and thirty feet wide.[5] All in all it was a very impressive structure.

The station became the entrance to the Assembly for the vast majority of those attending the conferences. The Southern Railway offered reduced fares to those traveling to the Assembly. Unfortunately, for those who arrived during the second summer there was still the necessity of either walking across the dam or having someone with an automobile or a shay meet the train. This would change by the end of the summer. The depot became a hub of activity particularly during the several times a day that trains arrived. Campers attending Camp Junaluska for summer camps would arrive at the station. Pullman service was available and was widely used. It was also an asset to the surrounding community, particularly as it related to freight shipments. Many local farmers used it as a shipping point for their tobacco, lumber, and other products. Likewise, it became a pick-up point for merchandise ordered by both summer residents and others.

For more than thirty years, the Junaluska Depot was hub of activity for the Assembly. The arrival of a passenger train was an exciting event. At the height of its use, there were six arrivals and departures a day. Many fascinating stories had their setting at the depot.

On the morning of May 9, 1917, as engineer Andy Enloe eased out of Waynesville at the head of a long freight train, he could hardly have imagined the tragic events that lay ahead. Riding to his left on the fireman's seat of the engine was Loyd Enloe. Andy, no doubt enjoyed having his twenty-one-year-old cousin working with him. Behind them was a second engine with Clint Burt as engineer and O. H. Bradshaw as fireman. Behind the two engines stretched a long string of boxcars. Unbeknown to these men, at about that same time a very cantankerous bull belonging to farmer Garrett Reeves found a weak spot in the fence and escaped from his pasture near the Junaluska Depot. He made his way to the tracks in a sharp curve called the "white cut" in the side of a hill. There he decided to challenge the oncoming freight. With the train bearing down on him, he pawed the ground, lowered his head, and charged. By the time Enloe spotted the bull, it was too late to stop. They collided head on. The cowcatcher of Enloe's engine failed to toss the bull to the side. Rather he was dragged under the train causing the lead engine to derail. Both engines left the track and came to rest in an adjacent field. Enloe's engine fell on its left side, but Burt's remained upright. A steam line broke and young Loyd was severely scalded by the escaping steam. He was moved from the accident site to the nearby Junaluska Depot where he was placed on an office table. A doctor was sent for. Shortly after the doctor arrived, Loyd Enloe died.[6]

The summer residents depended on the depot for a variety of reasons. Not only did many of them arrive and depart from there each year, but they used the freight depot as a receiving area for many of the items they needed including, in a few cases, Sears Roebuck kit houses. Several of these were assembled on the Assembly grounds and at least two of them still exist. Likewise, in the fall as they prepared to leave for the winter, many brought their pot plants to the depot where they would be cared for during the cold winter months. The next spring, when they arrived, they would go by and pick them up again.

More summer homes were under construction. These would add to the initial thirteen that were completed. Life was still primitive for their occupants, even with all that had been accomplished. There were no paved roads and, depending on the weather, the roads would either be a sea of mud or ribbons of choking dust. Water in the very early years came

A CROWD LINES THE RAILS OF THE *CHEROKEE I* ON LAUNCH DAY, AUGUST 17, 1914

THE FIRST BIG BOAT, *CHEROKEE I*

THE ARRIVAL OF A TRAIN WAS AN EXCITING MOMENT IN EARLY DAYS. AT ITS PEAK, SIX
PASSENGER TRAINS A DAY WOULD ARRIVE AND DEPART FROM THE JUNALUSKA STATION

THE JUNALUSKA DEPOT, BUILT BY THE SOUTHERN RAILWAY IN 1915

THE JUNALUSKA INN WAS THE LARGEST HOTEL BUILT AT THE ASSEMBLY. THE INN BURNED
IN 1918

from five springs on the north side of the lake. George Stuart owned
much of the land in a small cove just west of his summer home. There was
(and still is) a road which circled through this area. In the cove and near
Lakeshore Drive was one of the larger of the five springs, appropriately
called Stuart Spring. It was walled in and developed into an attractive area
and supplied water for the Stuart family and for other homes nearby. It
also provided a storage area for perishable foods such as milk and eggs.
This, along with the other springs in the area, became the iceboxes for
summer residents. Stuart Spring became a gathering place for those who
wanted to picnic or just enjoy the summer days. Likewise, some very
serious courting took place there.

Already there were families that would arrive in early June and spend
the entire summer at the lake. They were the vanguard of a summer
community that would quickly establish itself. Most of these were ministerial families. Mother and children would move in for the summer and
father would come and go as he could. The children would meet other

children who were present and friendships would develop that would be renewed each year as they returned for the summer season.

For the summer of 1914, a much expanded schedule of conferences was offered. In addition, there was a full repertoire of what were called "Chautauqua Features." In its second season the Southern Assembly hosted six conferences:

July 16–22:	*Epworth League Leadership Training Conference*
July 22–August 2:	*Sunday-School Conference*
August 4–7:	*Educational Conference*
August 7–11:	*Missionary Conference*
August 16–24:	*Bible Conference*
August 24–26:	*Deaconess Conference*[7]

Subsequent years would offer similar conferences. The numbers of conferences each summer varied from three to six.[8] Chautauqua offerings included:

The Neapolitan Orchestra and Miss Hallie Gasaway
The Ernest Gamble Concert Company
The Hawkeye Glee Club—male quartet
W. Powell Hale—impersonator
Charles Newcombe
Marvin Williams—comedian
The Knoxville Concert Company
The International Preachers Quartet
A lecture by George R. Stuart
An old-time spelling bee

This would set the pattern for the offerings at the Southern Assembly in the ensuing years.

The Chautauqua offerings varied also. In years to come, there would be such productions as lectures, stunts, magicians, and readers. At one point there was an address by William Jennings Bryan. Other features included travelogues, nature studies, and lectures on such subjects as health and self-expression. On still another occasion, the operetta *The Lost Princess—Bo Peep* was performed. It was such a popular presentation that reserved seats were sold in advance.[9] Another operetta was named *The House that Jack Built*. Still another was named, *Snow White and the Seven Little People*.

In 1914, the trustees named J. Dale Stentz as the business manager of the Southern Assembly. Stentz, brother-in-law of George R. Stuart, had been the song leader at the 1913 Missionary Conference with his wife, Mary, as the pianist. After their marriage, Stuart built a cottage for the newlyweds just behind Winona, his summer home. It was known for many years simply as The Honeymoon Cottage.

Elizabeth, another daughter of Stuart, had the honor of being chosen to christen the new boat *Oonagusta*.[10] This large vessel was constructed on the south side of the lake not far from the new depot. The boat was launched on August 22, 1914. It was operated by "Captain" J. T. Westcott. Westcott had been an officer in the Coast Guard. He would wear his coast guard uniform while operating the boat. One unsubstantiated story reports that the boat was powered by a Ford Model "A" engine. Not long after it was put in service the name of the boat was changed to the *Cherokee*. The primary purpose for the boat was to ferry guests and their luggage from the depot to the various hotels on the north side of the lake. It was also used for sightseeing. A moonlight cruise was one of its most popular excursions. In later years, a fake smokestack was mounted on the boat. Occasionally, a tub of dry ice would be placed under the stack and when water was poured on the ice it would appear that smoke was pouring out.

The lake was the prime attraction of the Assembly in many ways. It was of special interest because there were no natural lakes in Haywood County. Unfortunately, this very fact created a serious problem which continues until this day. Because it was the first still water that occurred along Richland Creek, silt that was held in suspension in the fast moving stream, would fall to the bottom of the lake. Thus the lake was continuously filling up and, unless dealt with, it would disappear. In a sense Lake Junaluska was slowly killing itself. Engineer James Seaver had become aware of this early on. In a report to the Board of Trustees in 1920, he called attention to an alarming amount of silt filling the lake. He went on to say that, in his opinion, dredging was the only answer. He stated: "It will only be a short time before the large boat will be unable to go above the narrows thus cutting off any travel by boat to the golf course."[11]

In 1916, a group met and formed a temporary organization for the purpose of creating an organization for women. This group was chaired by Mrs. Kate Shaw. A committee was formed to write a constitution and

THE ORIGINAL TERRACE HOTEL, LOCATED ON NORTH LAKESHORE DRIVE, WAS
COMPLETED IN 1920

bylaws for submission. The next summer the group came together, adopted the constitution and bylaws, and elected officers. It was initially called "The Junaluska Woman's Auxiliary." The group wasted no time making itself heard. At the August 20, 1918 meeting of the Board of Commissioners, there was a request from the Woman's Auxiliary that there be authorized a new hand laundry for the next season. In addition, there was a request for a competent janitor who would keep the public grounds clean and in order. Further, they expressed concern over the stock and hogs that were being allowed to run at large over the grounds during the absence of owners.[12]

Later, in 1919 the name of the organization was changed to "The Junaluska Woman's Club." Its first president was Mrs. Frank Siler.[13] The organization created at that time continues until this day and is a vital and important element of support for the Assembly, as well as a significant part of the social life of the community. (A list of presidents of the Junaluska Woman's Club will be found in the appendix.)

This was the period leading up to and during World War I. It is significant that the Assembly continued to function in the summer during the war years. There were reductions in the number of events, but there was no program book printed for the year 1918. As is always the case, the war

THE BELL TOWER, BUILT IN 1920 TO HOUSE
THE BELL GIVEN BY C. E. WEATHERBY

touched many lives that were involved with the Southern Assembly. In the early days, the Assembly grounds were relatively isolated. The only communication with the outside world was with one telephone located in the Public Service Building, the telegraph in the depot, by reading the newspapers that came on the train, or by word of mouth from persons arriving for conferences. When the train would drop off the daily newspaper at the station, a youth would row over to the depot, pick up the newspaper, row back, and ring the big bell located near the auditorium. Summer residents and persons attending conferences would gather in the auditorium and listen as someone would read the war news from the stage. Likewise, there would be those times when the youth would return with telegrams related to the death or wounding of someone. One such loss would impact the Herbert family in an unexpected way.

As recorded by Mrs. Herbert in the Crum history, their cottage was purchased in 1920 with funds received from the insurance of their son who was killed in France during World War I. Mrs. Herbert stated, "It became the property of all of us, a sacred memorial, and we named it Carlisle Herbert Cottage for the donor."[14]

In 1918, two subsidiary companies were formed to expedite private cottage construction and the building and operation of Assembly-owned hotels. The companies were called Junaluska Construction Company and Junaluska Hotel Company. Neither company lasted more than ten years. They were ultimately dissolved and their functions simply integrated with the general operation of the Assembly. The end of these companies may have coincided with the resolution of the lawsuit related to the paying of taxes.

The thousands of persons who had attended the first conferences at the Southern Assembly in 1913 underlined the need for accommodations

TOP: A GROUP OF UNIDENTIFIED YOUTH IN FRONT OF THE AUDITORIUM HOTEL, CIRCA 1919
BOTTOM: THE AUDITORIUM WITH THE ORIGINAL ADMINISTRATION BUILDING IN LOWER
RIGHT. NOTE BELL TOWER BETWEEN BUILDINGS

on the Assembly grounds. Only those persons lucky enough to have cottages built or under construction were able to stay on the grounds overnight during the sessions. The rest had to travel back and forth to Waynesville. The Public Service Building was well under construction in 1913 but, had it been completed, it would have held only a small fraction of those attending. Thus, the crucial need for further hotels was apparent.

There followed what amounted to a building boom for hotels. George Stuart completed his Epworth Lodge, J. M. Rhodes began construction on his College Inn, James Cannon began planning for his Virginia Lodge, and the majestic Junaluska Inn was slowly rising on the

THE PUBLIC SERVICE BUILDING WAS COMPLETED IN 1914 AND INCLUDED THE AUDITORIUM HOTEL

ridge overlooking the lake. Unfortunately, several of these hotels would experience hard times and tragedy.

When he left Nashville for the Educational and Press Conference to be held at the Southern Assembly, Dr. Stonewall Anderson, secretary of the General Sunday School Board of the Methodist Episcopal Church, South, could not have known that this conference which he had helped design would threaten his life. It was to be an interesting and exciting gathering of leaders and producers of Christian education materials. He, no doubt, was pleased that he would be staying at Junaluska Inn, a new grand hotel that had just opened the year before.

As reported, the Junaluska Inn had been several years under construction. There was really nothing like it in the area. Its architectural design was that of the great grand hotels of the 1800s. It had a porch that swept from one end of the building to the other. Its one hundred thirty rooms all faced the lake and most had private baths. All rooms had hot and cold running water. Its center façade featured huge columns which soared up past the second of its three floors. Two octagonal towers rose on each side of the center porch with flags flying above their conical roofs. It was a majestic sight to behold and a luxury to inhabit. Soon after its opening in the spring of 1917, it was obvious that it had established a reputation for gracious hospitality and wonderful cuisine. When the spring of 1918 arrived, its popularity was evidenced by the fact that it was well booked for the season.

THE JUNALUSKA INN WAS COMPLETED AND OPENED FOR GUESTS IN JUNE OF 1917. THE INN BURNED JULY 17, 1918

Dr. Anderson arrived at the Assembly the afternoon of Tuesday, July 16 and registered in the hotel. He received the key for room 235.[15] The conference began on Tuesday and that evening he retired to his room for a good night's rest. It was not to be. Around 2:30 in the morning, he was awakened to discover that the magnificent hotel was on fire. The fire had started in an unoccupied area on the lower floor of the hotel. It was well under way before it was discovered. The night was calm and the fire burned rather slowly. The Waynesville fire department responded quickly only to discover that, although there was a two-hundred-fifty-acre lake two hundred feet below the hotel, there was no water available at the structure and they had no way to pump water from the lake.[16]

Young Jackie Stuart, son of George R. Stuart, was awakened by all of the commotion. He remembered that a few days before, superintendent W. H. Stockham had asked him to go pick up four Old Town canoes at the depot and move them to the basement of the Junaluska Inn. Racing to the hotel and looking in the window, he could see the canoes with burning embers falling all around them. He rushed in and began to pull the canoes out. All were saved. Several days later, Stockham arrived and Jackie picked him up at the depot. After expressing dismay over the loss of the building, Stockham then remarked that he had lost his four new canoes. Jackie then informed him that he had saved the canoes, upon which Stockham gave him his choice of one of them in appreciation for what he had done.[17]

Due to the slow burning fire, the alarm went off and the guests were awakened and there was no loss of life nor any injury. Many lost their personal belongings, however. Summer residents opened their homes, along with other facilities of the Assembly to the displaced guests. Among them was the occupant of room 329, Dr. William P. Few, the first president of Duke University.[18]

Under construction at the time of the fire was the College Inn. Dr. J. M. Rhodes was the president of Louisburg College, a Methodist related

VIRGINIA LODGE, A HOTEL BUILT AND OWNED BY JAMES CANNON, WAS BUILT IN 1917. IT
WAS TORN DOWN IN THE MID-1940S

college located in Louisburg, North Carolina. Caught up in the enthusiasm surrounding the new Southern Assembly, he decided that he would
build a hotel on the Assembly grounds. He was able to secure a strategi-
cally located piece of property near the new auditorium. Work began on
the hotel but soon had to pause while Rhodes raised additional funds.
This happened several times during construction. Rhodes experienced
significant difficulties in fundraising to the point that his project received
the dubious title of "Rhodes's Folly." Although construction finally was
far enough along that a few guests could be accommodated, it appeared
that this hotel would have little chance of completion. After fire
destroyed the Junaluska Inn, the Junaluska Hotel Company contacted
Dr. Rhodes with a proposal that they purchase the still incomplete
College Inn. This was done. They then completed the construction of
the hotel and renamed it the Terrace Hotel. It became very popular due
to its proximity to the auditorium. In 1973, due to the move toward a
year-round operation of the Assembly, the hotel was demolished to make
way for a new hotel which would be operational in every season. This
hotel was built in two stages and completed in 1979. The new structure
retained the name Terrace Hotel.

The year 1919 saw the opening of the Junaluska Golf Course. Located
at the west end of the lake, it became a very popular recreational feature
of the Assembly. There were only nine holes for many years. In its earliest

days, an old farmhouse was used as the clubhouse for the course. Finally in the 1950s, a clubhouse was built. In 1947, a highway which was known as the Waynesville By-pass was built between the golf course and the lake. This put an end to the practice of catching the Big Boat and riding from the hotels to the golf course. The land on which the course was built proved to be very valuable. Several controversies swirled around it at various times. Early on there was a crisis over the grazing of sheep on the fairways. In the early 1990s, the course was enlarged to eighteen holes. Later a new, much needed, clubhouse was completed.

CHAPTER FOUR

The 1920s

• • • • • • • • • • • • • •

It was not until 1921 that a permanent bridge was constructed over the top of the Junaluska Dam. In a report to the Board of Commissioners, A. I. Dietrich, then business manager, states, "A contract has been made with the Atlantic Bridge Co. of Charlotte for a steel bridge over the dam. The bridge will cost $13,382.50."[1] Prior to this, a temporary bridge had been built at the time the dam was constructed, which by 1920, was in poor condition. In fact, in a report to the superintendent W. H. Stockham, engineer J. W. Seaver stated,

At your request I examined the bridge across the dam and found, on close inspection, that there were a number of timbers which should be replaced at once if the bridge is to remain in service . . . if I were in responsible charge of the grounds I would at once close this bridge to all but foot travel, even if it involved removal of a section of flooring.[2]

The new bridge was ready for the 1921 season.
In the same report, Dietrich notes,

A suitable tower for the bell, which Mr. Weatherby gave to the Assembly is being built on the grounds near the auditorium. Rough Tennessee marble is being used in its construction. Funds for this work are being provided by the Sunday School Field Services of our church.[3]

The bell was a gift from C. E. Weatherby, whose house at the corner of Atkins Loop and Lakeshore Drive is believed to have been the first house completed in 1913. For several years, it sat on the ground by the auditorium. In a letter to the commissioners dated September 3, 1918, Weatherby stated,

[I] would like to call your attention to the large bell at the side of the auditorium. You have never done your part, which was to have it raised and a cover put on same. [I]will say that if it remains in the condition it is now in, it will soon be ruined and money thrown away.[4]

With the coming of the 1920s, the fire nemesis continued to plague the Assembly. Just east of the Terrace Hotel, the Auditorium Hotel in the Service Building had served as the only Assembly-owned hotel for the first four years of the Assembly's operation. It opened for regular business at the beginning of the 1914 season, though it had been pressed into service for the Epworth League Conference at the end of the 1913 season. The Public Service Building was truly an impressive structure; it was shaped like a horseshoe with white columns at each end and in the center. Since initially it was the only Assembly structure other than the auditorium, it had to serve many purposes. The entire lower floor was used for offices and businesses necessary for the operation of the Assembly. A tearoom was located there and was the only restaurant on the grounds. There was a telephone and telegraph office and the post office. Also in the building was a branch of the Junaluska Supply Company. From the earliest days the Junaluska

ONE OF THE EARLY POST OFFICES AT THE ASSEMBLY

IN THE TWENTIES, THE PORCH OF THE OLD MOUNTAINVIEW LODGE WAS A FAVORITE PLACE FOR STUDY

Supply, a typical general store, became the source of almost anything needed by summer residents. Owned and operated by Jerry Liner, the store saved these residents a trip into Waynesville when groceries or household items were needed. Liner had built a building near the depot, but continued to operate his branch in the Public Service Building. Likewise, the administrative office of the Assembly occupied one room in the structure. Its forty guest rooms were all on the second floor. While not large when compared with later hotels, it was most impressive standing as it did just across from the auditorium. Its original name, the Public Service Building, referred to the entire building while the portion of the structure which contained the guest rooms was known as the Auditorium Hotel.

During the off-season it was leased to the Snyder School for Boys, a private boys school based in Florida. This was a mutually favorable arrangement both for the school and the Assembly. It gave the students a change of scenery from the beaches of Florida to the mountains of North Carolina. It also gave the Assembly an additional source of much needed income and the security of having the facilities occupied during a portion of the off-season.

TOP: A TYPICAL SCENE DURING A CONFERENCE IN THE AUDITORIUM DURING THE 1920S
BOTTOM: A BUSY DAY AT THE ASSEMBLY DURING THE LATE 1920S

Certainly the students in the Snyder School liked the arrangement. Their visits to the mountains were filled with new adventures. Hikes in the nearby hills, overnight camping trips to Mount Junaluska, and basketball in the auditorium with the pews pushed back were all exciting changes. In the fall of 1920, the boys were housed in the second floor guest rooms of the Auditorium Hotel. On the afternoon of October 17th, some of the boys decided that they would engage in a mischievous forbidden act. They would smoke some cigarettes. They gathered in one of the upstairs guest rooms and somehow a fire got started in the room. Quickly the fire spread throughout the wooden structure.[5] As in the case of the Junaluska Inn fire, there was no way to get water to the conflagration. The big boat, *Cherokee I*, was making its way across the lake when those on board saw the smoke and flames. Captain Westcott beached the boat behind the auditorium to offer help but there was nothing anyone could do but watch the beautiful building burn to the ground. By late in the afternoon there was nothing left but smoke and embers. As in the case of the Junaluska Inn fire there was neither injury nor loss of life.

The loss of the two major hotels to fire within a period of two years was a severe blow to the Assembly. Following the Junaluska

THE JUNALUSKA CROSS STANDS ON INSPIRA-TION POINT OVERLOOKING THE ASSEMBLY

Inn fire, the Junaluska Hotel Company purchased the incomplete College Inn. They then completed the hotel, later adding an annex to the east side and opened it under a new name, Terrace Hotel. By 1917, James Cannon had completed his ninety room Virginia Lodge, located just west of the Terrace Hotel.[6] In later years, the name of this hotel was changed to Cherokee Inn. Likewise, in 1919 George Stuart built and opened a much larger Epworth Lodge, replacing his original hotel. His new facility was located at the rear of Stuart Circle. These additions aided in replacing the lost bed space and carried the Assembly over until the 1920s when several more such facilities were built.

In November of 1920, the Board of Missions of the Methodist Episcopal Church, South bought the land on which the Junaluska Inn had stood. Their intent was to build a structure to house missionaries who might be back in the United States for their year-long furlough. Construction began and the cornerstone for the Centenary Mission Inn was laid in early 1921. Upon completion of the building, some mission-aries did use the facility but, rooms were also rented to persons attending conferences and other events at the Assembly. The name of the inn was

TOP: THE BOAT HOUSE WAS BUILT BY THE BOARD OF EDUCATION OF THE METHODIST EPISCOPAL CHURCH, SOUTH IN 1918
BOTTOM: ORIGINALLY NAMED THE RELIGIOUS EDUCATION BUILDING, THIS BUILDING WAS LATER NAMED SHACKFORD HALL. SHACKFORD HALL IS ON THE NATIONAL REGISTER OF HISTORIC PLACES

later changed to Lambuth Inn to honor the memory of Bishop Walter Russell Lambuth, a missionary bishop who had been one of the platform speakers at the 1913 Missionary Conference.

In the summer of 1916, Dr. John W. Shackford, superintendent of the Department of Leadership and Teacher Training and the entire General Sunday School Board of the Methodist Episcopal Church, South came to Lake Junaluska. During this meeting, a new type of teacher training school was discussed, along with the plans for its promotion. It was to be a much higher level of training than had been offered in the past. It was

THE FIRST BOOKSTORE, LOCATED WEST OF THE AUDITORIUM

initially called the Standard Training School. It would ultimately evolve into what was later called Laboratory Schools. The first of such schools was set for the summer of 1917 at the Southern Assembly.

On the opening day of the school, John Shackford found himself with a huge problem. The number of participants far exceeded all expectations. Six hundred persons from every area of the church and from Cuba to the Pacific Coast descended on the Assembly for two weeks. These persons were to be taught in small class sizes. There were no classrooms. Classes met in hallways of hotels, on porches, under trees, and anywhere they could gather. Remarkably, the school was a great success.

The plan had been that the school at Junaluska would be held each year as a continuing model for other such enterprises across the church. Obviously, if this were to happen there would have to be classroom space provided. Thus plans for a temporary building began to evolve. Finally, a building was designed that would provide the classroom space and also be usable at other times by the Assembly. Funds for construction were made available by the Sunday School Board. A building containing seven class-rooms, along with a very large meeting/cafeteria room was planned. The

WHITFIELD LODGE AND THE SUNDAY SCHOOL CAFETERIA SERVED THE NEEDS OF THOSE ATTENDING SESSIONS IN SHACKFORD HALL. BOTH WERE DEMOLISHED TO MAKE ROOM FOR NEW STRUCTURES

THE INTERIOR OF THE SUNDAY SCHOOL CAFETERIA

building would have a large hallway from front to back. At the back of the building would be stairs leading down to the lake level and a dock for boarding the Big Boat. And so, in the summer of 1918, the Boat House was opened for the first time. For the next five years, though not really adequate to begin with, the Boat House served to give the Sunday School Board time to plan for better facilities for its expanding leadership education program.

At the General Conference of 1922, a greatly enlarged appropriation for the training program was requested. This amount was needed to fund the construction of a suitable building at the Assembly. Most believed that the General Conference would not be willing to grant all that was asked. But to their surprise, the Conference approved the entire amount. On a summer morning in 1922, John W. Shackford and W. H. Stockham, the superintendent of the Assembly, went for a boat ride. Their main purpose was to discuss the possible location of a new Sunday School Board building. The Board of Education was interested in a site on a ridge at the west end of the lake. This location would overlook both the upper and lower lake. The problem was that this property would be very expensive. Finally, Stockham made an interesting proposal. The Assembly would swap the Sunday School Board the desired site in exchange for the Boat House. They agreed, and within days planning and construction was underway. By the 1923 season, the new Religious Education Building was completed. Later this building was renamed Shackford Hall.[7] This building is now listed on the National Register of Historic Places.

Shortly after the completion of the Religious Education Building, several other structures were built to complete the education area. The Sunday School Cafeteria (which was a dining hall) and the Whitfield Lodge were built. These were both located in the area now occupied by the Jones Dining Hall and the parking lot just east of it. Likewise, the first Mountainview and Sunnyside Lodges were built. Sunnyside Lodge originally was located behind and to the side of the Sunday School Cafeteria. J. B. Ivey built the Lakeside Lodges during 1921–22. These all made it possible for students to come for leadership training and have all their housing and class needs met in the general area of the Christian Education Building.

It was only natural that with the development of an Assembly ground with a beautiful lake in the midst of some of the highest and most majestic mountains east of the Mississippi River that organized camping would soon follow.

The first camp seems to have been one called School Eureka. It began in 1915 and used the Epworth Lodge as its dormitory. It was very classical in its approach to camping; an educational camp offering courses in history, languages (six including Latin and Greek), mathematics, and nature studies. As its brochure states it was "designed for high school and college students who desired advanced standing or to make up deficiencies in special subjects."[8]

One year later, a most unusual relationship began between the Southern Assembly and an exclusive private camp for girls. The Junaluska Camp for Girls was not located on the grounds of the Assembly. Rather, it was located across the road just east of the lake and north of the railroad.[9] Miss Ethel McCoy owned and operated the camp. It had begun in 1912 in another location and moved to the proximity of the Assembly in 1916. While not on the Assembly property, it nevertheless featured the lake and other scenes in its publicity. Likewise, the camp paid a flat rate fee each summer as a gate fee, which would permit anyone related to the camp to have access to the grounds, swim in the lake, and participate in other Assembly activities. The camp also purchased water from the Assembly. This camp lasted for decades until the mid-1950s.

During World War I and the immediate years after, there was a military style camp for boys each summer. The campers dressed in military style uniforms, lived in army style pyramidal tents, participated in parades, and even received rifle instruction using 30 caliber U.S. rifles. The first record of this camp is in 1917 and it continued through 1924.[10]

In the early twenties, the commissioners attempted to transfer ownership of the Assembly to the Methodist Episcopal Church, South. In a letter sent in 1921 to all stockholders by J. Dale Stenz, the Assembly business manager, the following statement was made:

> *It has become increasingly evident from year to year that, in order for the Southern Assembly to attain unto the highest degree of success and to accomplish the purpose for which it was established, it must be recognized as belonging to the church . . .*[11]

The intent of this letter was to encourage stockholders to transfer their stock to the Board of Commissioners, who then would transfer ownership of the Assembly to the General Conference of the Methodist Episcopal Church, South at the 1922 General Conference. If it proved not practical for some of the stockholders, the stock could then be exchanged for lots at the Assembly. A form was enclosed for the stockholder to fill out indicating which of the above options he would choose.

This appears to be the first attempt to give the Assembly to the church. In a later communication with the General Conference, it was noted attempts to secure all of the stockholders cooperation had failed and it would be four more years before this might be accomplished. This report concludes by stating,

> . . . *The Commissioners of the Southern Assembly herewith request the General Conference to authorize the Board of Lay Activities to accept control of the Southern Assembly Corporation whenever the Commission of the Southern Assembly may have made the conditions of transfer satisfactory to the Board of Lay Activities.*

The Missionary Movement indicated concurrence provided "that the Board of Lay Activities be instructed not to accept the property unless it be free from debt."[12]

This requirement that the Assembly be free of debt before any agency of the General Conference would accept ownership would become the obstacle preventing transfer of ownership for decades.

The decade of the twenties was one of achievement and failure, progress and loss. Crowds in growing numbers continued to come to conferences and other events. Several of the more visible and notable structures were built. Even as this progress took place, the Assembly continued to slide ever deeper into the morass of debt.

On July 10, 1922, The Federation of Wesley Bible Classes of the Western North Carolina Conference, under the leadership of its president J. R. Pepper, presented a lighted cross which was placed on Inspiration Point overlooking the lake. Following the dedication service, the lights were turned on for the first time. According to an oft repeated and printed story when the lights were turned off in the fall, the commissioners received a letter from crews on the Southern Railway requesting that the lights be turned back on. In their letter they indicated that, as they passed the lake in the dark of night the cross reminded them of their duty and the One who watched over them. The Board granted their request and the lights remained on each night year round.[13]

Mr. and Mrs. T. L. McClees were familiar faces around the Assembly. They would have greeted persons checking into Epworth Lodge and later at the Auditorium Hotel. Still, later visitors staying at the new Colonial Hotel would have been welcomed by these gracious hosts. At different times, they managed all three hotels. After the Auditorium Hotel burned in 1920, they built a new hotel just under Inspiration Point. It opened in 1922 and was named Colonial Hotel. Its long porch facing up the lake was a choice place to gather after dinner to watch the sun set behind the mountains. The McCleeses continued to operate the hotel until 1954. The Assembly gained ownership of the hotel in 1971.[14] It was then extensively remodeled and upgraded. The purchases and improvements were funded by a series of gifts given by Mr. and Mrs. George Finch. All told, the Finches gave more than one hundred forty thousand dollars as an endowment to be used for purchase, improvement, and maintenance. The hotel became a favorite of many of the regular visitors to the Assembly. In 1989, it ceased operations and since has been used for housing for the summer staff.

In 1922, as reported earlier, J. B. Ivey built the Lakeside Lodges. There were two units, one behind the other and connected by a center section. This facility, along with others constructed by the General Sunday School Board, provided accommodations for persons attending the Leadership School classes held in the Christian Education Building, which would be completed the next year.

In late November of 1923, Bishop Atkins was in Little Rock, Arkansas to preside over the meeting of the Little Rock Annual Conference. On Sunday, December 2, he concluded the conference in the traditional Methodist manner by reading the appointments of ministers for the next year. The next day he relaxed with a friend. That evening after retiring he suffered a stroke. He lingered for two days and died on Wednesday, December 5th. His funeral was held in Waynesville, North Carolina on Friday, December 7th. Speakers at the service included Bishop Warren Candler, Dr. George R. Stuart, and John R. Pepper, among others.[15]

On May 11, 1926, while at his home in Birmingham where he had been pastor of First Methodist Church for eleven years, George R. Stuart died suddenly of a heart attack. He was sixty-nine years old. He had been in poor health for several months, had undergone a severe operation, and was thought to be recuperating nicely. He was looking forward to continuing his recovery while spending the summer at Lake Junaluska. The impact of his death reverberated through southern Methodism. His biographer, W. W. Pinson, relates it this way:

> *The city of Birmingham went into mourning when he died. When his body lay in the church banked with flowers, crowds flocked to the church to do him honor. The special train that was to carry his body to Cleveland, Tenn. for interment was to leave at 7 AM. At that hour the crowd was so great that the hour of departure was postponed till nine o'clock. Some eighty, including Church officials, accompanied the family on the sad journey. They laid him to rest in Fort Hill Cemetery, near to the home in Cleveland, Tenn., where with his loved ones he had spent so many happy hours.*[16]

His funeral was held at the First Methodist Church in Cleveland, Tennessee.[17]

It was a long road these two had traveled from those early days in that cold, two-room house the two men shared in Morristown, Tennessee. Along the way, both had made their mark on the Methodist Episcopal Church, South. One became highly respected as a Christian educator and later as an episcopal leader in the church. The other was well known as a great preacher, evangelist, and pastor who had ranked with the likes of Sam Jones and Billy Sunday. Their accomplishments through the years were many indeed and the lives they touched for Christ would number in the thousands. Nothing they accomplished, however, could outshine the legacy they left in the mountains of western North Carolina. Although there were many individuals who would be remembered for their contribution to the establishment of Lake Junaluska Assembly, these were the two men who caught the vision, and dreamed the dream when there was nothing and then lived to see it become reality. They were true visionaries whom God used to bring about his Bethel in the South and thus to provide a setting for the transformation and enrichment of unnumbered lives. Their influence will continue for years to come.

In the summer of 1923, Mabel Westcott, daughter of J. T. Westcott who was captain of the boat *Cherokee,* was elected Queen of Junaluska. This marks the beginning of a tradition that would become the high point of the summer for both the summer staff and the summer residents. The election of the queen would become the apex of the social season at the lake. Strict guidelines for the election process would evolve over the years. Ultimately, the rules required that the person had to have at least two years summer attendance at the Assembly. Serious campaigns promoting candidates for queen would follow. Following the election, the queen and her court (made up of the other candidates and their escorts) would participate in a gala coronation. For many years, this was accompanied by a boat parade that involved a long string of decorated boats pulled by the good ship *Cherokee*. Prizes were awarded for the best decorated boat. Westcott was the first queen and started a tradition that continued for fifty-four years.

On November 16, 1923, W. H. Stockham, the second superintendent of the Southern Assembly, died. The natural successor to Stockham was J. Dale Stentz. As noted earlier, Stentz had been first business manager for the Assembly. His hands-on approach to leadership had resulted in a growth both in the realm of physical development of the grounds and facilities and a growing awareness, on the part of the church, of the opportunities for spiritual development it afforded. Having married Mary Stuart, one of the daughters of George R. Stuart, he was well aware of the background out of which the Assembly had emerged. He was also well aware of the struggles (particularly financial) which were continuing. In a report to the commissioners, Stentz called attention to the deteriorating financial picture. There were storm clouds on the horizon.

In 1924, the Board of Trustees made a sixty-foot lot on Lakeshore Drive between the Assembly office and the Boat House available to Lamar and Barton Publishers for the purpose of building a bookstore. A log building with large, open porches was then constructed. This building became the Methodist Publishing House Bookstore and was completed in 1925. It quickly became a popular gathering place at the Assembly.[18]

In 1929, another attempt was made to give the Assembly to the church. In an effort to get around the church rule which stated that it could not accept the property as long as it was in debt, a new approach was suggested. If the Assembly could be deeded to a group of trustees appointed by the annual conferences east of the Mississippi River, they then might hold it in the name of the church until such time as the debt was repaid. The strategy was that if the property was in the name of the church, then it would be tax free. This would mean that the three thousand five hundred dollars per year which went to taxes could be used for debt retirement. The stockholders passed a resolution to this effect on August 14, 1929.[19] There is no record that the annual conferences ever followed through with the plan.

CHAPTER FIVE

The 30s

• • • • • • • • • • • • • • • •

O n a bright summer afternoon in 1931, persons on the grounds of the Assembly heard the unmistakable sound of aircraft engines and when they looked skyward they saw a twin-engine circling over the lake. It bore the insignia of the United States Navy. To their surprise, after circling several times it began to approach the lake as though it were planning to land there. Indeed, it did just that, touching down and finally stopping in the water near Colonial Hotel. It was piloted by the son of J. A. Baylor.[1] This son of one of the original home owners at the lake just wanted to visit his folks! Interestingly, twenty years later another seaplane landed on the lake and almost wound up stuck there. When it attempted to take off, the lake was still and smooth. The surface tension of the water would not allow the plane to take off. The plane taxied in circles to churn up some waves and then was finally able to break free.[2]

That same summer, the Assembly became the focus of wide-spread attention when the cast of the famous *Oberammergau Passion Play* arrived for two performances in Stuart Auditorium. The group had been brought from Germany to the United States for a tour sponsored by the Chautauqua Corporation with whom the Assembly still had a working agreement. The actor who played the Christ in the production was Anton Lang, who later became a noted wood carver in Oberammergau.[3]

From the earliest days, the constant problem which plagued the Southern Assembly was money. To purchase the land and construct the dam, buildings, and the infrastructure required a huge outlay of funds. More than two hundred thousand dollars was spent on construction of the dam, auditorium, and Public Service Building. The engineering and roads cost forty thousand dollars initially.[4] Every conceivable source of revenue was explored. The business community of Waynesville had committed themselves to raise a hundred thousand dollars for the project. Unfortunately, the commissioners actually received approximately sixty thousand dollars. In his autobiography, first superintendent James Cannon wrote, "Had I known what would have been the net value of the Waynesville subscriptions, I would not have agreed to have anything to do with the Southern Assembly."[5] The sale of stock raised considerable amounts, however this represented an obligation on the part of the commissioners to achieve a return on the investment. Additional funds were raised through gate receipts. As one reads the minutes of the commissioners, it becomes obvious that they had to borrow money from any and every source available. Even as early as 1910, there is the record of a loan of ten thousand dollars that was used to purchase land. The next year, there is another reference to a loan of two hundred thousand dollars for expense incurred in what was called the "general plan of work."[6] Dr. Cannon was able to negotiate a loan of one hundred fifty thousand dollars in the form of a bond issue. Later, in an effort to consolidate the indebtedness, a loan was issued by the Mercantile Trust Bank of St Louis in the amount of one hundred thousand dollars. As the end of the decade of the twenties approached, the popularity of the Assembly continued to increase. Unfortunately, so did the debt. In a 1930 brochure written by then superintendent Ralph P. Nollner the average income for the previous three years was $37,779.98. During that same period, the average expenses for the operation of the Assembly was $45,357.35, including taxes and interest. This figure does not include any amount for debt retirement.[7] The total indebtedness was listed as three hundred thousand dollars. The interest on the debt alone amounted to twelve thousand dollars a year. In another effort to link the Assembly more closely with the church, the stockholders also officially changed the name of the Assembly from the Southern Assembly to Lake Junaluska Methodist Assembly in 1929.

The new board continued to struggle with the deteriorating financial crisis. However, none of the relief measures brought any appreciable change in the situation. In June of 1932, the Mercantile Bank called its notes and forced the Assembly into bankruptcy. This could have been the blackest day in the history of the Assembly. The land could have been sold to pay the debts and the Assembly could have ceased to exist as a result of this action. Some have suggested that it would have been as difficult to sell the Assembly as it would be to sell a church building. Others disagree,

A NAVY SEAPLANE LANDED ON THE LAKE DURING THE SUMMER OF 1931

citing the possibility that it might have been used as a privately owned resort. That it did not cease to exist appears to have been providential. To the surprise of many, Jerry Liner was named as the temporary receiver. Liner was well known as the owner and operator of the Junaluska Supply Company, the local general store. One might speculate that it was in the best interest of the Junaluska Supply to have the Assembly continue to function, since a large portion of his customers were residents.

Whatever the case, he was a good choice to be the receiver. His recognition and popularity were widespread. He was an excellent businessman and yet was known as one of the local folks. Interestingly enough, one of his first acts was to open the gates and cease the practice of charging for admission to the grounds. Soon, the fears of an imminent sell of the property began to diminish. It became apparent that the court would make an effort to allow the church to redeem its institution. The summer continued on as usual.

The next year, Mr. James Atkins Jr. was named as permanent receiver. Atkins, the son of Bishop James Atkins, was an attorney in nearby Waynesville. It has been noted that he had great talent in mediation and conciliation and, as such, was a good choice.[8] He was able to achieve the time needed to raise funds and calm creditors. During the period of his leadership, the Assembly was able to move forward with improvements and the programs went on without interference. Those attending the conferences in the summer would have hardly noticed any change. Atkins and others were constantly seeking ways to reduce the debt. One of the most original of these was to plan what was called Vanishing Parties. In 1932, letters were sent to key persons across the church. They would be invited to a Junaluska Party. To begin with, there would be a party to which twelve couples were invited. Each of these would contribute one dollar toward Junaluska debt retirement and also invite others to a similar party. This time, however, only eight couples would be invited. They, in turn, would invite four couples to the next party. Atkins calculated that each of these parties would raise four hundred ninety-two dollars. There is no record that any amount of money was raised in this fashion. In fact, there is no record that the parties were even held!

Although the depression was at its peak, the attendance remained high. Many of the leaders refused to accept honorariums. In 1934, the General Conference continued its support of Junaluska and the Western Methodist Assembly at Mount Sequoyah in Arkansas, with a grant of fifteen thousand dollars.[9] It was a false sense of normalcy, however. The debt was still there and the possibility of further action was lurking just around the corner. For there to be any hope for the Assembly to continue as an instrument of the church, at least one hundred thousand dollars earmarked for debt retirement had to be raised. For several years, the Assembly continued to operate under the guidance of Atkins. Ultimately, the bankruptcy court set August 15, 1936 as the deadline for payment of the debt. On May 1, 1936, the College of Bishops took action. Citing the importance of the Assembly to the church, they passed a resolution which stated that "immediate steps should be taken to liquidate the indebtedness . . ."[10] They proposed a campaign to raise funds and directed that a preacher be selected by the bishops to oversee the effort. As a result of this action, Dr. William A. Lambeth, pastor of Wesley Memorial Church in High Point, North Carolina was chosen to direct the campaign. It was a daunting task, particularly in the early thirties.

The Save Junaluska Campaign, as it came to be known, was a relatively high pressure campaign, although no strict quotas were imposed upon the conferences. Nevertheless, the bishops did suggest formulas for each conference. It was generally understood that the conferences closest to the Assembly would have the responsibility for the largest contributions. As a result, the Western North Carolina Conference was asked to raise an amount equal to nine percent of the pastor's salaries, while the North Carolina Conference would raise an amount equal to six percent. The other conferences east of the Mississippi River were asked to raise an amount equal to three percent. As a result of Lambeth's experience in fundraising and organizational skills, the campaign caught on and enthusiasm ran high. Contributions came from every quarter. Children, youth, and all ages of adults were caught up in the excitement. The *North Carolina Christian Advocate* reported that St. Joseph Afro-Methodist Episcopal Church in Durham contributed twenty dollars while a youth conference at Lander College in South Carolina also sent a contribution.[11] In spite of the far-reaching response, when August arrived there was still not enough funds to cover the debt. On August 13th, Dr. Lambeth announced that only sixty-two thousand dollars had been raised. Time was running out! The issue was still in doubt. In an unusual move, the Mercantile Bank agreed to extend the deadline in order to give Lambeth still additional time to receive funds. Finally, in early September it was announced that the goal had been reached and Junaluska had been saved to the Methodist Episcopal Church, South.

On October 21st, the Mercantile Trust Bank received a check for one hundred thousand dollars, which paid the indebtedness in full. For the first time since its inception, the Assembly was free of debt! Finally, the way was now open for it to become the property of the church. The property was then legally transferred to Bishop E. D. Mouzon, Bishop Paul Kern, and Dr. W. A. Lambeth to hold in trust for the Methodist Episcopal Church, South until the General Conference. The conference convened in 1938, at which time the property would be tendered to the church as a gift.[12]

The General Conference of the Methodist Episcopal Church, South met in Birmingham, Alabama from April 28 to May 5, 1938. On May 2, Dr. Few and Dr. Lambeth reported to the conference that the Assembly was now debt free and offered it to them. The General Conference then passed a resolution accepting the offer providing that the College of Bishops name a Board of Trustees of fifteen members. These persons had to have the confirmation of the General Conference. The resolution further stated that the Assembly property would never again be mortgaged and that the operational and program expenses could not exceed the support funds granted the Assembly by the General Conference for the preceding year. These conditions were met and the Assembly officially became property of the church. The next year, when the Methodist Church was formed by a union of the Methodist Episcopal Church, the Methodist Episcopal Church, South, and the Methodist Protestant Church, the Assembly became a property of the new denomination.[13]

Not everyone was happy about the fundraising efforts to save the Assembly. Nor were they happy with the proposal to unite the three major Methodist bodies. In the November 13th issue of the *Commercial Appeal* newspaper of Memphis, a letter from Mrs. Anne Gertrude Wiley of Greenville, Mississippi was published under the heading, "Lake Junaluska Playground of High-Salaried Officials of the Methodist Episcopal Church, South." The letter was a reply to one written by Bishop John Moore and published in the *Nashville Advocate*. In her letter, Mrs. Wiley stated, "He does casually refer to a $400,000 debt just paid off, but does not mention the many, many thousands paid in the past years on this pet of the Bishops." She goes on to express her disdain for the leaders of the church who were bringing about the merger.[14]

From the earliest days, it had been the intention of the Laymen's Missionary Movement and later of the stockholders and commissioners that the Assembly would be the property of the church. It was always considered to be an adjunct to the ministry of the MEC,S. Many of those who attended conferences and other events assumed that it was the official Assembly ground of the MEC,S and owned by the church. The fact that it was a private corporation and that there were stockholders was rooted in the belief on the part of the founders that this was the best, most practical, and perhaps the only means of raising the capital necessary for the purchase of land and the development of the campus. When the Assembly legally became the property of the church, it was the fulfillment of the vision and the intent of the founders.

Following the acceptance of the Assembly by the General Conference, the required Board of Trustees was named. Those who made up the first board included: E. A. Cole, J. B. Ivey, C. C. Norton, T. B. Stackhouse, Bishop W. W. Peel, Bishop Paul B. Kern, H. A. Dunman, W. S. F. Tatum, L. W. Wells, W. P. Few, W. A. Lambeth, the bishop of the Western North Carolina Conference, and the secretaries of the Boards of Missions, Education, and Lay Activities. One of the first actions of the board was to name W. A. Lambeth as president, superintendent, and treasurer without pay. They also named Mrs. Katherine Ray Atkins as assistant superintendent and treasurer. Mrs. Atkins was daughter-in-law of Bishop James Atkins, having married his youngest son, Hilliard. It is significant that among other positions created, they named Lucius M. Pitts as pastor of the Negro people and director of the Gilbert Center. This was done on the recommendation of Paine College, an African American educational institution.

CHAPTER SIX

The 40s

• • • • • • • • • • • • • • •

T he fact that the board named Lucius M. Pitts, an African American, as pastor of the Negro people and director of the Gilbert Center is significant. This is the first indication of a concern for African Americans in any official action related to the Assembly. Earlier there were hints of concern on the part of Assembly property owners. From the beginning, many families brought their African American servants when they came to spend the summer. Thus, there was a black presence on the grounds. While in most communities the African American population was treated as though they were invisible, it is obvious that this was not the case at the Southern Assembly. One is aware of a concern for these persons who, while they were there in a servant role, nevertheless were God's children and should be nurtured and their spiritual needs provided. Possibly the earliest reference is to be found in a letter written by E. Jane McDonald expressing concern for the Negroes and calling for construction of a Negro center at the Assembly. Unfortunately, this letter has been lost.[1] On a postcard dated October 17, 1939, Rev. H. D. Hart asks, "Has any progress been made on plans for the recreation center for colored people? We want to help with it when it is started."[2] Likewise, in 1939 the Junaluska Board of Education agreed to accept responsibility for the salary of a director for Negro ministry at the Assembly. They specified that this person would be from Paine College in Augusta, Georgia and that the college would choose the individual.

The original location of the ministry was in a small room in one of the Assembly buildings. This proved totally inadequate. In a census in 1943, the number of African Americans on campus was listed as one hundred thirty-three.[3] Probably the number from early days was close to

A EUROPEAN STYLE RAILROAD ENGINE USED IN THE 1955 FILMING OF THE HOLLYWOOD
MOVIE *THE SWAN* IN FRONT OF THE JUNALUSKA DEPOT

one hundred. Immediately, there was a desire to build a separate building for the ministry. Several cottage owners became involved in raising funds for such a facility.

Among the strongest supporters of the ministry and the facility were Mr. and Mrs. J. B. Ivey. In reply to a letter asking about progress on plans for the building, Mrs. Hilliard Atkins reported that the decision had been made to locate the building on a lot, "below the cafeteria."[4] The building was completed in the summer of 1941 and the Negro ministry moved in.

The structure was named for Dr. John Wesley Gilbert, a noted African American educator. Dr. Gilbert had accompanied Bishop Walter Russell Lambuth on a mission trip to Africa. The mission was a joint effort on the part of the Methodist Episcopal Church, South and the Colored Methodist Episcopal Church.

The two men and their team of nearly sixty Americans went to London, on to Belgium, and from there they sailed to Dakar, arriving on October 24, 1911. After a short stop in Dakar, they went up the Congo River and landed in Luebo. They set out further, crossing rivers, swamps, passing through villages, and altogether traveled 750 miles and visited 200 villages. Gilbert provided an

THE GILBERT CENTER WAS BUILT IN 1941 AND WAS LOCATED JUST WEST OF THE
SUNDAY SCHOOL CAFETERIA

important service to Lambuth and their cause, as he translated materials into
French and did some work with several dialects.[5]

As the two departed for Africa, Gilbert is reported to have asked
Lambuth what their relationship would be. Lambuth replied that they
would be as brothers.

The building included a large open, pavilion-type area which was
used for both worship and recreation. For worship purposes the building
could seat approximately two hundred persons. A piano was furnished by
Mrs. F. H. Aldrich. In addition, under the same roof were living quarters
for the minister and a storage room.[6]

In his report on the 1942 ministry, Director of the Gilbert Center Rev.
Louis Lomax gives the schedule of activities: Sunday worship—9:00 AM,
Church School—Tuesdays at 9:00 PM, Recreation on Thursdays at 9:00 PM,
and a music interest group on Friday evenings.[7] The ministry continued
well into the 1950s.

On April 24, 1940, Jerry Liner's Junaluska Supply building was
destroyed by fire. It was a Sunday morning. Around 9:30 someone noticed
smoke coming from a finishing room in the lumber area. Although they
used every fire extinguisher in the building, the fire quickly spread to the

TOP: THE INTERIOR OF THE BEAUTIFUL MEMORIAL CHAPEL
BOTTOM: THE FIRST CHILDREN'S PLAYGROUND WAS LOCATED JUST EAST OF THE AUDITORIUM

main store. The Waynesville Fire Department responded promptly, but the lake was too low (having been drawn down for maintenance) and when they attempted to draw water from Richland Creek the debris clogged up the pumps. A call went out to the Asheville Fire Department but it took forty minutes for them to travel to Junaluska. By that time, the fire had such headway that nothing could be done.[8]

As indicated earlier, the Junaluska Supply was truly the general store for the Assembly. It was built in 1921 and was located just before one turned into the main gate of the Assembly which, at that time, was located at the east end of the lake. The store faced south toward the railroad tracks. Advertisements in several earlier publications note that this was the primary source for groceries, clothing, building materials, hardware, and all manner of other items. It also served as the service station carrying gasoline, kerosene, oil, and repair parts for automobiles.

The loss of the store was a great blow to the summer residents, but not for long. Within three months, Liner had rebuilt it. On Saturday, July 20, 1940 the new nine thousand-square-foot structure opened. At the time of its construction, it was the largest store in North Carolina west of Asheville. This time it faced the lake. The new store offered all that the old one had plus some new features. It had a lunch counter in it. Its basement housed the building supply department. It also contained the Junaluska Post Office at one time. The front of the store was built to reflect the art-deco style which was popular in the thirties and forties. As in the past, it continued to be the supply source for just about all the needs of the summer residents and later those who became year-round residents.

In 1977, the store closed its doors and the building was purchased by the Assembly. It became known as the Liner Building. The lower level was then used for the annual flea market sponsored by the Junaluskans organization. The upper lever housed the year-round clothing outlet sponsored by the Junaluskans and the original home of the Heritage Center, which was the repository for the Southeastern Jurisdictional Commission on Archives and History. It was demolished to make room for the new Lakeview Condominiums.

The outbreak of the war had little effect on the operation of Junaluska Assembly. The program books indicate that most events and activities went on as usual. At one point, Dr. Lambeth was asked by a reporter whether the Assembly would close because of the war. His response, printed in the *Waynesville Mountaineer* was a resounding, "There'll always

A GROUP OF LADIES SURROUNDING ELEANOR ROOSEVELT DURING HER VISIT IN 1944

be a Junaluska," referring to a popular wartime song, "There'll Always Be an England."[9] However, several interesting details hint at difficult times. In the 1943 program book, visitors were cautioned to check with their gasoline ration board to determine if they could secure enough ration coupons for their trip. If not, they were advised to use the train or bus.[10] The 1945 program book is much abbreviated due to continuing wartime restrictions. It is obvious that there were repairs that had to be postponed until the end of the war primarily, one would assume, because of the difficulty in obtaining materials.

In spite of this, in 1942 a partial concrete floor was poured in the auditorium and one hundred thirty-two theater seats were installed. After the war, the project was continued and in 1946, one hundred additional seats were installed.

On July 27, 1944 a headline in the Waynesville paper proclaimed, "Mrs. Roosevelt to Be at Lake Junaluska for Two Talks July 25–26."[11] The coming of the wife of the president of the United States captured the interest of and excited the entire community. She was one of the featured speakers at a jurisdictional meeting of the "Department of Christian Social Relations of the Southeastern Jurisdiction of the

Woman's Society of Christian Service." She was introduced by Mrs. M. T. Tilley of Atlanta, Georgia. She spoke on the subject, "Postwar Problems" to an estimated crowd of three thousand five hundred gathered in Stuart Auditorium. The next morning, she participated in a forum on social action, which was held at Mission Inn. During one of her speeches, she is quoted as having said, "The brotherhood of man has got to be more than a phrase; it's got to be a reality or it is not true."[12] That afternoon, she was given a sight-seeing ride on the big boat, the *Cherokee I.* A photo taken during her cruise shows her sitting on the upper deck flanked by a uniformed police officer. Another photo shows her standing in front of the Junaluska cross with a large group of women. She also gave a speech to the Waynesville Chamber of Commerce.[13]

In June of 1945, J. B. Ivey wrote in the *Junaluska News*:

> *Surveyors were busy recently in surveying the cut off from the road to Waynesville leaving the highway above the Junaluska railroad station and cutting across the golf course to the Soco Gap road. This will shorten the road to Cherokee Reservation and the entrance to Smoky Mountain National Park by twenty-five miles. This road by Soco Gap is already well graded from Soco Gap to Cherokee, and will be paved as soon as road building is given the green light.*[14]

For many, this was the confirmation of rumors that had made the rounds of the Junaluska community for several years. Prior to the outbreak of war in 1941, the North Carolina State Highway and Public Works Commission had done preliminary studies for a new stretch of highway that would cut the distance from Asheville to Cherokee. It was to be known as the Waynesville By-pass. The outbreak of hostilities put the project on hold. After the war had ended, the project was revived. The new highway would leave the old Asheville highway at about the area known as Tuscola, cut through the western end of the Assembly, and connect with the highway from Waynesville to Soco Gap at an area known as Dellwood. The news of this new road met with enthusiasm on the part of the Assembly leadership, as well as most cottage owners. J. W. Fowler, then superintendent of the Assembly, stated in a letter to Dr. J. Q. Schisler, executive secretary of the Board of Education of the Methodist Church, "We have had nothing happen to us in recent years comparable

THE ORIGINAL MAIN ENTRANCE TO THE ASSEMBLY AT THE EAST END OF THE LAKE

to this and I am confident it will send through these grounds as many as twenty-five thousand tourist cars each year."[15]

In return for the easement through the Assembly grounds, the state highway department agreed to pave the Assembly road from the Terrace Hotel to the point where it intersected the new highway.[16] A new gate would be located there. Upon completion, the new highway had the effect of turning the Assembly campus around. What had been the rear of the grounds was now the front. The playground, most youth activities, the Gilbert Center, and other facilities deemed noisy were located at what had been the back. This gate served as the west entrance until 1977 when the present main gate was constructed.

In 1947, after years of negotiation, the Assembly purchased land on the south side of the lake which belonged to Florida Southern College. The area included some forty lots. The trustees agreed to pay the college seven thousand five hundred dollars for the land. Today, this includes the area between Harmon and Harrell Drives.[17] A year earlier, a group of ministers from the Holston Conference had purchased the original trailer camp at the west end of the lake and began to develop what they named Holston Village.

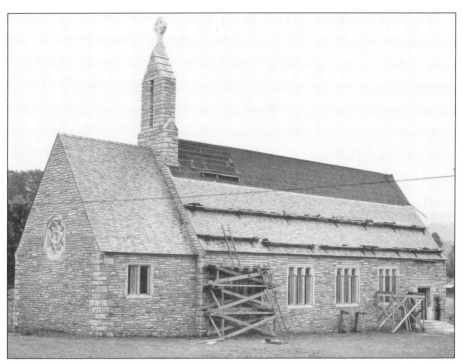

TOP: THE MEMORIAL CHAPEL UNDER CONSTRUCTION, CIRCA 1947
BOTTOM: THE MEMORIAL CHAPEL. THE BUILDING WAS COMPLETED IN 1949 TO HONOR THE
MEMORY OF METHODISTS WHO SERVED IN WORLD WAR II

By 1948, travel by railroad was diminishing fast. Automobiles that were using improved post-war highways and the continued growth of air travel were replacing the train as the preferred mode of travel. The Southern Railroad announced that service from Asheville to Murphy, the Murphy Branch, would be discontinued. On July 13, the last passenger train departed from the Junaluska Depot and the days of excitement at the Junaluska Depot came to an end.

The end of passenger service marked the end of an era. For more than thirty years, the depot was a gathering place for both visitors and summer residents. Newspapers were available at the station having been dropped off the trains. A telegraph office was located there. Various groups would meet there. It was the custom of summer residents to move their pot plants to the station for care during the winter. The next spring they would pick them up when they arrived for the summer.

The station would continue to operate as a freight depot for more than a decade. Finally, even this ended. It was during this period that the depot became a movie star. It was used in 1955 in a scene filmed for the movie *The Swan*. Portions of the movie—which featured Grace Kelly, Alec Guinness, Louis Jourdan, and Agnes Morehead—were filmed at the station that had been temporarily transformed to resemble a mountain railroad station in a Bavarian region of the Alps. The *Waynesville Mountaineer* reported that an old 1880 locomotive was moved to the Assembly from Baltimore, Maryland and used in the scene.[18]

An article printed in the *Waynesville Mountaineer* in 1943 was headlined "Cottage Owners Raise $25,000 for Proposed Chapel."[19] It reflected a suggestion by Dr. Elmer T. Clark, then president of the Junaluska Cottage Owners Association, that the organization spearhead an effort to raise funds for a chapel to honor those Methodists who had served in the armed forces. The group embraced the idea and took it to the Board of Trustees. The Board named a chapel committee made up of Bishop Paul B. Kern, Dr. Clark, Dr. F. S. Love (who had recently been named as the new superintendent of the Assembly), Bishop Costen J. Harrell, and Mr. Edwin Jones.

A design was agreed upon which called for a chapel that would be of English Gothic architecture. It would be made of local granite and would have a Celtic cross atop a granite turret. Early estimates called for the structure to cost approximately one hundred thousand dollars, including its stained glass windows. In an effort to raise the necessary funds for construction, local churches of the jurisdiction were asked to send in the names of those members who served in the armed forces. These names would be placed in a Book of Memory that, in turn, would be placed in a separate structure to be called the Room of Memory. They were also asked to contribute one dollar for each name submitted. More than ninety thousand names were received. If the churches had followed through with the request, the funding would have been assured. However, the income fell far short of the amount needed. Others, however, sent names without funds.

In a letter sent to F. S. Love, Elmer Clark said,

I have today sent Jerry Liner the following telegram:

"Suggest you proceed to stake off the chapel. Put rock on ground and lay foundation with understanding we can stop if committee so decides October twenty-third. Members contacted all agree but no meeting has been held. Consult Love."[20]

Construction then began. Both the funding and construction had to overcome many hurdles in the next several years. These are well-documented, along with a beautiful interpretation of the symbolism of

THE CURRENT PLAYGROUND IS AT THE WEST END OF THE LAKE AND IS PART OF THE WILSON CHILDREN'S COMPLEX

the structure both inside and out in a well-written book by Charles W. Brockwell Jr. Unfortunately, the book is now out of print although occasionally used copies become available.[21]

After a great deal of frustration, the chapel was finally completed and opened on the Fourth of July 1949. Bishop Paul Kern presented the building to the Board of Trustees on August 4th. Admiral William N. Thomas, retired chief of chaplains for the United Stated Navy, a resident of Junaluska, and a member of the Board of Trustees, was named as the first dean of the chapel.

The Room of Memory was not completed until 1951. At that time, the Book of Memory was placed in the room. Since its opening, other items have been placed there, including a portrait of Admiral Thomas and a photograph of the Keesler Air Force Base Male Chorus that sang at the formal opening. A photograph of Glen Draper who was, at that time, the director of the chorus and later became the music director for the Assembly is displayed as well.

On May 23, 1952 Elmer Clark wrote Edwin Jones, then the chairman of the Board of Trustees of the Assembly a letter in which he stated:

> I have the original painting by Howard Chandler Christy of "The Great Commission." . . . I have thought of placing it in the Memorial Room of the Chapel, where it would attract thousands of visitors. . . . There is a space in the Memorial Room for it, and there probably should be something of deep spiritual significance there in addition to the book of names.[22]

Howard Chandler Christy was a highly respected painter of note. His painting entitled *The Signing of the Constitution* hangs in the rotunda of the United States Capitol in Washington.

The *Great Commission* was then hung in the Room of Memory where it remained until 2006 when it became apparent that it was deteriorating due to lack of climate control in the building. There were also security concerns as it was determined that the painting was extremely valuable. It now hangs in the main lobby of the Terrace Hotel.

To this day, Memorial Chapel remains a place of meditation and worship. It is used for communion services each Sunday in the summer as well as other worship experiences. Occasionally concerts and funerals are held there. It is most popular as a wedding chapel. Many visit the Room of Memory each year and find the names of family members who served during World War II.

In 1954, Airman First Class Glenn Draper was originator and director of the Keesler Male Chorus, made up of airman stationed at Keesler Air Force Base in Biloxi, Mississippi. The group had received national recognition for their presentation of Handel's *Messiah*, which was broadcast on NBC. After hearing the group, Major General Charles I. Carpenter, chief of Air Force Chaplains, informed Draper that in July he was going to dedicate a little chapel in North Carolina and wanted him to bring his singers to sing at the service. He would even send two planes to fly them up there. Thus it was that Glenn Draper came to Lake Junaluska for the first time. When General Carpenter informed Draper that the Keesler Air Force Base Male Chorus was to sing for the dedication of the Memorial Chapel at Lake Junaluska Assembly, Draper could have hardly known that this performance would affect the rest of his life.[23]

On July 4, 1954 the chapel was dedicated. During the service of dedication, the chapel was given the official name The Memorial Chapel of the Methodist Church. Dean Thomas presided over the service. Also participating in the service were Bishop Costen J. Harrell, Dr. Elmer Clark, and Major General Charles I. Carpenter. Music for the service was provided by the Keesler Air Force Base Male Chorus under the direction of Sergeant Glenn Draper.[24] The following year the chorus was invited to return to the Assembly for the celebration of the Fourth of July.

In the meantime, in May of 1955 shortly before his discharge from the Air Force, Draper had a life changing experience. It came in the form of a dream. In this dream, he saw himself as a old man who had become extremely successful. He saw himself with a large house and two cars. When he wondered how he had become so successful, God told him that it was because he had left God out of his life. He remembered his commitment as a young boy and prayed that God would forgive him and take over the direction of his life. He asked God to open doors and promised that if he did, he would walk through them.[25]

Draper did, in fact, bring the Male Chorus that summer and, after the Sunday morning worship service, Dr. J. W. Fowler approached him and indicated that he felt led to offer him the position of music director for the Assembly. Draper replied that he would consider it. A short time later, remembering his dream and seeing this offer as one of those open doors, he sent Fowler a telegram in which he stated, "Am definitely interested in accepting your offer. A letter is on the way."[26] A subsequent article in the 1956 edition of the *Junaluska News* was headlined "Glenn Draper is New Minister of Music at Lake."[27]

ONE OF THE EARLY SINGING GROUPS AT THE ASSEMBLY

In Draper's early years at the Assembly, the choir for worship services was made up of volunteers. The first musical group led by Draper was a quartet in 1956. For several years, quartets were the official singing group of the Assembly. When needed, he would recruit additional singers from those at the lake. When the singers produced their first album entitled *Hallelujah, Amen* in 1966, Glen even recruited a few extra singers.

Later, Dr. Manning Potts, then superintendent, approached Draper with the idea of establishing an artist series. His desire was to include vocal and instrumental soloists in concert. While the seeming return to the Chautauqua format seemed appealing, it was not well received and attendance was disappointing. Draper suggested at the end of the season that if the funding for the series could be used to hire exceptional singers and they sang, music people would like it and it would be a success. This was done and the Junaluska Singers was formed. The results in the next year were that the auditorium was filled and the response was enthusiastic. The Junaluska Singers became an ongoing feature of the summer season and continues to this day. Their contribution to the worship experiences and their concerts are extremely popular. Their 4th of July concerts, along with concerts in the fall and at Christmas, have become traditional. They have produced many records, tapes, and CDs. Draper remained music director of the Assembly and the Junaluska Singers for fifty-five years.

In 1944, Edwin L. Jones became a trustee and in 1948, he became chairman of the Board of Trustees of the Assembly. Jones was the owner and president of J. L. Jones Construction Company of Charlotte, North Carolina. His company was one of the outstanding construction firms of the Southeast. Among their projects had been several of the United States consulates in foreign countries. He was a lifelong Methodist and was a dedicated supporter of Junaluska. With his expertise and resources in the construction field, he was responsible for a great deal of physical improvement of the buildings during his twenty years as chair. It was reported that during Jones's tenure as chairman of the trustees, the capital assets of the Assembly increased from one-half million dollars to more than two million.[28] It is said of Jones that many of the promissory notes that funded construction of buildings during this period had but one signature on them, that of Edwin L. Jones.

Jones was a strong-willed individual who left no doubt who was in charge of the trustees. His forceful leadership led to many improvements at the Assembly. But he was also a formidable person to differ with. Compromise was not one of his strong suits. This trait led to several periods of conflict where controversial issues were concerned as we shall see later.

THE JUNALUSKA SINGERS IN THE MID-70S

At the General Conference of the Methodist Church held in Boston in 1948, the ownership of the Lake Junaluska Methodist Assembly was transferred to the Southeastern Jurisdiction. At this point in the life of the Assembly, it primarily served those who lived in the southeastern portion of the United States. There were other assemblies, camps, and conference centers that were used by other areas of the church. It was felt that it was inappropriate for the general church to support this one while it did not support the others. The actual wording of the legislation reads:

> [the General Conference] transfer(s) all rights, titles, and interest in and to the Lake Junaluska Assembly, Inc., including the right of confirmation of its Trustees, to the Southeastern Jurisdictional Conference, together with all privileges, functions, powers, discretions, and authority incident or appertaining thereto as fully as the General Conference has the right and power to transfer the same.[29]

Thus, the Assembly became the property of and an agency of the jurisdiction and remains so to this day.

The transfer of the ownership to the jurisdiction ushered in a new era of strength and growth for the Assembly. When the Jurisdictional Conference of 1948 convened in Township Auditorium at Columbia, South Carolina on July 30th, one of the major agenda items was the acceptance of Lake Junaluska Methodist Assembly and matters related to its operation. Ownership of the Centenary Mission Inn was transferred to the Board of Missions of the jurisdiction. A new and expanded Board of Trustees was approved. Whereas the Assembly, in the past, had been given four thousand dollars by the General Conference, that appropriation was now increased to twenty-five thousand dollars. More significantly, the conference authorized a capital funds campaign which would be called the Greater Junaluska Campaign. The results of that effort are very evident, even decades later.[30]

CHAPTER SEVEN

The 50s

• • • • • • • • • • • • •

The Greater Junaluska Campaign that was called for by the Jurisdictional Conference began to take shape in the months that followed the conference. The conference had named Luther W. Wells to head the effort. The bishops of the Southeastern Jurisdiction were solidly behind the development of the Assembly. At a meeting held at Buck Hill Falls, Pennsylvania in December of 1949, they proposed a plan of action which called for heavy involvement of the bishops and their cabinets. The goal for the campaign was set at six hundred thousand dollars, half of which would come through the local churches. Likewise, the district superintendents were instructed to set up dinner meetings at which pledges would be received. Each district was given an apportioned amount, which was arrived at by the bishop and cabinet. The campaign was to be completed by the end of 1951. It was an intensive effort and it exceeded its six hundred thousand dollar goal.[1]

The funds received were put to good use. Among the projects it funded were the construction of the Junaluska Apartments, the painting and renovation of the Terrace Hotel, the completion of flooring and seating in the auditorium, the Room of Memory at the Memorial Chapel, and the rebuilding of the bridge over the dam.

The Greater Junaluska Campaign ushered in a decade of building and improvements on the grounds of the Assembly. The western end of the Assembly was greatly changed during the fifties. Mountainview and Sunnyside Lodges were replaced. The name Sunnyside was given to a new structure located beside Mountainview rather than in its old location. When the old structures were demolished, the material from them was used to construct several new cottages on Liberty Road.

TOP: THE PRESENT TERRACE HOTEL, ON LAKESHORE DRIVE, WAS COMPLETED IN 1977 AND
REPLACED AN EARLIER STRUCTURE BY THE SAME NAME
BOTTOM: THE PRESENT TERRACE HOTEL AT TOP, THE HARRELL CENTER BELOW, AND THE
GEORGE R. STUART AUDITORIUM ON THE RIGHT

In his report to the Board of Trustees on July 18, 1951, H. G. Allen wrote:

*All of you know that the Assembly does not have an adequate Administration
Building. We work under great handicaps, especially during the winter. The
Administration Building should include not only office space, but a ladies
parlor, real estate room and space large enough for the Jurisdictional Historical
Collection, and, also, Dr. Elmer Clark's library, which he has generously offered
to donate to the Assembly.*[2]

There could be no doubt that a new such building was in order. The
original Administration Building, located between the auditorium and
the log bookstore, had been built in the first decade of the Assembly's life
and was woefully inadequate. The board looked favorably on Allen's
suggestion and at its next meeting held on November 15th, it was
announced that the planning for the building was complete and that
construction had begun. The hope was that it would be completed by the
following June when the season opened.

Not only did this happen, but the *Junaluska News,* in its 1952 edition,
stated: "Dr. Allen reported at the close of the season that . . . the new
Administration Building, costing $30,000 was paid for."[3]

At the west end of the lake, a new dining facility replaced the old
Sunday School Cafeteria. On August 16, 1958, in a meeting of the
Buildings and Grounds Committee, Chairman W. Hugh Massey proposed
that the new cafeteria be named the Edwin L. Jones Dining Hall, and that
a suitable plaque be placed in the building "as a tribute to the splendid
leadership and great contributions of Mr. Jones to this and other Assembly
improvements."[4] The proposal was well received and so ordered.

In 1953, after many years of planning, construction began on a children's
ministry building for the Assembly. Located at the west end of the lake, it
became an addition to the other buildings that are dedicated to the ministry
of Christian education. There was a need for a building that would be
designed to meet the needs of children and the leaders of children, both in
the local church and those who were on the grounds of the Assembly. One
of the foremost advocates of the construction of such a facility was Dr. Carl
King, who worked untiringly on the project. King was the executive secretary of the Western North Carolina Conference Board of Education. The
building was named for Minnie E. Kennedy and Mary E. Skinner, both of
whom were directors of Children's Work for the General Board of

FROM LEFT: J. W. FOWLER, ASSEMBLY SUPERINTENDENT, RICHARD NIXON, VICE PRESIDENT, BILLY GRAHAM, AND EDWIN JONES, CHAIR OF ASSEMBLY BOARD OF TRUSTEES

Education of the Methodist Church. On July 3, 1953, the building was formally opened. Dr. King presided and tributes to Miss Kennedy and Miss Skinner were presented by Dr. Harry Denman and Dr. J. Q. Schisler.[5]

The following year, the building, now debt free, was dedicated on August 8. The invocation was given by Bishop Costen J. Harrell and the dedicatory address was given by Bishop Clare Purcell.[6] The building included the J. B. Ivey Playground, which had been moved from the area east of the auditorium.

In the ensuing years, several enhancements were made to the area, including the Sue and Mary Dizer Nursery wing in 1963 and additional classrooms in 1968. The later addition was named for Dr. Carl King, who died in 1966. It then became the Kennedy-Skinner-King Children's Building. In 2004, the entire complex was enlarged and enhanced, following a gift by the family of Earl Wilson, chairman of the Junaluska Board of Trustees during the 1980s. The entire J. B. Ivey Playground complex is known as the Earl and Martha Wilson Children's Complex.

The matter of guest rooms at the Assembly continued to be a problem. The old Cherokee Inn was now gone. Terrace was the largest hotel with Lambuth as the newest. In a letter written to Superintendent Fowler in October of 1953, Edwin Jones wrote:

TOP AND BOTTOM: J. B. IVEY, FOUNDER OF IVEY DEPARTMENT STORES IN NC AND AN
EARLY SUMMER RESIDENT OF THE ASSEMBLY ENTERTAINING CHILDREN WITH MAGIC

TOP: THE CENTER PORTION OF THE LAMBUTH INN WAS BUILT IN 1921 AND IS LISTED ON THE NATIONAL REGISTER OF HISTORIC SITES
BOTTOM: THE PRESENT LAMBUTH INN WELCOMES GUESTS WITH AN ELEGANCE OF EARLIER DAYS. THE INN IS ON THE NATIONAL REGISTER OF HISTORIC PLACES

The largest item in our development program from the very beginning was a hotel or an addition to one of the present hotels. We finally agreed that we could build 40 or 50 more rooms to Lambuth Inn, fireproof, each with private bath and each as modern as they can be and have deluxe accommodations. The theory was that Lambuth Inn had enough public spaces, lobby, dining room kitchen, etc. and all the money would be spent for hotel rooms except on the ground floor where we would have more class rooms that are badly needed. The Trustees are very anxious to get this addition built to Lambuth Inn.[7]

The Board had approved the construction of a wing on the west side of Lambuth, plans were accepted and work was begun. Construction continued throughout 1954–55 and the new addition was ready for the 1956 season. An article in the *Junaluska News* in early 1956 stated:

A beautifully designed addition is being erected at Lambuth Inn providing forty-four new rooms with private baths and wall-to-wall carpeting. . . . The building is of fire-proof construction having an exterior of light colored brick and it blends architecturally with the original building. The artists have suggested that the original building be painted the same color as the brick in the new section with white trimming.[8]

Among the construction projects of the fifties, that were also funded by the Greater Junaluska Campaign, were the Administration Building, the Paul Kern Youth Center, the west wing of the Lambuth Inn, new Mountainview and Sunnyside Lodges, the Edwin Jones Dining Hall, and a new swimming pool,

In May of 1953, Art O'Neil, a junior at Millsaps College in Jackson, Mississippi, received an air-mail letter which was totally unexpected and not welcomed. The letter, written by H. G. Allen, began,

I am sorry to have to report to you that the County Health Authorities have prohibited swimming in our Lake for the present. This is due to the fact that now, as it has been in the past, the sewer from Waynesville and Hazelwood has been flowing in our Lake and the bacteriologist's reports show it polluted beyond passing health requirements.

We have been authorized by the Executive Committee of the Board of Trustees to bring suit against Waynesville and Hazelwood for damages and also force them to remedy the situation.

The letter went on to state that, as a result of the action of the Health Department, lifeguards would not be needed for the 1954 summer season.[9] Similar letters were sent to several other young men who had been chosen as lifeguards for the 1954 season. O'Neil served the Assembly that summer as director of Religious Activities and Recreation earlier in the year.[10] As such, he was responsible for all matters related to the waterfront. For the 1953 season, persons at the Assembly were bussed to Canton, North Carolina to swim at the YMCA.

The problem of sewage entering Richland Creek, which flowed into Lake Junaluska, had been known for some time. Efforts to work with the two municipalities involved had failed to result in any solution to the problem. Finally, in 1953 the Haywood County Health Department closed the lake to swimming. At a called meeting of the Board of Trustees on August 1, 1953, Edwin Jones announced to the group that the lake had been closed to swimming by the Health Department for sanitary reasons.[11] Lake Junaluska was (and still is) the largest body of water in Haywood County. There are no natural lakes in the county. The concept of swimming in the cool waters of a mountain lake was a great drawing card from the very beginning of the Assembly. Thus, the closure of the lake was a huge blow. Several attempts at compromise with the Health Department failed. Likewise, a proposal to wall off a portion of the lake and chlorinate the impounded water was rejected as impractical and too expensive. The only solution was to build a swimming pool.

After a long process of study and consultation, a new pool was constructed in time for the 1954 season. The pool extended out into the lake at the location of the old swimming area. By building it in this location, the bath house which was built in 1946 could continue to be used. The design of the pool was such that the water level in the pool was the same as the water level of the lake. This gave a casual onlooker the impression that swimmers were still swimming in the lake. Unfortunately, because of water pressure, the lake would have to be lowered each time the pool was emptied for maintenance.

O'Neil was typical of the youth that worked for the Assembly during the summer season. The summer staffers were from the entire Southeast. They would arrive as soon as possible after summer vacation began. Their pay was low and after their expenses, they did well to break even. But they also had a very special summer experience. They were truly jacks of all trades. In a letter to his parents, O'Neil wrote:

I am in charge of recreation for the Lake and am in charge of Sunday School and MYF for young people. I am responsible for repairing the negro place of worship (Gilbert Center) and organizing them into a Sunday school and church. I have to work up and mimeograph the bulletins on Sunday and be in charge of ushers and collection on Sunday. I also publish a recreation Bulletin each week. I am in the midst of raising $250 in donations for fire works for our 4th of July show. I really have been busy.[12]

Busy indeed! In his role as director of recreation, O'Neil also had responsibility for the operation of the Big Boat, a new boat just completed the year before. The original *Cherokee*, built in 1915, served well, but after more than thirty years of service had deteriorated greatly. By the late forties, it leaked profusely and had many other mechanical problems. There was still a need for a large boat, although railroad passenger service had ceased in 1948. In 1951, inquiries were made to several commercial boat building companies concerning the possibility of their building a boat. Finally, the decision was made to allow Ben Sloan, the son of the builder of the original boat, to build its successor. The new boat was built in a specially constructed shed on the south side of the lake. The boat would be the largest boat built inland in the state.[13]

By the summer of 1951, the boat was completed and, as a part of the Independence Day festivities, it was launched on July 4th. Queen Barbara Russell presided over the event. Linda Sloan, the daughter of the builder, christened the boat with water from the River Jordan and proclaimed it the *Cherokee II*. The keynote speaker for the christening was Admiral Thomas.[14]

In a letter to Mrs. T. W. Aldred dated August 19, 1950, H. G. Allen, Assembly superintendent, wrote: "We have for some time had a tentative engagement with Billy Frank Graham for a series of services at Junaluska, however a meeting in the far west was going to absorb his time and he will not be here."[15]

This letter obviously is in answer to a request on the part of Mrs. Aldred and refers to the famous Los Angeles Crusade which is credited with launching Graham as a national figure in evangelical circles. In future years, Graham would preach at the Assembly on at least six different occasions.

On August 19, 1952 he preached in Stuart Auditorium at the evening service. During his visit, he was informed of the need for replacing the roof. He asked for a special offering during the service for this purpose.

The superintendent later wrote to Graham, in which he thanked him for his visit and message. He also added, "The offering for covering the roof of the auditorium amounted to more than eight hundred dollars. We appreciate very much your willingness to help us with this cause."[16]

He returned in 1955 to appear on the platform with Vice President Richard Nixon. He introduced Nixon. The appearance of Nixon generated great excitement among not only the Junaluska community, but the entire western North Carolina area. The auditorium was filled with an overflow crowd. Nixon, Graham, the Assembly Board of Trustees, and other dignitaries were entertained with a dinner held that evening at Lambuth Inn.[17]

Graham shared the pulpit with William Sangster, a famed British clergyman, during the Candler Camp Meeting in August of 1956. His first sermon was on August 10.

Dr. Graham returned to preach in Stuart Auditorium on July 7, 1963. In a letter to James W. Fowler dated October 3, 1962 from W. G. Haymaker, special assistant to Dr. Billy Graham, he wrote "... we are definitely placing Sunday evening, July 7, 1963 on his schedule and we have every reason to believe this will stay put."[18]

On August 8, 1963, a special service was held to honor Dr. Harry Denman, long-time head of the General Board of Evangelism of the Methodist Church. Billy Graham was invited to appear. To his surprise, it was also a service to honor him. Citations by the Board of Trustees were presented to both Denman and Graham at that time. The citation for Graham read, in part:

"The Board of Trustees of the Lake Junaluska Methodist Assembly honors and congratulates Dr. Billy Graham for his notable service in extending the Kingdom of God through evangelism in many nations and for his Christian character and personality ..."[19]

In the light of the above, it would appear that Dr. Billy Graham preached at Lake Junaluska Assembly on six occasions. He was well received on each occasion.

The same could not be said for Dr. Nels F. S. Ferre. His inclusion in the leadership for the Candler Camp Meeting in 1955 as leader of the Bible Study resulted in a firestorm of protest. Ferre, a native of Sweden, was a noted theologian, a graduate of Boston University, Andover Newton Theological Seminary, and Harvard, and the author of several theological books. He was a very popular speaker and had earlier spoken to a Methodist Women's group at the Assembly. The printed brochure for the 1955 Candler Camp Meeting described him in these words: "Dr. Ferre . . . is at his best in this field. New insights and rare inspiration await you at this hour each morning. Recently *Newsweek* included Dr. Ferre in the list of the ten greatest preachers in America."[20] However, in 1953 he had written a book entitled *The Sun and the Umbrella*. In this book, he raised questions concerning the divinity of Jesus. When the publicity for the 1955 Candler Camp Meeting was circulated, there was an immediate reaction by many persons who felt that his theology was not in keeping with Methodist beliefs. The Assembly trustees received letters from both the grassroots of southern Methodists and also the leadership of the church.

In a letter to Edwin Jones, J. A. Baldwin said, "Unless you write me soon that he has been taken off the program, I will get out 1000 letters immediately to the other speakers on the program, the Board of Directors of Junaluska, newspapers, preachers and laymen, telling them the real situation."[21]

Jones feared that this kind of reaction would result in loss of giving on the part of some of the strongest supporters of the Assembly. On the other hand, there were those who strongly supported the invitation. Jane McDonald, in a letter to Jones written on August 17, 1955, eloquently stated her opposition to the action of the trustees and pled for academic freedom which would allow Ferre to speak.[22] Jones named an ad hoc committee to deal with the matter. The group met and decided that Ferre would not be allowed to speak. Later, on July 10, this was reported to the board. The minutes of that meeting read:

Dr. Nels Ferre had been secured to lead the Bible Conference, but because of so much opposition, a special group of the Executive Committee has asked that this phase of the program be cancelled and Dr. Denman has done so. . . . Dr. [E. H.] Blackard insisted that whatever action was taken be done in a diplomatic way; and Henry Gamling insisted that we take a definite stand and without apology. . . . The vote was taken by raised hands and was unanimously adopted.

Dr. Elmer Clark insisted that the blame for securing the man not be put on the program committee. Neither should this committee be blamed for the cancellation. . . . Dr. George E. Clary, (Executive Secretary of the Southeastern Jurisdictional Council), defended Dr. Ferre, stating that he had spoken before several other Methodist groups including the Woman's Society of Christian Service; and that he made a mistake in asking him to come. . . . President Jones expressed his joy and thrill that the Board has taken a definite stand and that our Bishops have led us wisely and spiritually.[23]

When the matter came before the annual meeting of the board, there was a great deal of discussion. Minutes from the meeting held July 30, 1955 record:

It was pointed out that Dr. Ferre is a Congregational Minister and that many of his writings show that he at least leans toward Unitarianism. The passage read by Bishop (Costen J.) Harrell was from "The Christian Understanding of God" and related to Dr. Ferre's treatment of the deity of and also the virgin birth of Jesus Christ.[24]

A lengthy discussion followed and the board voted to uphold the action of the Executive Committee. At that time, Bishop Harrell suggested that it was not he who initiated the action to withdraw the invitation. Likewise, the program committee should not be blamed. Dr. Clary defended Dr. Ferre, saying that he had spoken previously to several Methodist groups. Mrs. E. U. Robinson declared that Dr. Ferre had spoken to the WSCS at the Assembly earlier and everything was of the highest order.

Following this action, Bishop Marvin Franklin of the Mississippi Conference wrote to Edwin Jones commending him for their action. He wrote, in part, ". . . I just want you to know that I appreciate your high ideals and your fine leadership."[25]

The *Nashville Banner* reported the action of the board in an article along with several other newspapers. Their treatment of the issue fueled further controversy.

In an effort to ameliorate the situation, it was decided that the Assembly would send Dr. Ferre his honorarium check, along with a letter withdrawing the invitation. Upon receipt of the letter, Dr. Ferre returned the check along with a letter which began, "Enclosed please find your thirty pieces of silver . . ."[26] A great deal of confusion and embarrassment resulted from Ferre's return of the honorarium check. Correspondence flowed between Fowler, George Clary, Jones, and others.

The entire experience was a great embarrassment to the Assembly and the church. Perhaps it was best summed up in a letter from George

Clary to James Fowler in which he stated, ". . . the most unfortunate situation of Dr. Ferre has given us at the Lake 'a black eye' with many of our people. Any thing we can do to ease the tension I think would be wise."[27]

If the Ferre matter had been an embarrassment to the Assembly, it was quickly overshadowed by the completion and opening of the World Methodist Building and the Ninth World Methodist Conference held at the Assembly in 1956.

Elmer Clark had a dream and it was a big one. In his dream, the World Methodist Council would not only have one of its worldwide meetings at the Assembly, but it would also locate its international headquarters there. One might have assumed that since the Methodist movement had begun in England and the first meeting of the parent organization of the Council was held in London, that its first permanent headquarters would be located there. This was certainly not an assumption of Clark, who was the editor of the Methodist Board of Missions periodical *World Outlook*, a historian in his own right, and a huge supporter of Lake Junaluska Assembly.

The World Methodist Council is one of the first ecumenical Christian world communions. It traces its origin back to the Ecumenical Methodist Conference, which was held in London in 1881. At that time, four hundred delegates from thirty Methodist bodies gathered at Wesley's Chapel. It was, initially, a loosely organized group of persons representing churches whose origin was rooted in the teachings and ministry of John Wesley. Following the 1881 conference, it was decided that the group would meet every ten years. The meetings were held until the outbreak of World War II. After the war, the first meeting was in 1947. At the next meeting, held in 1951, two significant decisions were reached. The name of the organization was changed to The World Methodist Council and this council would meet every five years. The proceedings of the Eighth Ecumenical Council contain the following:

"On the recommendation of the Executive Committee, which met in London on August 24 and 25, the name of the organization was changed to WORLD METHODIST COUNCIL."[28]

At the same meeting, it was decided that the next meeting would be held in the United States in 1956. The specific location, as well as the time, place, and nature of the meeting was referred to the executive meeting for final determination.[29] This was the opportunity for which Clark had been waiting. Both Clark and Edwin L. Jones were on the executive committee of the World Methodist Council, having been elected to the group at the 1951 meeting. Jones would serve as treasurer. In subsequent meetings of the Executive Committee, it was decided that the meeting would take place August 7 through September 12 at the Lake Junaluska Methodist Assembly.

Prior to the 1956 World Methodist Conference, the administrative offices of the Ecumenical Conference had no permanent location. Clark and others felt that there was need for a physical location for the headquarters of the council. They began to promote the idea. Fundraising began, and in a letter to Elmer Clark, dated November 16, 1951, H. G. Allen, the superintendent of the Assembly wrote:

I hereby extend to you and the Executive Committee a most cordial invitation to make the Assembly its headquarters and to use a room in our new Administration Building for your offices until the "Archives Building" is finished.[30]

Letters were written to church leaders encouraging their support. In one such letter, Jones states:

This Archives Building is something that will reflect great credit to the Assembly in years to come, and will attract the type of scholar and research person to the Lake who otherwise would never come, as well as provide a place of interest and study for those who normally come, and will also focus on world-wide Methodism the fact there is a Lake Junaluska and it has a headquarters for world-wide Methodism.[31]

It was the intention and the hope of both Elmer T. Clark and Edwin L. Jones that the arhives building would be constructed without the use of any of the World Methodist Council funds. A brochure was produced which outlined this sincere effort. It contained drawings of the proposed building, along with the estimated cost, which was fifty thousand dollars, and a request for donations. At the beginning of the brochure, the need for the building was presented along with the following statement:

It is proposed to erect at Lake Junaluska, North Carolina, a Methodist Archives and History Center which will be the administrative headquarters

of the World Methodist Council and the Association of Methodist
Historical Societies.

*The enterprise has been endorsed by the World Methodist Council through
both the World and the American Executive Committees, the Association of
Methodist Historical Societies, the Board of Trustees of the Lake Junaluska
Assembly, and the College of Bishops of the Southeastern Jurisdiction. It will
be the only official and national center of its kind in the country.*[32]

The project generated a great deal of enthusiasm. Donations, large and
small, poured in. Jones gave generously, but there were many gifts, some less
than ten dollars. Each was carefully recorded and a letter of thanks was sent.

By summer of 1955, the first phase was complete. Clark had an extensive collection of material related to the history of Methodism which he
immediately placed in the museum. In addition, he was able to procure a
large collection of Wesleyan artifacts from Cliff College in England. A
Methodist news release dated October 1955 stated:

*What is believed to be the largest collection of John Wesley Art objects has
arrived here from England; it was announced by Dr. Elmer T. Clark, secretary
of the World Methodist Council.*

*The objects pertaining to Wesley, 18th century founder of Methodism, will be
added to Dr. Clark's personal collection of Wesleyana for display in the new
archives and headquarters building of the World Methodist Council and the
Methodist Historical Societies, now under construction at Lake Junaluska.*

*Formerly the "Eagles collection" at Cliff College in England, the group
included 58 large busts of Wesley, 53 miniature busts and statuettes, and 57
medallions, plaques, and cameos with Wesley's likeness.*[33]

Excitement grew as the opening of the conference grew near. The
1956 edition of the *Junaluska News* proudly announced that the Ninth
World Methodist Conference would be held at Lake Junaluska Assembly.
An article entitled "Ninth World Methodist Conference Set at Lake began:

*The largest body of Methodists from other lands that ever assembled will come
to Lake Junaluska next summer when the Ninth World Methodist Conference
meets. . . . The whole group, including those from the United States will*

number around 1500. They will represent forty Methodist bodies from around seventy-five different countries.[34]

On August 27, 1956 the Ninth World Methodist Conference convened. There were more than one thousand members and delegates in attendance. In addition were unnumbered visitors. Clark jubilantly proclaimed that it was probably the largest world meeting of Methodists ever held.[35] During the opening sessions, greetings were read from President Dwight D. Eisenhower, who stated "We should work for peace with the same vigorous, single-minded purpose of John Wesley ..."[36] Other greetings and communications from international leaders to the 1956 World Methodist Conference included: Vice President Richard Nixon; the president of Korea, Syngman Rhee; the Queen of Tonga, Salote Tupon; the President of the Republic of China, Chiang Kai-Shek; and others.[37]

The World Methodist Building was enlarged in 1960. Later still, on November 2, 2000, the Come-Up Lodge, located west of the World Methodist Building, was moved and construction began on a replica of the boyhood home of John Wesley at Epworth, England. The building, a replica on the exterior only, is occupied by the administrative offices of the council, while the entire original building is currently occupied by the museum.

The construction of the World Methodist Building and the location of the International Headquarters of the World Methodist Council at Lake Junaluska Assembly remains one of the most significant events in the history of the institution. In 1967, Dr. Elmer Clark, first executive director of the World Methodist Council, died. Clark's zeal for history and his organizational ability contributed to the establishment of organizations dedicated to the preservation of Methodist heritage that reached across oceans and secured the history of Methodism in America. In recognition of his leadership, a rustic chapel in the Susannah Wesley Garden adjacent to the World Methodist Museum bears his name.

On Saturday, October 2, 1954 eleven ladies[38] gathered at the home of Mrs. Everett McElroy with a single purpose in mind that would result in years of natural beauty for the Assembly. On that day they formed the Tuscola Garden Club. The eleven became the charter members of the club. The next year, the club became a member of the Federated Garden Clubs. The stated object of the club was to promote interest in home, garden, and community beautification.

THE CRAFT HUT ON FIRE JUNE 31, 1958

Dr. Jack Fellows enjoyed his job as director of the Lake Junaluska Assembly Craft Program. It kept him busy in the summer months and yet did not involve a great deal of physical exertion. An automobile accident six years earlier had left Fellows with a disability that required him to wear a steel back brace and made it difficult to walk. Most of his time was spent in the little craft hut across the street from the Memorial Chapel. That is, until Thursday, July 31, 1958 when he attempted to open a window and knocked over a can of lacquer which spilled onto a nearby kiln and caught fire. The fire spread rapidly over the log building trapping Fellows inside. With his way blocked and his disability restraining him, he looked around desperately and spied the bathtub in the bathroom. Lowering himself into it he turned on the water in an attempt to keep from being burned. At the same time, he began to cry for help. A passerby (unknown to this day) heard his cries, entered the burning hut, and dragged him to safety. Fellows was not injured, but the craft hut burned to the ground.[39]

Would it be possible to have a national meeting of Methodist Youth at Lake Junaluska? Troy Barrett was thrilled by the idea. He was considering inviting the National Conference of Methodist Youth to have a meeting at

Lake Junaluska Assembly. Barrett, the director of the Methodist Student Movement for the North Carolina Conference, was exploring the possibility before actually inviting the group. On July 28, 1948 he wrote to Superintendent F. S. Love:

We would like to know if this National Conference of 125–150 youth and adults (whites, negroes, Japanese-Americans, Nationals, and Internationals) from all points of the United States could gather at Lake Junaluska sometime between August 25 and August 30, and share fellowship and ideas, enrichments and training, and plan the activities, projects, and policies of the National Conference of Methodist Youth?[40]

Barrett had good reason to want to test the waters before issuing the invitation. Since the end of World War II, there had been a new sensitivity to the issue of racial equality in the United States and more particularly in some Methodist circles. Any suggestion of change, particularly but not exclusively in the South, had been met with immediate and strenuous opposition. Already there had been occasions where the presence of African Americans at the Assembly had brought about strong opposition.

The situation on the campus was complicated by the fact that the Assembly did not own all of the buildings. Lambuth Inn was owned by the Board of Missions of the Methodist Church, while Shackford Hall was owned by the Board of Education. Thus the Board of Trustees had no control over the policies regarding these two facilities. These two agencies were encouraging interracial meetings. The relationship of the buildings to the Board of Trustees was largely unknown by the laity of the local churches. On more than one occasion, there was an outcry of opposition when it was discovered that there had been African Americans staying at Lambuth and attending meetings in Shackford.

Thus, when Barrett received a reply from Love, it was not what he wanted to hear, but probably what he rather expected. In his letter, Love said:

. . . you can well understand that in an institution like this the inter-racial feature of the conference presents something of a problem. . . . I have been under fire this summer from over the church because of incidents arising out of the Christian Student Regional Conference and also our School of Missions. . . .[41]

The Assembly had long been concerned about the needs of African American persons.[42] The Gilbert Center, while it in no way promoted equality, nevertheless was an expression of concern for the welfare of the black presence on campus. It continued into the fifties and overlapped the effort for total integration.

The position of the Board of Trustees was that they were responsible to the owners, i.e. the Methodists of the Southeastern Jurisdiction, and that they would follow the lead of the local churches as far as their position on integration was concerned. In 1961, Edwin L. Jones published a paper entitled "Lake Junaluska Assembly, Year A.D. 1961." In it, he attempted to state the position of the board with regard to the pressure to integrate. He stated:

> *Since Junaluska is supported by and for the members of the Southeastern Jurisdiction, its trustees have no moral, ethical, or legal right to subject them to conditions at Junaluska which they are unwilling to support at home. . . . This is not a discussion of the ethics, nor theology, or of the race question. It is a statement of fact as to the responsibilities of Junaluska Trustees . . .*[43]

For more than a decade, the trustees had been dealing with extreme pressure on both sides. On the one hand, there were the boards and agencies of the general church, along with other groups pressing for total integration. On the other hand, there was pressure from local churches, particularly in the South, and pressure groups dedicated to retaining segregation throughout the culture, along with church leaders who felt that to integrate would lead to financial disaster. The whole issue was augmented by individual lay persons with strong feelings on both sides.

As early as 1949, Bishop Arthur J. Moore wrote to F. S. Love in reply to a question of accepting an integrated group at the Assembly:

> *I feel we are going a little too fast in the matter of trying to accommodate our Negro friends at Junaluska . . . the impression is abroad that we will take mixed groups and I think we dare not run ahead of public opinion in that matter.*[44]

Likewise, Bishop Costen J. Harell expressed himself in a letter written to the Hon. J. B. Ricketts in 1950:

I cannot foresee in the future any time when the lake will be operated on an inter-racial basis. It is my understanding that the board will tighten its rules in this matter.

The executive committee met last week, and there was a long discussion of the question you have raised. The Executive Committee made a positive rule that there would be permitted no inter-racial mingling in any of the grounds or buildings controlled by the trustees—this includes social halls, the beach, the play-group, etc.[45]

In August of 1962, Fowler wrote in his superintendent's report to the Board of Trustees:

I am reporting this to you so that you may understand that we are now confronted with serious decisions because, in the minds of many Methodist Christians the matter of race relations is of the greatest importance. . . . It seems that the range and scope of reconciliation have now become very narrow where it is a serious matter of—if we don't segregate we are damned, and if we do segregate we are damned—therefore, I beseech you, Brethren, that you consider this situation prayerfully, sincerely, giving to us the benefit of your finest judgment, tempered by Christian Convictions . . . Members of the Central Jurisdiction seem to be taking the position that they will not participate even on an invitational basis in conferences at Junaluska unless they can come on an unbiased basis. . . . We have some reason to believe that the Central Jurisdiction is exerting pressure upon the Board of Missions to withdraw its patronage and participation except in those areas where members of the Central Jurisdiction and others can be entertained on an unbiased basis.[46]

Leading the effort to bring equality to the campus were two major groups within the church, the Board of Missions, and the Board of Education. As stated earlier, each of these boards owned major buildings on the campus. Likewise, each sponsored major events that, traditionally, had met at Junaluska. Within the two boards were such groups as the Woman's Society of Christian Service and several youth organizations, including the Methodist Youth Fellowship and the Methodist Student Movement.

In 1963, after the General Board of Missions of the Jurisdiction decided to invite the Central Jurisdiction conferences to the annual SEJ Missionary Conference at the lake, the trustees informed the chair of the SEJ Missions Conference, Dr. Edward L. Tullis, that they would not allow the integration of the Missions Conference. Upon receiving this information, the Missions Conference voted to meet the next year at another location. Following this, the Trustees Executive Committee informed the Conference that they could not integrate, nor could they leave the Assembly. (The SEJ Missionary Conference was one of the largest conferences at the Assembly each year.) The Conference officers then reminded the committee that the Executive Committee had no say in either matter.

The Executive Committee then offered a compromise: The Missionary Conference could invite the Central Jurisdiction conferences provided they all stayed at the Colonial Hotel, took their meals there, and did not use the swimming pool.[47]

Tullis, who was later elected a bishop, relates in his memoir *Our Faith Journey*:

> I told him [Jones] that that was entirely unacceptable. For a few minutes I took the ugliest dressing down I ever had in my life, and then my Irish background arose and to keep from saying something I might regret, I walked out. The next day an embarrassed administrator met with the entire Conference and told us we could integrate in 1964.[48]

The issue of integrated swimming became the flash point of both the effort to and the opposition against integration at the Assembly. As early as 1950, there is a record of opposition on the part of the Methodist Student Movement to segregated swimming at the Assembly. An open letter from the steering committee of the MSM Regional Training Conference states:

> **Resolution:** *Due to the facts that the Board of Trustees of the Lake Junaluska Assembly prohibit interracial participation in use of its swimming facilities, and that we desire to maintain a group unity within our interracial conference, we move that this conference recommend that all its registrants united in abstaining from utilization of the swimming area.*[49]

The letter goes on:

> Here at Junaluska we have heard and seen dramatized the missionary strategy of Methodism in other lands. Here, we covet the privilege of translating that gospel in terms of community living.[50]

Also, in June of 1951, Al Weston, chairman of the Caravan Training Steering Committee, expressed similar feelings and the committee had passed a similar resolution.

With the construction of the new swimming pool in 1954, the youth sought to pressure the board to integrate the facility. Each year when the various youth groups gathered, they boycotted the swimming pool. The segregated pool became the symbol of the Assembly's resistance to racial equality on its campus.

Both the pressure to integrate and the opposition seem to have reached its high in 1960. Over and over the MSM committee and others had asked for the right to have all of its attendees use the pool. Each time they were denied. Finally, in 1960, these words appeared in an article reporting on the National Conference on Race published in the *Daily Motive* newsletter during the MSM Conference in August.

> *This resume of the National Conference report on race relations stands in marked contrast to the practices of segregation in the swimming pool here at Lake Junaluska. In protests, past regional conferences have refused to go swimming. This year the steering committee recommends that each student consider carefully his own decision as to his own policy regarding the segregation ruling. The Committee realizes that this decision may take one of two forms: a "swim-in" in which groups of white and negro students may go to the pool together and seek admission or a decision not to swim at all . . .* [51]

This resulted in two attempts by integrated groups to enter the pool. These, in turn, resulted in the pool being closed temporarily. This swim-in received extensive publicity, which resulted in strong reaction from proponents and opponents. Their positions hardened and any possibility of compromise seemed dim indeed. Yet things were about to change.

In 1962, Gayle Graham Yates was the newly elected president of the National Conference of the Methodist Student Movement. A graduate of Millsaps College, a Methodist liberal arts College in Jackson, Mississippi, Yates had been the president of the Southeastern Region of MSM before becoming national president. Following a meeting with the National MSM Council, she wrote a letter to Edwin Jones in which she stated:

> *. . . the presidents of the Southeastern states of the NCMSM and the NCMSM Council have asked me to write you asking permission to appear*

before your Board when you meet at Junaluska August 4–5 . . . requesting (as we have done before) that you change the policy that now exists, which does not allow interracial groups to swim at Junaluska.[52]

The reply from Jones was surprisingly cordial. He indicated that a special committee of the Board of Trustees would meet with her group on Monday, July 30, 1962. He invited the group to be the guests of the Assembly. Then he added:

We assure you that our committee will meet your committee with an open mind. We also are glad to discuss with you the organizational set up of the Southeastern Jurisdiction under the organic plan of Union of the Methodist Church and its control of and purposes for Lake Junaluska, which it owns.[53]

The meeting was held as planned. Representing the Methodist Student Movement were: Gayle Yates, Ron Gaddis, Charlene Rushton, Gene Bennett, Phyllis Ann Moore, Charles W. Rinker Jr., John Robert Zellner, Bill Corzine, and Charles Lipthrett.[54]

Representing the Board of Trustees was: Edwin Jones, Dr. Carl King, Admiral W. N Thomas, Bishop Paul Hardin Jr., and Hugh Massie. Bishop Hardin presided. Also present was Mrs. Ila Campbell, secretary to Superintendent J. W. Fowler. Mrs. Campbell served as secretary and took the minutes. We are indebted to Mrs. Campbell whose minutes are almost verbatim and give us an unusually clear picture of what transpired that day.

The meeting was frank and open. At one point, Massie pointed out that the swimming pool was now the only facility which was not integrated.

Bishop Hardin noted that the College of Bishops was charged with the responsibility of holding the Methodist Church together while at the same time steering her through a "great revolutionary expansion." He went on to point out that the Gilbert Center was gone and that everything was integrated except the pool, seeming to imply that the Gilbert Center was a symbol of racism. He then asked if we were going to "cut the line right here and let the church be torn and possibly destroyed or are you going to try to hold the church together?"[55]

The issue of economics was raised. There were differing opinions of what the economic impact of pool integration might be.

Miss Phyllis Anne Moore stated: "If the pool were integrated I would feel totally a part of this wonderful organization. . . . How can we explain to the negro students that they can't swim? They will think that they are not wanted."

At this point, Dr. Carl King made a most unusual suggestion. He suggested that there was a possibility that the pool might be turned over to the MSM conference from four to six-thirty each afternoon during their conference. That the leaders of the conference would have total control and the Assembly would not be involved. He went on to say that this was a personal question and had not been discussed with the rest of the committee.

Yates replied that she did not believe this group would recommend any action that would apply to any group of people in our church and exclude another. She noted that they, too, were Methodist and, with one exception, all from the SEJ. She said that, in their opinion, the moral question of the pool remaining segregated was of national concern.

Dr. Yates, remembering the day comments, a "gentle retired admiral, a chaplain (Admiral William N. Thomas) whispered to me, 'That's all you are going to get, Gayle!' teaching me a major lesson in how to compromise."[56] Both groups gave tentative assent pending approval of their respective boards. Mrs. Yates went on to comment that "the pool is a small issue and is only symbolic of segregation which we do not want to exist in our church."

Finally it was generally conceded that Dr. King's suggestion was a step forward toward resolving the matter.[57]

On August 4, the Board of Trustees met at Lambuth Inn and Bishop Hardin reported on the meeting including the plan tentatively agreed upon. There was a lengthy discussion of the whole issue and there seemed to be no agreement on how to handle the problem. The board recessed for lunch. When the board reconvened for the afternoon session, Admiral Thomas made the following motion:

> . . . that the plan presented by Bishop Hardin be adopted, namely, the committee recommends that during the week of the Methodist Student Movement Conference, August 23–29, the swimming pool at Lake Junaluska be turned over to the Methodist Student Movement Conference for the use of their registered delegates each afternoon between the hours of 4:30 and 6 PM except Sunday.

The motion was seconded by Dr. Carl King. After further discussion, the motion passed with one negative vote. After more than a decade the matter of the swimming pool was settled!

As the news became public, appreciative words came from many. The boards and agencies of the church were unanimous in their compliments. Similar messages were heard from leaders of various youth organizations.

Still, the board was unwilling to take an uncompromised step to lower all the barriers at the Assembly. Frustration continued to mount in the church and within the board. Finally, J. P. Stafford, a layman and board member, wrote a letter to Jones which summed up his (and others) feelings. Saying that he would not be able to attend an upcoming meeting he wrote:

Our basic trouble seems to be a determination on the part of the controlling elements of the Board to stall change as long as possible.

The race trouble is merely a symptom of our real sickness in this day when daring and duty to the future must be partners. We are dragging out the agony of decision on each bit of progress except in finances. No one is really satisfied, but the slowest and they are not very happy.

As a Christian organization we are like the politicians yielding only under pressure and not from principal.

Ed, I am a Mississippian.... . I have been living in the Mississippi Delta for 43 years . . . I was born and raised with all the prejudices of the times. BUT—a new day is here and we must have the courage to live in it or be the rear guard standing for what we cannot in conscience defend. . . .

I wish we could get together as a Board and really think in terms of the long range future of the Assembly, instead of being such lovers of the Status Quo that we hesitate to do what needs to be done except as it is forced upon in the same way. Expediency usually gets you by the minute to kill you on the hours.[58]

Following the meeting, J. W. Fowler replied to Stafford:

The Trustees also overwhelmingly voted to sustain the administration in its management of the Assembly regarding the entertainment of the few Negro people on the grounds. This has been quite an amazing experience for Mr. Jones for he had not realized that the attitudes were changing so rapidly.[59]

Still later upon receiving a copy of Stafford's letter to Jones, Fowler again wrote to Stafford: "I want to commend you for a forthright and courageous and truthful appraisal of the situation. Your expression to Brother Jones confirms what forty-two of the Trustees voted at our recent meeting."[60]

Finally, on August 1, 1964, the Board of Trustees approved a resolution by the Christian Education and Recreation Committee which stated that "Junaluska hereby removes all restriction in entertaining registered guests, delegates, and residents under the supervision of the Superintendent and staff."[61] While this appears to be short of total integration, in practice it was indeed just that. By 1971, Superintendent Edgar Nease was able to write Dr. Robert Lundy the following:

> It would be of interest perhaps for all concerned to know that Lambuth Inn was perhaps the first integrated facility in Western North Carolina and has led in integrating all other facilities throughout this area. No thought is given to any man's color whatsoever. We intend to serve all men irregardless to race, for the Assembly belongs to all Methodists of the Southeastern Jurisdiction irregardless of race.[62]

While segregation is long a thing of the past at Lake Junaluska Assembly, the effect of those difficult days still lingers on in the minds and attitudes of many of those who were deeply hurt by past actions and attitudes. Nevertheless, the Assembly has changed. Today, all persons are welcome and visitors to the Assembly are greeted at the strikingly beautiful Bethea Welcome Center. This symbol of openness, hospitality, and welcome is named for Bishop and Mrs. Joseph Bethea and is the first major building on the campus to be named for African American persons. Likewise, today 15 percent of the year-round staff and 20 percent of the summer staff of Lake Junaluska Assembly is made up of ethnic individuals.

CHAPTER EIGHT

The 60s

• • • • • • • • • • • • • •

There was a need for a new craft building to replace the one that had burned in 1958. Shortly after the fire, the Buildings and Grounds Committee of the Board of Trustees reported:

> We have received an anonymous gift in the amount of three thousand dollars ($3,000) to start a fund for a new Craft House. The Committee was asked by the Superintendent to locate a new site suitable for the erection of the Craft Center. . . . If this Committee (the Executive Committee) authorizes us to do so, we will proceed in getting architect's plans and shall proceed to obtain further contributions . . . [1]

The next year, Bishop John Branscomb of the Florida Conference died. Branscomb had long been a supporter of the Assembly and a trustee. After his death, there was a movement to name the new craft building in his memory. Funds were raised, a design was approved, and construction began. When completed, the building had three thousand five hundred square feet of floor area and contained craft rooms to provide facilities for all manner of creative crafts, including ceramics, leather, jewelry making, painting, and weaving. The Branscomb Arts and Crafts Building opened for the season of 1960. A bronze plaque was placed on the building. It was inscribed:

Arts and Crafts Building
Erected in Memory of
BISHOP JOHN W. BRANSCOMB
May 11, 1905–January 16, 1959
Devoted friend and trustee of the Lake Junaluska Assembly

THE ALLEN-BRANSCOMB ADMINISTRATION BUILDING

A year later in a Board of Trustees meeting, it was decided that the arts and crafts building was not a suitable enough memorial for Bishop Branscomb. In the minutes of the August 5, 1961 meeting we find:

> *Upon the motion of Bishop Harrell, seconded by Henry Gramling, it was recorded that the consensus of the body is that some adjustment should be made for a more worthy memorial. [for Branscomb] This was left in the hands of the Executive Committee.*[2]

The board also decided that the building would be changed from an arts and crafts center to central offices for apartments and lodges.

The Executive Committee later made the decision that Branscomb's name would be made a part of the name of the new Administration Building. The decision was that the Administration Building would be known as the Branscomb Administration Building.

In their report to the Board of Trustees on August 8, 1959, the Buildings and Grounds Committee listed a new building to be built on the site where the old Administration Building and adjacent bookstore had been as one of their top priorities. With the construction of the new Administration Building, the area was now available. In their report, the committee indicated that the size of the building would be determined by the funds allotted.[3] There was a significant need for such a building. The old bookstore was woefully inadequate. Likewise, the Boat House was nearing the end of its useful life and when it was gone, the Tea Room would have to be relocated. It was not long until the plans were complete and construction began.

By the following summer the building was completed. The 1960 edition of the *Junaluska News* included a headline which read, "New Harrell Center Honors Great Junaluskan." The accompanying article read, in part:

> *Bishop Costen J. Harrell, retired, of Decatur, GA is being honored by the Trustees of Lake Junaluska Assembly by the naming of the new center for him. The Harrell Center will provide facilities for all of the services formerly offered in the old Administration Building, Book Store, and the old Boat House Building. . . .* [4]

The completion of the Harrell Center gave the Assembly a new central core. Located, as it was, just across the street from the Terrace Hotel and next to the auditorium, it quickly became a gathering place for persons attending conferences. The Tea Room located on the lake level

THE HARRELL CENTER, BUILT IN 1960, HOUSES THE COKESBURY BOOKSTORE, THE HERITAGE CENTER, JUNALUSKA LIBRARY, AND A FIVE HUNDRED-SEAT AUDITORIUM

offered food and fellowship. There quickly developed a custom for persons in the auditorium to gather for ice cream and other refreshments when the services ended.

On the afternoon of Sunday, August 29, 1965, Dr. and Mrs. Wilson Weldon had visitors. They had had a lot of company recently. It had been a little more than a month since their daughter Nanci had died following a long and courageous battle with cancer. A highly popular girl, in 1961 she had been elected Queen of Lake Junaluska Assembly. In her coronation speech, Miss Weldon had stated of the Assembly, ". . . I just hope she [the Assembly] will continue to grow to become a place where the social classes and the castes of the old South are forgotten, but where Southern charm, friendliness, and hospitality are preserved . . ."[5] This statement summed up not only her love of the Assembly, but also her sensitivity to the issues of her day and her love for people. In many ways, she was typical of the youth of the sixties. On the one hand, she was a gracious southern girl having been presented to Charlotte, North Carolina society. On the other hand, she was very concerned about the needs of society and very much involved in the movement for social change. At one point, she was arrested for being involved in a civil rights demonstration in Hillsboro, North Carolina. After graduating from Duke, she focused her life on the less fortunate of the Atlanta slums by serving through the Methodist Church as a US-2 inner city missionary. Shortly thereafter, she was stricken with cancer. Throughout her illness, she never once relinquished her concern for others and shortly before her death attended the 1965 Methodist Student Movement Conference in Greensboro to lead a discussion group on the mission of the church in the inner-city. Upon her election as queen, the *Junaluska News* had described her with these words: ". . . she personifies the characteristics of beauty, grace, charm, and Christian principals that have always been typical of her choice for this most coveted honor."[6]

The group that called on her parents that summer Sunday included Sam Banks, chairman of the Education and Recreation Committee of the Assembly. He was accompanied by Mrs. Melford (Daisy) Wilson; Bill Finger, president of the Lake Junaluska Assembly Youth Council; and Bob Toenniessen, Youth Staff representative. Also included were Assembly Superintendent J. W. Fowler and Mrs. Fowler. Banks explained that there were many persons who wanted a memorial for Nanci at the Assembly. There seemed to be a great deal of interest in a gymnasium. The gymnasium would be named the Nanci Weldon Memorial Gymnasium and

A LARGE CROWD AT A SERIES IN THE GEORGE R. STUART AUDITORIUM, CIRCA 1965

would be located at the west end of the campus. The cost was projected to range from twenty thousand to fifty thousand dollars. At that point, a total of $1,384 had already been contributed for a memorial. In a letter to the Executive Committee of the Board of Trustees, Fowler stated, "Mr. Banks explained that this was a movement prompted by the devotion of the people and the appreciation of the people of Nanci's contribution to the life and spirit of Junaluska . . ."[7] The Weldons were very much in favor of the project, and later the Assembly trustees also agreed to the memorial.

When the proposed memorial was announced, contributions flooded in from many sources. Within a short period of time, construction began and the new Memorial Gymnasium was used for the first time in the summer season of 1967. Less than two years later, the entire cost of $54,748.28 had been raised. A dedication service was held June 4, 1969. Leading the service was, long-time friend of the Weldons, Bishop Earl Hunt. A bronze plaque unveiled that day reads: Nanci Weldon Gymnasium—in memory of—Nanci Leila Weldon, Dec. 18, 1941–July 24, 1965—initiated by youth of Junaluska, Built with Gifts of Friends.

Dr. Lee Tuttle, in addition to being executive secretary of the World Methodist Council, was a lover of roses. Thus, it was not a surprise to Mrs. George Finch, chairperson of the Beautification and Grounds Committee of the Assembly, when he approached her with the idea that he would like to plant roses across the street from the World Methodist Building. In her report in the late summer of 1962, she records:

More or less a personal project sponsored by Dr. [Lee. F.] Tuttle was that of the planting of magnificent roses along Lakeshore directly in front of the [World] Methodist Building. Dr. Tuttle agreed to plant the roses there if the space were allotted to him, and this was done and it is expressly understood that Dr. Tuttle is able to expand the rose program as he desires to do so having roses extend all the way from the Harrell Center to Harrison Memorial . . .[8]

Thus began the Rose Walk, which now includes more than two hundred rose bushes and reaches from the Harrison Colonnade along the lake to the Harrell Center. It has received accolades of national note for its beauty and has brought joy and peace to many.

From the early days of the Assembly, a fee was charged to enter the grounds. The first gates at both ends of the lake included a gate house. There a gate boy would stop each car or bus and collect the fees. To be a gate boy was to be someone very special in the eyes of the young people who worked at the Assembly during the summer. Many applied . . . few were accepted. The fees ranged from fifty cents a day to seven dollars fifty cents for an entire season. The amount was unchanged for more than thirty years. From the beginning, there were problems collecting the fees. There were other entrances to the grounds which were not gated. Persons wishing to enter without paying the fee could use these. Others who were in leadership roles objected. In a special recommendation from D. Trigg James, executive secretary of the SEJ Council and program director for Lake Junaluska Assembly, there had been a recommendation that the practice of requiring ground fees to be paid for faculty and employed leaders of the various educational conferences be discontinued.[9]

On February 27, 1969, at a meeting of the Trustees Executive Committee, Henry Gramling, chairman of the Hotels and Public Accommodations Committee, brought a recommendation that gate fees be collected at the hotels, bath house, children's building, apartments, lodges, etc, and not at the gates, and that an information booth only be maintained at the West Entrance. In discussion which followed, it was agreed to rename these fees "Activity Fees" and that they be added to the hotel bills and collected when the bill was paid. It was also agreed that these rates be put in all correspondence concerning rentals, etc.[10]

Other changes were taking place. Some reflected the changing times. The minutes of the Board of Trustees meeting held on August 3, 1963 stated, "It was decided to allow Sunday afternoon recreation from

2 to 5 PM."[11] This included the swimming pool and thus, for the first time, Sunday swimming was allowed.

One striking change was about to take place. The 1966 issue of the *Junaluska News* bore the headline: "Junaluska May Become Year Round Facility." The article that followed stated:

> *Many Boards and Agencies of the Methodist Church have expressed an interest in holding fall, winter, and spring meetings on the Assembly Grounds. Since Lambuth Inn is fully winterized and could accommodate groups of up to 250, the Trustees and Management look with favor on extending the season provided enough conferences can be booked to make it a break-even proposition.* [12]

One of the most significant influences in moving the Assembly to a year-round institution was the beginning of Interpreter's House. In the spring of 1967, Interpreter's House opened in Lambuth Inn. This innovative and unconventional program was the inspiration of Dr. Carlyle Marney. Marney was pastor of the Myers Park Baptist Church in Charlotte, North Carolina. After preaching a series of sermons on contemporary church life, he determined to leave his pulpit to help pastors and laypersons develop into authentic disciples. He was convinced that the church was too concerned with itself and its success. He dubbed the situation a "dreadful crisis in modern Christianity." The church was too turned inward. "It survives to keep itself going. It is no longer sought. It is a subjective, inward, defensive, closed, self-concerned corporation and it is a moral failure on the broad scale. If this continues it is the death of Christianity." He was later to say that he had literally preached himself out of the pulpit in that series of sermons. The term "Interpreter's House" was drawn from a reference in John Bunyan's *Pilgrim's Progress*. Ironically, earlier Marney had come under fire for agreeing with another controversial theologian, Nels Ferre.[13]

In an article written for the *Waynesville Mountaineer* newspaper, Clifton Metcalf wrote:

> *One of the South's most respected Baptist leaders has been named director of an ecumenical center for ministers and laymen being organized at the Lake Junaluska Methodist Assembly. . . . The center which will be known as Interpreter's House, will utilize the Assembly's Lambuth Inn on a year-round basis, service men of all faiths and races. . . . It will be a "way-station" where*

clergy and laity may search for meaning in their own lives, probing a conviction upon which Dr. Marney has based his ministry: lay people must find their own manhood [to] become the ministry of the church in the world. . . . It's not a school, not a seminary, and we don't intend it to be a university, although it will utilize some brilliantly trained men from the best universities and seminaries in the country. . . . We have discovered that something terrible happens to a pastor 10 to 20 years out of school. He has "bought" his culture. He is no longer a real chaplain. Mostly he blesses the things that are already there.[14]

The participants would commit themselves to a three-week seminar which consisted of introspection, participation in work projects, and recreating their concept of the church. The seminars would be ongoing throughout the year and would be interdenominational, and bi-racial in nature.

Interpreter's House became a very important and popular source of continuing education for ministers of several denominations. It also provided a continuing year-round schedule of events and made possible the transition from a summer-only seasonal facility to a year-round operation. It was noted throughout the church for its bold and comprehensive approach to ministerial renewal and social sensitivity.

Unfortunately, Interpreter's House only lasted for a little more than a decade. On July 3, 1978, Marney was walking back to his office at Interpreter's House after visiting with friends along the hall when he suddenly collapsed. He had died of a massive heart attack. In six days, he would have been sixty-two years old. His untimely death signaled the end of Interpreter's House. By the end of the year, Interpreter's House ceased to exist.

Two years before the death of Dr. Marney, two of his co-workers in Interpreter's House had felt called to move into another area of in-service ministry for clergy. In recalling this later, Dr. Mark Rouch wrote of himself:

During the summer of 1976 Dr. Mark Rouch, a member of the staff of Interpreter's House came to the decision that a new center for continuing education at the Assembly was needed. He met with Dr. Sarah Workman, a colleague at Interpreter's House and the Rev. Hugh Eichelberger, pastor of Grace-Covenant Presbyterian Church in Asheville, NC for discussions about the proposed center. Similar discussions continued through the year and into the fall of the next year.

They decided that the center would be named the Intentional Growth Center continuing a concept of intentionality in human growth in ministry. Dr. Rouch had worked with this concept at Interpreter's. They also decided that the center would be an independent, not-for-profit educational organization. It would develop three program emphases: 1) personal-professional growth for pastors and others in ministry, 2) organizational effectiveness in which persons would be able to enhance their leadership and other skills, and 3) enhancement of family life.

Recognizing the potential of such a center and the need for a stronger continuing education program at the Assembly, Dr. Mel Harbin, executive director of the Assembly, asked Rouch to serve as a consultant for the Assembly's continuing education program. The support and connection with the Assembly was crucial to the development of the center. Another factor was the availability of the Atkins Memorial House, which had formally been designated as the home for the director, but which was not occupied. This house, originally built by Bishop Atkins, was given to the Assembly by his widow. After a new residence for the Assembly director was built in 1964, Miss Dille Ousley purchased the house and gave it to the SEJ as a memorial to Bishop and Mrs. Atkins to be used as "a place of spiritual retreat for active and retired missionaries, deaconesses, ministers and other guests."[15]

In a document used to promote the center, we find this historical reference:

> At the time of the founding Mark Rouch was invited by Mel Harbin to be a consultant with the Assembly in continuing education and was paid a retainer for that service with the idea that in addition to directing the center he would work with the Assembly in the development of its own continuing education programming.

> In 1979, conversations were begun with Dr. Harbin, Dr. Wright Spears and others about the possibility of the Intentional Growth Center becoming more closely related to Lake Junaluska Assembly. At the beginning of 1980, a formal relationship was established in which financial matters would be reviewed by the Assembly auditors; there would be close contact on program development; and the Center would attempt to work as much as possible on behalf of the Assembly in providing continuing education programming.[16]

The concept upon which the Intentional Growth Center operated was best stated in their purpose statement, which was circulated in several printed forms. It read:

Purpose statement:

1) To enable persons to discover their own identity as human beings and the sources of their growth;

2) To enable persons to grow mentally, emotionally, and spiritually, and to provide special skills for their life journeys;

3) To help persons function effectively in their families, churches, and all other relationships of life; and

4) To enable persons to develop a lifestyle which is uniquely Christian, including intentional involvement in Christian ministry.[17]

Dr. Rouch retired as director of IGC in 1988. His successor was Dr. Jim Warren. Dr. Warren retired in 1999 and his successor was Dr. Larry Ousley.

As noted earlier, the building of the Waynesville By-pass in 1947 ushered in great changes in the physical layout of the Assembly grounds. By the sixties, large numbers of persons were entering through the gate built at the western most end of the lake. This end of the lake was not particularly scenic. The portion of the lake from the apartments to the gatehouse was very shallow and was filled with cattails. Indeed, it had been dubbed by many, "Cattail Marsh." In the October 31, 1963 report, the Buildings and Grounds Committee reported that a new "causeway west entrance road would be made possible by pumping 80,000 yards of silt into the west end of the lake."[18] In order to do this, a causeway would have to be built to hold back the water. The effect of building the causeway would mean that the extreme western end of the lake would be filled and dried. This was done and the area became a large athletic field.

With the coming of the year 1963, the Assembly was fifty years old. It had come a long way in those first fifty years. From a beautiful mountain farm valley had come a remarkable complex of auditorium, meeting rooms, recreational areas, and guest facilities. That lovely pastoral scene had changed into a campus which, in the summer, buzzed with activity. More important, where there had been cattle and corn, there were now persons who were coming to know new friends, falling in love with one another, and finding new meaning in Christ. A celebration was in order.

On July 28th, the Golden Anniversary observance began with the opening of the Jurisdictional Laity Conference. It was fitting that the celebration would begin with the laity conference since it had all begun with the resolution at the Laymen's Missionary Conference. In the opening services, Bishop Paul Garber spoke at the morning worship hour and the Honorable Brooks Hays, assistant to the president of the United States, spoke that evening. The members of the Assembly trustees and the Southeastern Jurisdictional Council were also involved in the services.

The observance continued throughout the conference. Daily themes included Junaluska and Christian Education, Junaluska and Christian Service, Junaluska and the Laymen, Junaluska and the Ministry, Junaluska and Youth, and Junaluska and Old Timers.

Among those who spoke were: Bishops Roy Short, James Henley, Walter Gum, and Costen J. Harrell. Other speakers included: Dr. Billy Graham; Col. John Glenn of NASA; Dr. Conwell Snoke of the General Board of Missions; The Honorable James Avery Joyce, author and lecturer; Dean Robert Cushman of the Duke Divinity School; and Dr. Henry Sprinkle, editor of *World Outlook*.

In addition, entertainment included the Transylvania Symphony, The Carolina Chorallites, and the Pensacola Air Force Academy Flag Team.[19]

During the 1960s, the Haywood County Board of Education made the decision to consolidate the several county high schools into two large campuses. One would be located in Canton, North Carolina and the other in Waynesville. Inquiry was made into the possibility of acquiring the Junaluska Golf Course property for the location of the Waynesville campus. Fortunately, the Board of Trustees was able to persuade the school board to look elsewhere.

During 1967, there was an addition to the campus of the Assembly that continues to be controversial to this day. In his report to the Board of Trustees, Dr. Fowler reported that "speed breakers" had been installed in several locations. The speed bumps, as they came to be called, created a large negative response. Although they are disliked by many, there is general agreement that they effectively reduce speeding on campus.[20]

As reported, the *Cherokee I* was in service for thirty-seven years before being replaced by the *Cherokee II*. Unfortunately, the second Big Boat was not as well constructed as its predecessor. By the early sixties, it was obvious that the *Cherokee II* had many problems. The matter came to a head when the insurance carrier informed the Assembly that it could not continue to insure the craft. The minutes of the Board of Trustees meeting held on October 6, 1966 include the following:

The administration expressed:

> . . . *concern for the operation of the Big Boat and expressed a hope that another could be secured to replace the* Cherokee II *which is no longer seaworthy. Discussion followed as to approximate cost of such a vessel and the Supt. was instructed to continue his efforts to secure a boat that would suit the needs of the Assembly if the price could be afforded* . . .[21]

Several options were explored, including the possibility of purchasing a war surplus navy craft. Finally, a decision was made and a press release issued in March of 1967 stated:

> *The Lake Junaluska Assembly announced today that it has purchased a new pontoon cruiser which will be in operation on the Lake this summer. The new boat will be named CHEROKEE III and will take the place of the old CHEROKEE II which has now been retired. . . . This is the same type of boat that was such a popular favorite at the recent New York World's Fair and is used exclusively at Homosassa Springs, Florida.*[22]

In 1967, the Board of Trustees named Dr. J. Manning Potts to head the Assembly. He was given the new title of executive director of Lake Junaluska Assembly.

In 1968, an organization which was destined to become one of the major support groups for the Assembly was born. An article in the August 9 issue of the *Waynesville Mountaineer* entitled "Lake Trustees Name Hugh Massie President" included the following:

> *Tonight, a new program will be launched—Lake Junaluska Associates—made up of those people who will give $100 or more per year for the expansion of Lake facilities. The goal is 1000 members and already 200 have joined. The $100,000 per year will be used during the next four years to add new facilities and improve existing ones, Massie said.*[23]

In its initial effort, more than thirty thousand dollars was pledged to the associates. The associates organization was endorsed by the SEJ Council, the Jurisdictional Conference, and the Board of Trustees of LJA. A steering committee was appointed by the bishops of the jurisdiction with two members from each annual conference. The group elected Dr. Wilson O. Weldon as president, George Proctor as vice-president, and Rev. H. Levy Rogers as secretary.[24]

During the next year, the first associates banquet was held and the membership grew to three hundred twenty-five members. In the ensuing years, the associates has continued to grow and its support of its many projects has been a huge asset to the growth and enhancement of the Assembly.

Each year in August, the associates meet for a weekend of business and entertainment. One feature of the event is a concert by the Junaluska Singers. Another feature is the presentation of the annual Chief Junaluska Award, which is presented to an individual who has made "outstanding and continuous contributions to Lake Junaluska."[25]

After four decades of service to Lake Junaluska Assembly, the associates had raised more than three million dollars for its projects, which have included a new trolley, rebuilding of the Rose Walk, the building of the amphitheater, the replacing of the original Junaluska Cross, the beautification of the campus, placing the cross and flame emblem on the back of Shackford Hall, and many other such contributions. Its membership is now more than eight hundred.

In the summer of 1969, the Assembly welcomed a very special guest, Dr. Helen Kim, president of Ewha Woman's University in Korea. Ewha had been founded by Methodist missionaries in 1886. She was educated at Ewha and later at Columbia University in the United States. She became the first Korean woman to earn a doctorate. A leader in the struggle for the rights of women, Dr. Kim became president of Ewha in 1931 and by the time of her retirement in 1961, it was the largest women's university in the world.[26]

Dr. Kim was at the Assembly to see the new Korean Room at the Lambuth Inn. Dr. and Mrs. J. Manning Potts had initiated a project to transform the old Sun Parlor at the Inn into a beautiful room which would exhibit art objects from Korea. The room was formally opened with a ribbon cutting during ceremonies in June of 1969. Dr Kim died only a few months later in February of 1970 at the age of seventy-one.

In 1972, Dr. Clara Howard was honored by the International Prayer Fellowship as a member of the Founding Group and her devotion as a missionary in Korea for forty years. In a special service in the Korean Room, tribute was paid to Dr. Howard. Howard donated mementos and treasures from Korea to the Korean Room.[27]

In 1984 during a restoration of Lambuth Inn, the Korean Room was moved from its original location to the International Prayer Chapel. This was altogether fitting since the International Prayer Fellowship was born in the Upper Room Building of Ewha University in May of 1966. At that time, Dr. Kim, Dr. J. Manning Potts, and Dr. Harry Denman knelt in prayer for international peace, the healing of divisions, and for world brotherhood. Out of this meeting came the International Prayer Fellowship. The Prayer Chapel maintains an oriental atmosphere. The silk wall coverings were donated by Dr. Kim and shipped from Korea to Junaluska. Additional Korean artifacts, along with a Korean Room exhibit, are on display in the museum of The Heritage Center located in the Harrell Center on the Assembly campus.

In April of 1968, during what was termed a Uniting General Conference, The Evangelical United Brethren Church and the Methodist Church merged and a new church, The United Methodist Church, was formed. As a part of this new church, a new commission was formed by merging the Historical Society of the Evangelical United Brethren Church and the Association of Methodist Historical Societies. It was to be known as the General Commission on Archives and History.

The specific legislation which accomplished this is found in the *Journal of the 1968 Uniting General Conference* and reads:

> *The Commission on Archives and History shall be incorporated under the laws of whatever state the Commission may determine, and as such it shall be the successor of the Association of Methodist Historical Societies, Lake Junaluska, NC, and the Historical Society of the Evangelical United Brethren Church, Dayton, Ohio. The Commission shall take note that the historical materials, relics, and equipment in the World Methodist Building, Lake Junaluska, are owned jointly by the Association of Methodist Historical Societies and the World Methodist Council, and at the time of incorporation, the commission shall confer with the American Section of the World Methodist Council and shall decide whether it is feasible to continue the joint ownership in the United Methodist Church. The instrument of incorporation shall provide for the commission to own real property and to receive gifts and bequests and the process of incorporation shall be consummated as soon as feasible after the two churches have officially united.*[28]

The formation of the commission was applauded by both EUB and Methodist historians and others interested in the preservation of the two denomination's heritage. Dr. John H. Ness Jr., curator of the Historical Society of the EUB Church, said of the commission:

A new era opens. The past has been merely the prologue to the future. We trust that the Church will recognize its obligation for securing and preserving its record of history. Let us work together through the Commission on Archives and History to provide those tools that make the future more meaningful and free from the mistakes of the past.[29]

As noted earlier, when the World Methodist Building was proposed it was with the understanding that this building would not only be for the offices of the World Methodist Council but also for the repository for the Methodist Historical Societies. During fundraising for the World Methodist Building, it was stated that the building would also be the administrative headquarters for the Association of Methodist Historical Societies.[30]

Immediately, the question of where the commission headquarters would be located was raised. Naturally, the former EUB historians would want to keep their repository in Dayton and the former Methodists would opt for Lake Junaluska. The question was made even more difficult by the fact that the Junaluska site was shared by both the Historical Societies and the World Methodist Council. Indeed, as noted above, there was joint ownership of items of equipment.[31]

Two more general conferences, one in 1972 and another in 1976, were necessary before all of the details of the merger of the two denominations were completely worked out. The matter of the location of the commission was dealt with at both. In a document entitled "Headquarters-Commission on Archives and History" and presented by the Executive Committee of the new Southeastern Jurisdictional Archives and History, the following was stated:

The Executive Committee of the Southeastern Jurisdiction Commission on Archives and History views with deep regret the fact that the [General] Commission on Archives and History is operating two headquarters building offices several hundred miles from each other. This causes an unnecessary expenditure of funds for rent and for office personnel. We consider the funds allotted to the [General] Commission as alarmingly low. Indeed, we and others petitioned [without success] the General Conference for more funds even when we thought the operation would be from a single headquarters building.

We believe that Lake Junaluska is the proper place for the [General] Commission's headquarters. . . . At Lake Junaluska more Methodists gather during the course of the year for great conferences and gatherings, with . . . opportunity to visit a historical headquarters and archival building, than any other place in the world . . . .

Therefore, the Executive Committee of the SEJ Com on Arch and History, in session at Lake Junaluska on January 10, 1969, goes on record as saying to the [General] Commission on Archives and History, and to the UMC in general, that the Commission should have only one office and that the proper place for it is at Lake Junaluska in conjunction with the World Methodist Council.[32]

The matter was finally settled during the 1976 General Conference when the delegates adopted a proposal that established the Junaluska site as the official repository for Methodist archival material. At the conference, the words "Dayton, Ohio, and" were struck from the report of the Commission on Archives and History. The report (which was accepted) then read, "The commission shall have responsibility for and supervision of the archives and libraries at Lake Junaluska, NC and established by the United Methodist Church."[33]

The above was approved and the paragraph became number 1903 in the 1976 Book of Discipline.[34] The archives were finally officially located at the World Methodist Building. Unfortunately for the Assembly, this was not the end of the story.

In 1977, Drew University proposed that they build a new building to house the United Methodist Commission on Archives and History. The building would be complete with the latest climate controlled file and artifact storage. This would be a separate wing on a new library and would be added at no cost to the commission.

Drew University had a position of strength in that there were eleven persons with Drew connections on the new commission which comprised a total of thirty members. The Assembly countered with a proposal to build a new building for which they would have a campaign to raise the necessary funds for construction. Any funds not raised would be amortized by a lease-rental agreement, thus attaching a potential liability for the commission. The Methodist Publishing House initially indicated an interest and set up a study committee to gather data for a future proposal. Apparently, their effort got no further than the committee. On the other hand, the competition between Drew and the Assembly was very strong.

The offer of Drew University was presented in the form of a letter to the Commission on Archives and History, dated July 12, 1977. It listed five reasons for moving the archives to Madison:

1. Its historical relationship to the Church.
2. The strength of its library particularly its collection of "Methodistica."
3. Its campus and academic atmosphere.
4. The accessibility of major transportation facilities.
5. The offer to build a new wing on its library specifically for the Methodist archives.[35]

The Assembly, likewise, presented an impressive proposal. A presentation document consisting of fifteen bound pages was prepared. In his cover letter to Bishop John Warman, who chaired the commission, Wright Spears stated:

> *This proposal is made with deepest appreciation for the fact that the Association of Methodist Historical Societies under the direction of Elmer T. Clark was brought to Lake Junaluska in 1951. In 1968 it became known as the Commission on Archives and History. It has never had any other home. We feel that it has a strong compatibility with the World Methodist Building Headquarters and the Lake Junaluska Assembly where many agencies of the church come for their training programs.*[36]

The presentation booklet went on to argue that the location should not be associated with a larger institution, but should be autonomous rather than a part of a university.[37]

As both institutions continued to vie for consideration by the commission, Dr. Paul Hardin III, president of Drew and the son of Bishop Paul Hardin Jr., sent a letter to Mel Harbin, Wright Spears, and Bishop Paul Hardin with a proposal that he hoped would break the deadlock. He proposed that Drew and the Assembly work out a joint proposal that would have any duplicate archival material reside at Lake Junaluska and the Madison campus, along with copies (via microfilm or other means) of other material deemed most needed which would be made and sent to the Assembly. In effect, the Assembly would become a branch location for the commission.[38]

In a letter to Dr. Hardin in answer to his proposal, Mel Harbin, super-intendent of the Assembly wrote:

> *We deeply appreciate the brotherly manner in which you have made your proposal. You have certainly been fair in explaining your position, but at this time we feel that it is to the Assembly's best interest to make a separate proposal for the Archives to remain here. We feel there are a goodly number of cogent reasons for the Commission to vote to keep the Archives here at the Assembly . . .*[39]

Harbin was convinced that Lake Junaluska Assembly had the best case of any. In a letter to Dr. Larry Tise, the director of the North Carolina Division of Archives and History, he stated:

> *I have reason to believe that if we could put up a new building at the present location where Archives and History are now housed, that we would have the strongest position of any to keep in North Carolina this important aspect of the Church.*[40]

After many frustrating delays, the decision was made in a meeting of the new Commission on Archives and History on Saturday, September 9, 1978. The proposal presented by Drew University was accepted. Funding seems to have been a primary issue, along with the perception that the overall offer from Drew was more attractive. It was deemed by the commission that to have the commission located on the Drew campus would be less expensive than at Junaluska.[41] The repository for the archives of the new United Methodist Church would now be relocated at Drew University in Madison, New Jersey.[42]

For several years, the Southern Railway Depot had stood empty and abandoned alongside the tracks on the south side of the lake. After the passenger service had ended in 1948, it remained as a freight depot for several years. Finally in 1966, the Southern Railway closed the freight service over the strenuous opposition of several Assembly residents and others.

By 1969, the old depot was abandoned and up for sale. Dr. John Holler from Columbia, South Carolina bought it with the intention of moving it to the top of Utah mountain and using it as a summer home. This proved to be impossible. It was estimated that the weight of the station was thirty tons. It actually weighed more than seventy tons, primarily because of its tile roof. Elmore Bailey then purchased the depot and had it moved to a site a few hundred yards away on South Lakeshore Drive. As the depot was being moved, a wheel broke and it blocked the road. After a week, it was finally moved to its new location on South Lakeshore Drive and converted into a private house.[43] Later, the converted depot became the home of retired Bishop Edward Tullis.

CHAPTER NINE

The 70s

• • • • • • • • • • • • • • •

As noted earlier, from the very beginning the Assembly facilities were owned by many individuals and groups. Begun by a group of laymen and owned by a corporation formed by this group, the dam, auditorium, and two hotels were owned by the original group. Other buildings, built as years went by, were also owned by the corporation. At the same time, individuals were involved in the construction and ownership of accommodations. The very first guest facility, opened in 1914, was Epworth Lodge—built and owned by George R. Stuart. Virginia Lodge (1917, later Cherokee Inn), was built by James R. Cannon. Lakeside Lodge (1921–22) was built and originally owned by J. B. Ivey. Later, there were several owners through the years. The Centenary Mission Inn (1921, later Lambuth Inn) was built by the Board of Missions of the Methodist Episcopal Church, South while the Religious Education Building (later Shackford Hall) was built by the Board of Education of the Methodist Episcopal Church, South in 1923. Colonial Hotel (1922) was built and operated by the T. L. McClees family. There were numerous other privately owned boarding houses, lodges, and inns including James Atkins's original summer home. Most of the youth camps were initially owned and operated privately or by church agencies.

This fragmented ownership caused problems for the Assembly management, as we saw in the case of the integration struggle. There was also the fear that private ownership could result in a change in the spiritual climate of the campus. Beginning in the 1950s, there was a real effort of the part of the church to obtain ownership of the major facilities. During 1950, the Assembly became the owner of Camp Adventure. Earlier in 1948, after Cherokee Inn (located just west of Terrace Hotel) had been demolished, the Assembly purchased the land on which it stood.

IN 1973, THE OLD TERRACE HOTEL WAS DEMOLISHED TO MAKE ROOM FOR A NEW TERRACE HOTEL

During the seventies, Colonial Hotel and Lakeside Lodges were purchased. By the end of the seventies, the Assembly had obtained owner-ship of the majority of the public buildings on the Assembly grounds.

At a meeting of the Executive Committee of the Board of Trustees held on November 1, 1971, Dr. Edgar Nease shared a draft resolution to be presented to the 1972 Southeastern Jurisdictional Conference which would create a major fundraising campaign designed to raise monies for capital improvements at the Assembly.

The need was significant. There were serious maintenance matters, which included dredging silt that was continuing to accumulate in the lake. The silt problem, first identified by engineer James Seaver in 1920, had continued as he had said it would, and the lake was slowly filling. Likewise, the infrastructure, particularly the sewer system, now approaching sixty years old was beginning to break down. These were pressing matters. As early as 1962, one of the urgent needs for the Assembly, as reported by Edwin Jones, was a new Terrace Hotel.[1] In addi-tion, there were additional needs at Lambuth Inn.

The original 1921 building was in desperate need of repair. The two additions, one on each side of the original building, never quite fit. There

THE GEORGE R. STUART AUDITORIUM, CIRCA 1970

were differences in hallway connections necessitating a step up or down along with other problems.

Besides this, it was becoming very apparent that while there had yet to be any specific decision, the Assembly was rapidly moving to a year-round operation. Already, Interpreter's House had used Lambuth Inn well beyond the summer season with significant success. Unfortunately, Lambuth did not have adequate heating and Terrace had no heat at all. On top of this, attendance at events was increasing and additional guest rooms were desperately needed. Nease proposed that there be a capital funds effort which he called the Junaluska Improvement Fund. The resolution called for each church in the jurisdiction to give an amount equal to one dollar per member payable over the four years of the upcoming quadrennium. There would be four major projects funded by the program:

Center Section of Lambuth—& small auditorium—$1,500,000
New Terrace Hotel—$1,500,000
Dredging—$250,000
New Sewer Lines—$200,000

The method of raising the funds would be left up to the individual conferences. Some suggestions were included however. Possible ways: budget, special drives, personal subscriptions, and various organizations in local church.

A great deal of discussion followed. Mr. R. P. Caldwell suggested another name for the project. He felt it would be better to name it The Junaluska Development Fund. The committee agreed and the name was changed.[2]

Further provisions of the resolution included:

(A) All monies would be paid to the treasurer of the jurisdiction and be remitted monthly to the Assembly;
(B) No monies could be used for anything but capital improvements; and
(C) Promotion and publicity would be financed through the regular budget and the Associates program.

    The Executive Committee, and later the entire Board of Trustees, approved the resolution and submitted it to the Jurisdictional Conference.

When the resolution was perfected, it then became the responsibility of Dr. Nease to include it in his report to the Jurisdictional Conference. He presented this on Thursday, July 13, 1972. The conference accepted his report and the resolution, making it a part of the total financial program for the jurisdiction. Thus, the way was open for the campaign to begin. It would indeed have the force and backing of the jurisdictional administration.

Quotas were set for each of the conferences and, in addition, a Special Gifts Committee was named with Dr. Wilson Weldon named as the chairman. This committee would seek gifts from a list of donors who were deemed able to make significantly large contributions. A brochure entitled "New Hope for Tomorrow" was printed and circulated throughout the jurisdiction. The folder outlined the program, pointing to the needs and giving estimated costs for each facet of the improvements. The estimated cost of the new Terrace Hotel was one and a half million dollars.[3]

As the funds began to come in, the planning moved forward. The most visible and popular feature of the project was the new Terrace Hotel. Several designs were offered by various architects. Some designs were examined and rejected. The design accepted by the trustees was offered by Six Associates, Inc. One of the most interesting aspects of the design phase was that Dr. Nease asked for and received suggestions from persons from all over the jurisdiction, including its leadership, rank, and file Methodists and property owners at the Assembly. He got a great many replies. Among these was one from Mrs. Mary Gatewood, who said that the new hotel should have ". . . long porches with that breathtaking view . . . railings on the porches on which men could prop their feet! I don't know that this had any spiritual effect, but it seemed to mean a lot of solid comfort."[4] Another interesting suggestion was that there should be "small bachelor rooms with shower stalls . . ." This came from Dr. Harry Denman of the General Board of Evangelism.[5] Still another from Mrs. Nowelee Green suggested that a fireplace be in the lobby ". . . that, to me, adds so much warmth (not literally) but friendly warmth, conducive to fellowship."[6] Many of the suggestions were included in the design, although there is no evidence that there were any rooms designated for bachelors! Finally the day came when the *Birmingham Christian Advocate* ran an article with a headline entitled, "Terrace Hotel Coming Down." The accompanying picture shows a crane with a wrecking ball crashing into the old hotel. The article states, "After some sixty years of service to people who came . . . the hotel has closed its doors and been torn down. Thousands of people have enjoyed its wide porches and breezy hallways through the years. It was a favorite honeymoon spot for some; for others a great place to stay year after year to renew acquaintances with Methodist friends across the Southland . . ."[7]

The new hotel was built in two stages. The first stage was comprised of the guest rooms from the fourth floor up. The Special Gifts Committee sought gifts to cover the furnishing of the one hundred bedrooms. The rooms were then identified as memorials, honors, etc. The second stage included the street entrance, lobby, dining hall, classrooms, and auditorium. The initial estimate of construction time called for the hotel to be completed by the summer of 1976. This proved very optimistic.

A headline in the April 28, 1976 edition of the the *Waynesville Mountaineer* newspaper stated, "Terrace Hotel Construction Delayed." The article began, "Despite rain, sleet, and snow during the winter, some progress has been made . . . in the construction of the first phase of the new Terrace Hotel. The progress made, however, is not as much as had been hoped for, say officials.[8] The article further states that, to date, $1,071,386 of a goal of $2,969,389 has been raised.[9]

THE COLONIAL HOTEL BUILT IN 1922 AND OWNED BY THE T. L. MCCLEES FAMILY

The first phase was finally completed in 1977, with a temporary lobby built to serve until completion of the second phase. This enabled the guest rooms to be used during the years between the stages. Likewise, the old annex was allowed to remain and was used during the period between the two stages. The second phase opened in 1980.

While construction of the hotel was proceeding, so were the other projects in the development program. A news release dated February 22, 1974 stated: "A contract has been signed to remove some 350,000 cubic yards of silt from the upper section of Lake Junaluska. Work will start at once with a completion schedule in early fall. The project will cost over 400,000 . . ."[10] Likewise, the upgrading of the sewer system continued throughout the seventies. Much of the sewage system work was done in cooperation with the city of Waynesville, whose treatment plant handled Assembly sewage. At one point during the decade, the Assembly paid 10 percent of the cost of operation of the Waynesville plant.

By 1976, it was apparent that (at least at the early stage of fundraising) there would not be enough support for the improvements to Lambuth Inn and that portion of the Development Program was abandoned. Six Associates had done preliminary work on the project and they were paid for the work they had done. Quietly, this item of the total project was given up. However, the work was still very much needed at the hotel, as we shall see.

At a meeting of the Board of Trustees held on February 13, 1976, engineer Dr. Langfelder gave a disturbing report regarding the condition of the dam. He reported that he had examined the dam and discovered that the water-proof-membrane covering the face of the dam had failed and water was percolating through the dam. As it did so, it went through a freeze-thaw cycle causing a deterioration of the structure. If this continued, ultimately the dam would fail. He further recommended that a new face be built and also extensive repair on the buttresses. He estimated that the cost for repair would range from three hundred fifty thousand dollars to four hundred thousand dollars. Feeling that they had no choice, the trustees authorized the repairs.[11] The lake was lowered and a coffer dam was built to hold the water away from face of the dam.

At the October 15th meeting of the trustees, the engineers were present with a progress report. They stated that the buttresses were in better condition than they had originally believed. When asked when the coffer dam would be removed, they stated that it was their plan to leave it in place when the water was raised. It would be under water and not seen. They also indicated that the entire project should be completed by March of 1977.[12]

March came and went and the project was still not complete. Finally, the engineers reported to the trustees that the project would be completed no later than June 15th, at which point the frustrated trustees requested that every effort be made to have it finished by June 3rd.[13]

The Junaluska Supply building (by now known as the Liner Building) at the east entrance to the Assembly had been empty since the business closed. At the trustees meeting on March 25th, it was reported that the Liner Building was now on the market. The asking price was forty thousand dollars. It was suggested that the board should act quickly to negotiate the purchase of the property. R. P. Caldwell moved that the Assembly purchase the property. The motion was seconded by Granville Crockett and passed unanimously.[14] A portion of it was then leased to the Jurisdictional Commission on Archives and History for future use at a repository and a museum which they planned to name The Heritage Center.

From its construction in 1922, the Colonial Hotel had been privately owned by its builders, Mr. & Mrs. T. L. McClees. At an early point in the history of the Assembly, it had been the accommodation of choice for many persons. Like many of the early structures, it had deteriorated over its fifty years of life. As early as 1948 the McCleeses had discussed selling the hotel with F. S. Love. Then in 1951, their daughter, Nellie, had written to Superintendent H. G. Allen offering to sell the hotel to the Assembly for forty thousand dollars. Allen, in reply, indicated that he would carry her offer to the trustees. He did this along with a recommendation that they not buy the facility's.[14] Two years later, she again approached the Assembly, this time offering to sell for thirty thousand dollars. Finally in 1954, McClees sold the hotel to Mrs. Jack Bowen and Mrs. Ralph White.

Later, in his report to the Board of Trustees meeting held on August 7, 1971, Superintendent Edgar Nease wrote:

> One of the biggest improvements has been the acquisition of Colonial Hotel and the renovation program. Two-thirds of this establishment has been completely redone giving us lovely dining, kitchen, and lobby facilities and 20 new rooms with private baths. To Mr. & Mrs. George Finch, who made this acquisition and renovation possible, the LJA shall be eternally grateful.[16]

For the next eighteen years, the newly renovated hotel was a popular destination for many visitors to the Assembly. In 1989, it was closed as a hotel and designated as housing for the summer staff.

The mid-1970s saw significant changes, endings and beginnings for the Assembly. Over the years, the rules concerning the election of Queens of Junaluska changed at times. The most significant came in 1973. Whereas in the past, residents of the summer community and summer staffers voted to choose the person to be named queen, that summer only the youth would have a vote. Thus it was that on Friday, August 10, Miss Sylvia Ann Harkness was crowned Queen of Junaluska. Harkness would have the distinction of being the only African American queen so named.[17] The same evening, Fred McWhorter was crowned king and was the only person ever named King of Junaluska. Four years later, on Thursday, August 4, 1977 Miss Rose Ann Haire was crowned Queen of Junaluska. She would be the last of fifty-four such queens. Various reasons have been given for the end of the tradition. Most are conjecture. In truth, things were different after more than fifty years. There was less of a summer community atmosphere at the Assembly. Cultural and social changes were taking place. The close-knit interaction among those who spent the summer at the lake was not the same. Fewer and fewer families were in residence for the entire summer. Youth who worked on summer staff did not tend to be the children of summer residents to the degree they had in years gone by. The old criteria just didn't apply anymore. Thus a grand tradition came to an end with little fanfare. The world was changing, and so were summers at the Assembly.

Likewise this was the year that the Junaluska Associates announced their first recipient of the Chief Junaluska Award. Bishop Paul Hardin was named Chief Junaluska during the annual Junaluska Associates weekend. This award, which is given annually, recognizes those persons who have made significant contributions, including financial, services, and promotion, to the Assembly.[18]

Another acquisition by the Assembly during the seventies was the Lakeside Lodges, built in the twenties by J. B. Ivey. The property had changed ownership several times. In the early seventies, the Bruce Gannaways, a clergy couple in Florida, owned Lakeside which consisted of the two lodges, a dining hall, and a house which they called the "motel." They had operated it in the summer for eight years. During a Laity Conference, four Methodist laymen from Florida decided to attempt to purchase the Lodges, demolish them, and build a group of condominiums on the site. In a letter to the trustees, the spokesman for the group, John A. Wall, proposed the purchase. Hugh Massey, chairman of the trustees then wrote to Wall thanking them for their interest and informing them that the Assembly needed the property for future housing.[19] The trustees then purchased the four structures, along with the 3.5 acres from the Gannaways for seventy-five thousand.

Since the creation of the Waynesville By-pass through the west end of the campus in 1947 and the building of the causeway entrance in 1963, more traffic entered the Assembly at that location than at any other. An impressive entrance gate was needed at that location, although there were no longer entrance fees.

Trustees' minutes recorded:

On August 3, 1974, at a meeting of the Trustees, Dr. Wright Spears, Chairman of the Buildings and Grounds Committee, reported that the Committee discussed a proposed new gate in the western side of the grounds. An offer has come from the Home Owners Association that it would be glad to undertake this as a project. Architects have drawn plans . . . Dr. Spears made this in the form of a motion and it was seconded by George Proctor. The motion passed unanimously.[20]

The new West Gate was completed and dedicated on Wednesday October 12, 1977 at 5:00 PM. The presentation of the gate was given by Mrs. Tom A. Wooding Jr. and the acceptance was by Drs. Spears and Paul Worley. The dedicatory prayer was given by Bishop L. Scott Allen.[21]

At the same August Trustees' meeting, Dr. Spears reported that Dr. H. G. Allen had given a gift of twenty-five thousand dollars to be used to enlarge the Branscomb Administration Building. Plans had been drawn for an annex and also for improved parking in the rear of the building. The estimated cost was forty thousand dollars. The annex would increase the available space by four additional offices. Dr. Nease suggested that the addition be named the Allen Annex. He further suggested that the auditorium offering on Junaluska Sunday be allocated for this purpose. The board passed a motion to accept the proposal.[22]

On August 2, 1975 at 2:30 PM a service of dedication for the new Allen Annex was held; Bishop Paul Hardin presided. The presentation of the new wing was made by Dr. Edgar Nease and W. Hugh Massie, chairman of the Board of Trustees accepted the annex on behalf of the Assembly.[23]

As noted earlier, there were privately owned cottages on the Assembly grounds from the beginning. Indeed, the Assembly had encouraged this. This was one of the many means of raising the capital needed for construction and maintenance of facilities. For the first four or five decades, these cottages were used as summer homes almost exclusively, but later many became year-round residences. Also, as one might expect, the homeowners began to meet for the purpose of fellowship, support, and dealing with matters unique to property owners. No one seems to know when the first such owner's meeting took place. At first they were very informal gatherings. In his book, *The Story of Lake Junaluska*, Mason Crum has a delightful description of these early meetings:

> *When I came here thirty years ago, they were holding them and getting a peculiar kind of excitement and satisfaction from them. The cottage owners meeting has become a kind of indoor sport. As in all good families, there must be a time and place for setting things in order, and talking over weak points, and even fussing a little. Just so the cottage owner's meeting, held once or twice a year, is the place for the big family stock-taking and grievance airing. There is something slightly comical about the average cottage owner's meeting, the humor arising from the fact that it has no authority whatever. We talk ourselves blue*

in the face, have a good time telling what is wrong and what ought to be done,
and then go home satisfied that we "told them so."[24]

As years went by, the meetings became more frequent and better organized. The organizations bore several names. It appears that the first title was the Cottage Owners Association. This name was later changed to the Lake Junaluska Home Owners Association. In the late seventies, the Home Owners Association began what was called First Wednesday Coffees. These were times of gathering at which items of interest and concern might be discussed informally.

In 1979, Paul Worley served as president and Clay Madison was vice president. The leadership of the association felt that they needed to broaden the support of their efforts by adding more members. Thus, in 1980 they offered a plan to reorganize the group. Included in the plan was a change of name from Home Owners Association to The Junaluskans and to include in its membership friends and neighbors who might be interested in building a supportive community, whether they owned property or not. The plan was adopted on May 7, 1980. Worley and Madison continued as officers of the new organization.[25]

Almost a decade later, a newspaper article in the *Waynesville Mountaineer* stated that a movement was underway for the town of Waynesville to attempt to annex Lake Junaluska This news was met with mixed feelings and strong concern on the part of many home owners. It was felt that as a result of the reorganization of the Home Owners Association, there was no group to speak authoritatively for property owners. The owners met on October 21, 1989 to address this issue. At the meeting, John J. Miller read a paper which observed that the Junaluskans Organization had evolved from a homeowner's organization into "a social and service oriented organization welcoming anyone to be a member whether they owned property or not."[26] The result was the forming of a new organization whose purpose was to deal with matters unique to persons owning property at the Assembly. The constitution for the organization was ratified at the meeting. It was named the Lake Junaluska Property Owners Organization (LJAPOO). The first president was Clay Madison.

In another matter related to property ownership and residency at the Assembly, the idea of condominiums had been in the minds of several persons for several years. It appeared to some that the time was ripe for there to be another option beyond buying or building a home at the

Assembly, should one desire to live on the campus or a second home for vacation and/or attendance at the many events held there. Likewise, there were those who saw in the building of condominiums a ripe business opportunity. The trustees, on the other hand, were very cautious and cool to the idea. It was the desire for such an undertaking that had precipitated the invoking of the "right of first refusal" clause at the time of the Assembly's purchase of Lakeside Lodge, as noted earlier.[27]

Several studies were done to determine the feasibility of such construction. Some were by private groups. At a meeting of the Trustees Executive Committee held on October 11, 1978 the Buildings and Grounds Committee asked for authorization to be granted for a feasibility study for consideration of possible condominiums to be constructed on the Liner property and that an architect be hired. On motion of Bishop Mack Stokes and second by Dr. Allgood, the motion passed. An ad hoc committee was then formed with Lachlan Hyatt as chairperson. Their conclusion was that such a project was, indeed, feasible.[28]

However, when a resolution giving the Executive Committee authority to build condominiums on the Liner property near the southeast entrance to the Assembly was brought to the Board of Trustees, it was soundly defeated.[29]

In spite of the opposition, the concept refused to die. Later Hyatt reported that the Ad Hoc Condominium Committee had made significant progress since their previous meeting. He further reported that they had hired Mr. Michael Miller of the firm of Adams, Hendon, Carson & Crow P.A. of Asheville, along with Glen Brown the Assembly Counsel. Miller had written an eighteen-page opinion letter in which he stressed the interrelated and supportive roles of the board and the proposed Junaluska Housing, Inc. Hyatt further stated that there was a list of fifty-five expressions of interest in a condo at Lake Junaluska.

Another resolution was then brought to the board, which gave the Executive Committee authority to make further studies redevelopment of condominiums on Junaluska property, to formulate plans for the development and construction of same. Further authority was given to select the location and purchase from the Assembly such lands as needed. They were also given permission to borrow such funds as needed for the project. It was stipulated that the project must be self-supporting. The resolution called for the Executive Committee of the Trustees to make further studies as deemed necessary for the development of condominiums.

It further called for the organization of a "wholly owned subsidiary corporation of the Assembly . . . which would plan, develop, and contract for construction of condominiums and the sale of individual units therein . . ."[30] There would be seven directors selected from the jurisdiction appointed by the president of the Board of Trustees. It called for the project to be self-supporting. It further outlined the duties, restrictions, and details of the corporation. In addition, there was a further recommendation that the Executive Committee be given the sum of sixty thousand dollars as a contribution from the Assembly to the corporation.

It noted that the corporation would be subject to the will of the Executive Committee of the Board of Trustees. Upon motion of Earl Wilson and second by Bishop Edward Tullis, the resolution passed unanimously and Junaluska Assembly Housing, Inc. was born.[31]

Early in the life of the Assembly, Mr. and Mrs. H. E. Adams, residents of Florida, built a large summer home at a prominent location near the junction of Lakeshore Drive and Whitfield Way. It was an impressive house which had commanding views of mountain vistas in three directions. As a result, they named it Tri-Vista. Long-time residents remember that they built tennis courts on the grounds and allowed others to use the courts long before there were any Assembly-owned courts. Junaluska Housing chose this as the location for their new condominiums. The house was moved to a site on nearby Rogers Cove Road.

In May of 1984, a groundbreaking ceremony was held. A photo in the Junaluska Associates newsletter shows Dr. Wright Spears, Norman Paschall, Lachlan Hyatt, and Dr. Mel Harbin breaking ground for the new Tri-Vista Villas.

An intensive marketing campaign began and there was immediate response on the part of potential condo owners. Units were selling briskly. There were to be some bumps in the road, however. In 1986, the Internal Revenue Service ruled that Junaluska Assembly Housing, Inc. was not tax-exempt. Their ruling was appealed and a letter from the office of Chief Counsel of the Internal Revenue Service, dated October 27, 1986 indicated that the tax ruling came on October 21, 1986 recognizing Junaluska Assembly Housing, Inc. as exempt from federal income tax. The letter is signed by Director Robert P. Ruwe.[32]

By the fall of 1985, the condos were complete and the new owners were moving in. Unfortunately, this was not the end of the problems for the condominium project, as we shall see in a later chapter.

For many persons the sixties and seventies were the halcyon years of the Assembly. Those were the days of the great jurisdictional meetings that filled the auditorium and attracted much interest and publicity. Such events as the Candler Camp Meeting, SEJ Laity Conference, the Jurisdictional Minister's Week, the Prayer and Bible Conference (sponsored by The Upper Room Ministry), the Music Week, the Youth in Missions Conference, and others consistently drew bus loads of participants from local churches throughout the Southeast. In subsequent decades, the emergence of similar events located in and initiated, planned, and supported by annual conferences along with changes in travel and communication resulted in smaller crowds and, in some cases, the demise of events. There were then more opportunities for training, inspiration, and spiritual growth and many were simply closer to home. However, many persons still look back wistfully to those glory days.

CHAPTER TEN

The 80s

· · · · · · · · · · · · · ·

In February of 1979, Superintendent Mel Harbin received a very disturbing letter from Susan Emmons of Raleigh. Emmons was reporting on her recent stay in Lambuth Inn. In it she complained about the food, heat, and general condition she found there.[1] Her unhappiness was justified. Other guests at the hotel had similar complaints. The venerable old hotel was in bad shape. When the Junaluska Development Campaign began, it was a given that the restoration of the hotel would be one of the included projects. As reported earlier, the hotel project was abandoned due to a lack of funds.

The 1980 Southeastern Jurisdictional Conference gave new life to the project. The conference continued the Junaluska Development Fund for another quadrennium and subsequently their budget included a grant of two hundred thousand dollars for Junaluska Assembly. They also requested that the district superintendents make the Lake Junaluska Advance a priority item for the charge conferences in 1980 and 1981.[2] Now the churches of the jurisdiction would continue financial support. This action, coupled with the success of the new Junaluska Associates program, assured that the plans for the restoration of Lambuth Inn (which had been all but abandoned in the late seventies) could be revived. With the new funding given by the Jurisdictional Conference, the proposal was then revisited.

Initially there was concern over whether the board was obligated to give the project back to Six Associates, the company that had designed the new Terrace Hotel and had done preliminary design work on Lambuth, or if they were free to hire another group. However, Glen Brown, legal counsel for the Assembly, indicated that when the initial project for Lambuth Inn was abandoned in 1976, the Assembly paid Six Associates for their work to date and thus there was no further obligation. Six Associates agreed and relinquished any further claim.

A local Waynesville firm, Foy and Lee Architects, was retained and in April of 1982 they presented a document to the trustees which outlined the plans for the project. It stated that the purpose of the project would be ". . . to upgrade the existing center section of Lambuth Inn in its entirety, to improve its function as a conference center facility, to upgrade furnishings and systems as needed in both wings, and to effectively combine all three sections into one operational unit."[3] Among the requirements was that the building be accessible to the handicapped so as to make it completely usable by senior citizens and for groups with special needs.[4] Another stipulation was that the Korean Room would be relocated from above the front porch to the third floor. As a part of the project, the existing stairways would be removed and replaced.

At this point, Foy and Lee estimated the cost of the project to be $244, 246. The timeline for the effort was from December of 1982 until April of 1983. It was not until the spring of 1984 that the project was completed.

Another important feature of the Lambuth Inn project was the earlier creation of the Gilbert Room. A headline in the July 14, 1980 edition of the *Waynesville Mountaineer* read: "Gilbert Room Honors Black Methodist." It went on to state:

> *With the dedication of the John Wesley Gilbert Room at Lambuth Inn on July 9, a name important to Methodist History was reclaimed at Lake Junaluska. . . . For years at the west end of the grounds stood the Gilbert Center, where blacks held separate worship services. When churches became integrated the little center disappeared but the name of Gilbert lived on in the hearts of folks who knew his story.*[5]

A large room at the west end of the first floor of the hotel was designated as a memorial to Dr. John Wesley Gilbert. As noted earlier, Gilbert accompanied Bishop Walter Russell Lambuth on a mission endeavor to the Belgium Congo in Africa. Later, the building at the Assembly designated for ministry to African American persons was named for him. The building was removed in the sixties to make room for the Junaluska Apartments. It was deemed most appropriate that recognition for the contribution of Dr. Gilbert be a part of the building named for Lambuth.

Dedication of the Gilbert Room was held July 9, 1980. Participating in the dedication service was Dr. Clayton Calhoun, former president of Paine College. Dr. Wright Spears, president of the Lake Junaluska Assembly trustees, presided. Dr. G. Ross Freeman, executive secretary of the Southeastern Jurisdictional Council, unveiled the portrait. Bishop Frank L. Robertson, president of the College of Bishops, accepted the memorial. The invocation was given by Dr. Israel Rucker, director of the Southeastern Jurisdictional Commission on Race Relations and Ethnic Minority Concerns.

Following the completion of the Lambuth restoration, application was made to the United States Department of the Interior for the inn to be placed on the National Register of Historic Places in the United States. On September 29, 1982 Dr. Harbin received a letter from John J. Little, Deputy State Historic Preservation Officer which contained the certificate stating that Lambuth Inn had been entered in the National Register of Historic Places. In the letter, Little mentioned that the National Register had been called ". . . a roll call of the tangible reminders of the history of the United States."[6] Earlier, Shackford Hall had been so designated also.

Likewise, by the early eighties it was becoming very apparent that something would have to be done about Lakeside Lodge. The complex of two guest houses with a dining room between had been constructed in the early 1920s by J. B. Ivey. The accommodations were spartan, but adequate for the early days of the Assembly. As time moved on, the old facility deteriorated and on several occasions there were expressed concerns about conditions and safety. At the September 1984 meeting of the Board of Trustees, member Mrs. Twick Morrison noted that, "after a visit by the Children and Youth Committee, it was determined that the descriptions of the fire hazard and health hazards at Lakeside Lodge were not exaggerated."[7] The committee went on to recommend that Lakeside Lodge be closed permanently at the end of the summer. The trustees voted to approve the recommendations in principal and to refer the matter to "respective committees for implementation."[8]

As early as 1978, Foy and Lee developed a cost analysis and other preliminary plans for a new Lakeside Lodge. As in the case of Lambuth Inn, the project had been put on hold. Now with new funding assured, the Lakeside project could also be revived. By the fall of 1984, it was reported that the new Lakeside Lodge was under construction. The projected cost was seven hundred twenty thousand dollars. The new facility was completed and opened in 1985. With the completion of the new Lakeside, the major components of the Junaluska Development Campaign were considered completed.

Bishop Roy Clark had a serious concern as he traveled to the meeting of the Board of Trustees in December 1980. He perceived that there was a lack of support for the Assembly by many of the local churches. Thus, when he presented the report of the Promotion and Program Committee, which he chaired, he expressed this concern. He further stated that he was seeking ways to improve communication so that local churches might better understand the role of the Assembly. He suggested that an advisory committee be named for the Intentional Growth Center as a means of drawing it into a closer relationship with the Assembly. The report from the committee called for the naming of such a committee along with an advisory committee for the music program.[9] These issues were discussed but no action was taken.

In a later meeting of the board, Bishop Clark noted that there was, in fact, a need for an advisory council for the Assembly, which would be made up of one person in each district in the Southeast. This council would become a communication link between local churches and the Assembly. Building on this suggestion, Norman Paschal suggested that there needed to be a Committee on Communication and Interpretation.[10]

When the board gathered in November, Clark reported that the bishops had approved the formation of the committee with the understanding that the district superintendent and district lay leader would jointly designate a member of the council from each of the districts in the jurisdiction. This committee would provide a channel of communication for information and interpretation between the Assembly and the United Methodists of the jurisdiction. The committee members would be related to the Board of Trustees through the Committee on Communication and Interpretation. They would be persons on the District Council on Ministries and would act as Lake Junaluska representatives to collect things we ought to hear and take back things we would like to send. Clark further pointed out that the term "advisors" was used because they wanted to convey the idea that Junaluska is listening, thus Junaluska Advisors.

As a follow-up of these suggestions, during the November meeting of the Board, the Committee on Communication and Interpretation was formed with board member Dr. George Gilbert as chairperson. A new position, director of public relations, was created and Marie Grasty was named to this post.[11]

By the summer of 1982, the new Committee on Communication and Interpretation reported that one hundred sixty-three districts in the Southeastern Jurisdiction had named advisors. There remained forty-seven districts that had not been heard from. As 1982 came to an end, there were one hundred fifty-five Junaluska Advisors. Training sessions were to be held in all conferences. The first of these was held in December of 1982 in the Holston Conference. The plan was that by the first of June in 1983, all conferences would have had training sessions and the Junaluska Advisory Council would be a reality. Bishop Clark's initial concern had resulted in a significant channel of communication between the Assembly and the local church.

Reverend Brooks Little was the curator of the Upper Room Museum in Nashville, Tennessee during the seventies and early eighties. Little also had great affection for the Lake Junaluska Assembly and its heritage. On one occasion, while walking along the sidewalk adjacent to the Upper Room Building, he happened to glance in a trash dumpster nearby. He noticed an object that appeared to be a printer's plate for a press. On closer examination, he discovered the name "Junaluska" on the plate. Rescuing it from the dumpster, he later took it to a printer who printed a copy of the material on the plate. It turned out to be a map of the available lots at the new Southern Assembly and was dated 1912. Little, who had an intense interest in history, and particularly the history of the Assembly, saved the plate. He continued to collect other materials related to the Assembly. This collection continued to grow until he had a closet full of Assembly artifacts.[12]

On September 19, 1981, Little along with Marynell Waites, a member of the Jurisdictional Historical Society, and Charles Brockwell, a member of the new Jurisdictional Commission on Archives and History, in conversation, shared their concerns about the need for preserving and disseminating the history and heritage of Methodism in the Southeast. Out of this came a document entitled, "The Southeastern United Methodist Heritage Center—A Plan for the Southeastern Jurisdiction Council on Ministries."[13] The plan called for there to be established a site whose mission would be "to represent, and to interpret the Southeastern United Methodist heritage to all the ethnic constituencies of the

Southeastern Jurisdiction and to the public at large."[14] To accomplish its purpose, the center would have several functions:

- It would be a museum of SEJ United Methodists and also of Lake Junaluska;
- It would provide assistance to genealogical researchers;
- It would be a repository for the archives of the SEJ; and
- It would encourage scholarly research and publication in the history of the Wesleyan denominations in the Southeast.[15]

It was proposed that initially it would be housed in the first floor west wing of Lambuth Inn or in the Liner Building, site of the second Junaluska Supply Company. Later, it would move to a building built specifically for the center.

The Board of Trustees voted to name a Heritage Center Feasibility Study Committee, and did so. Its initial meeting was on November 10, 1982. At this meeting, Dr. Charles Brockwell was named chairman, Ben St. Clair, vice-chairman, and Mrs. Virginia Whitworth, secretary.

A study by this committee resulted in a decision that the plan was feasible. Furthermore, the committee proposed that the cost of the project would be one million dollars and would include allocations of $500,000 for 10-12,000 square feet of space and $500,000 for an endowment to provide utilities, maintenance, staffing, and operation. Funding would be received in the following manner: the Southeastern Jurisdiction would provide $500,000, foundations with United Methodist entities would be approached for $250,000, a Heritage Center Bi-Centennial Club would be formed to raise $250,000 and the Southeastern Jurisdictional Council on Ministries, and Lake Junaluska would budget $40,000 annually.

When the proposal was initially presented to the Executive Committee of the SEJ Council on Ministries during their meeting in March of 1983, it met with both skepticism and serious reservations. It was pointed out that some in the church might view this as a sour grapes move, coming as it did shortly after the decision to locate the general archives at Drew University. Likewise, it might be seen as competing with the new national repository and drain away needed financial support. In addition, there was expressed the fear that the Assembly trustees might get stuck with a mortgage should the venture fail.

Nevertheless, the committee adopted a motion to authorize the SEJ Commission on Archives & History to designate its repository at the new Heritage Center. This was conditional upon approval by the Assembly Board of Trustees. They also adopted a motion that the SEJ Archives and History be authorized to develop a plan for enhancing The Heritage Center as a museum, archival repository, and library. To accomplish this, there would be established a ten member Heritage Center Committee. They also agreed that the committee would be authorized to contact foundations and special donors to raise money.[16]

Finally, both the Jurisdictional Council on Ministries and the Board of Trustees of the Assembly endorsed the concept of The Heritage Center. The Heritage Center was born. Later in July of that year, the Southeastern Jurisdiction Historical Society established the SEJ Historical Society Bicentennial Heritage Club for the purpose of providing funds for current and future operating expenses of the SEJ Heritage Center. This organization later became known as the Heritage Center Associates. Brooks Little was named as the first director of the SEJ Heritage Center.

On January 21, 1983, sixteen thousand pounds of archival materials, including the contents of Little's closet in Nashville, arrived at the Liner Building. The Heritage Center now had a home.

From the beginning, it was understood that the Liner Building location was temporary. For the first six years of its existence, however, this historic building was its home. In 1986, Brooks Little resigned, giving advancing years and a desire to have more personal time as his reason. In December, The Heritage Center Committee named Francis Hart as the new director. Mrs. Hart served for six years and was followed in January of 1993 by Mrs. Gerry Reiff. After the retirement of Mrs. Reiff in 2002, Kimberly Boyd became director. Mrs. Boyd served until 2007. Brooks Little died in 2006 and Mrs. Hart died in 2008.

For more than twenty years, the Harrell Center had served both residents and visitors to the Assembly. Now there were even greater needs. There was a need for an auditorium larger than those in the hotels, but not as large as the two-thousand-seat George R. Stuart Auditorium, which was the largest auditorium in Haywood County. The auditoriums in the hotels could, at best, seat two hundred fifty persons in each location. The Cokesbury Bookstore needed more room. And now there was a new need. What would be the permanent location for the new

Southeastern Jurisdiction Heritage Center? One possibility, suggested by the Jurisdictional Historical Society, was to excavate under the new Terrace Hotel and use the space there. Dr. Ed Tullis then approached the chairman of the Historical society, Dr. Ken Lile, and suggested that the society develop a definite proposal for such action for the Committee on Buildings and Grounds.[17] Lile agreed to do so. Following consideration of this proposal, the Buildings and Grounds Committee decided that, after considering all of the needs that this was unsuitable. Finally after considering several possibilities and following much discussion, the decision was made to remodel and expand the Harrell Center and, in so doing, to provide the space for all the current needs.

The idea of expanding the Harrell Center had been floated around for many years. Now it seemed that this was the best solution to the many problems. Finally in the summer of 1986, Barry Rogers, the Assembly superintendent, wrote Rick Lee confirming that the Assembly would like for them to move forward with the plans for the Harrell Center addition.[18] Foy and Lee responded with plans which would include, in addition to the space for the Heritage Center, space for Cokesbury, an adult lounge, a registration area, snack bar (tea room), library, auditorium, restrooms, offices, conference rooms, storage, and a work room. The area designated for the Heritage Center would contain 3,192 square feet of space. This compared favorably with the 2,200 feet in the Liner Building. In order for them to provide this space, the Board of Trustees required that the Commission on Archives and History raise two hundred thousand dollars of the cost.[19]

The projected cost given by Foy and Lee was $1,483,517 though the completed cost actually was more than $1,500,000. On October 28, 1986 a contract for the project was signed and work began shortly thereafter.

On April 21, 1982 in the town of Hazlewood just west of Waynesville, the calm of a lovely spring afternoon was shattered when a terrific explosion and fire erupted at the Benfield Industries chemical plant at 3:20 PM. The resulting black toxic smoke settled on the town causing the evacuation of more than two thousand persons. Included in these were the residents of several nursing homes. A headline in the *Waynesville Mountaineer* told the rest of the story. It read "Chemical Plant Explosion Turns Hotel into Hospital." The article went on to tell of one hundred thirty-two patients of the nursing home that were moved to the two top floors of the Terrace Hotel. A nurse's station was created in the hall of each

THE NEW LAKESIDE LODGE ON LAKESHORE DRIVE REPLACED AN EARLIER LODGE
BY THE SAME NAME

floor and a member of the hotel staff had a portable refrigerator that was
converted into a medical storage chest. An eyewitness of the activity
reported that by 7:00 that evening, there was a line of ambulances in front
of the hotel as far as the eye could see.[20]

On November 10, 1982, Rev. & Mrs. Gail Bergstresser, owners of
Come-Up Lodge, located just west of the World Methodist Building at
Lake Junaluska, entered into a contract with Mrs. Norma Wright to sell
her the lodge. Mrs. Wright and her husband already owned and operated the Sunset Inn located in the original Atkins House and the
Providence Lodge just behind it. The Board of Trustees, having considered the location of the lodge decided to invoke the "right of first
refusal" clause in the Bergstresser's deed to purchase the lodge for the
Assembly. From the initial sale of property in the earliest days of the
Southern Assembly, every deed issued contained the same provision. In
its earliest form it read:

> *That the party of the first part (the Assembly) may at all times possess an*
> *accurate record of the owners of lots in its territory and be able to protect the*
> *community from undesirable residents the party of the second part (the owner)*

> *. . . will give notice to said party of the first part, . . . in writing of any purpose to transfer the estate in said lands, and shall give to the Treasurer of the said Southern Assembly an option in writing to purchase said lands, good for ten days whether it will purchase the lands and in the event the said part of the first part declines to purchase said lands, the party of the second part, . . . may sell said lands to any other purchaser, provided the amount paid by said purchaser shall not be less in the net sum . . . than the price at which the lands were offered to the party of the first part.*[21]

Mrs. Wright through her attorney, John S. Stevens, notified the trustees that if they did not immediately allow her purchase to take place, she would file suit. After consideration by the Executive Committee of the Board of Trustees, Glen Brown, counsel for the Assembly, was instructed to communicate to the Wright's attorney, John S. Stevens, that the Assembly would not relinquish the property. In a letter to Stevens, Brown stated, ". . . the Assembly feels that the entire structure of its real estate operation and the objectives for which it was organized are at stake in this matter."[22]

Wright then made good on her threat and on March 30, 1983, she filed a complaint in Justice Court naming both the Assembly and the Bergstressers as defendants.[23] The initial ruling was in favor of the plaintiffs. The case dragged on in the courts until March 20, 1986 when, on appeal of the initial ruling, Judge James U. Downs of the North Carolina Superior Court dismissed all claims against the Assembly.[24] Initially the Wrights indicated that they would appeal the decision, but later in June of 1986 withdrew their appeal.

Thus a serious court challenge to the Assembly's protective clause was met and a legal precedent was established which would, in the future, protect the first refusal clause against further challenges. Years later, the Come-Up Lodge was moved to Cokesbury Circle behind the Administration Building to make room for an additional building for the World Methodist Headquarters complex, thus confirming the wisdom of the action of the Assembly.

During the 1984 session of the Southeastern Jurisdictional Conference, one of the reports from the Committee on Financial Administration called for the College of Bishops to ". . . appoint a committee, or assign an existing committee, the responsibility to study 1. overlapping programs, 2. staff, 3. office location and other concerns that involve Southeastern Jurisdictional Funds."[25] The Conference adopted this report on July 18th. Shortly thereafter, the College of Bishops named an eleven member committee. The committee consisted of: C. P. Minnick (chair), Robert M. Blackburn, Foy Campbell, William J. Carter, Roy C. Clark, M. McCoy Gibbs, Clay F. Lee, Olive J. McLendon, Effie E. Miller, William W. Morris, and Alvis A. Waite Jr.

During the next quadrennium, this committee met seven times. Significantly at the March 1, 1986 meeting of the Board of Trustees, Bishop Minnick gave a detailed report on their progress to date. In it, he noted that the recommendations from the committee had not been finalized. But he did share some of their thinking at that point. It is significant to note that there is no hint of any disillusion of the Assembly Board of Trustees. In fact, he pointed out in his report that the Board of Trustees and the Assembly director would continue to be responsible for services related to and using the Assembly facilities.[26]

When the Jurisdictional Conference of 1988 convened, the committee presented their report. In this report was the proposal for a totally new administrative structure for the jurisdiction. The report observed:

One suggestion that came repeatedly from many different persons and groups was that good stewardship and effective service call for a unified jurisdictional administrative structure which would have responsibility for all functions presently divided between the Jurisdictional Council on Ministries and the Lake Junaluska Trustees.[27]

Responding to this, the plan of reorganization contained no provision for a Junaluska Board of Trustees, but rather in its place substituted a Junaluska Division which would be a part of the new Southeastern Jurisdictional Administrative Council (SEJAC). Likewise, instead of there being a superintendent of the Assembly, the chief administrative officer would be the executive director of the jurisdiction. Also included in the report was the recommendation that all administrative offices of the jurisdiction would be moved from Atlanta, Georgia to Lake Junaluska Assembly. SEJAC then named Reginald Ponder as the new executive director and Clyde Mahaffey as the chairman of the Junaluska Division.

While the reorganization of the jurisdiction was well intended, carefully crafted, and, in fact, did eliminate several areas of overlapping responsibility, it also created a rather unwieldy oversight group for the Assembly, some of whose members had little interest in the Assembly.

Thus, while the reorganization may have been good for the jurisdiction, it was not in the best interest of the Assembly as time would tell.

On Tuesday, July 12, 1988 at 2:00 PM, just prior to the convening of the thirteenth session of the Southeastern Jurisdictional Conference of the Methodist Church, a large crowd of bishops, conference delegates, and other interested persons gathered in front of Stuart Auditorium for the unveiling of a monument. The sculpture was a likeness of Chief Junaluska, the Cherokee Indian whose name provided a portion of the title of the lake and the Assembly. Planning for this recognition had begun four years earlier.

At the Assembly Board of Trustees meeting held December 6, 1984, the report of the Committee on Communication and Interpretation, chaired by Dr. Reginald Ponder, included a recommendation that the trustees "explore the possibility of erecting a marker (monument) honoring Chief Junaluska on the Assembly grounds."[28] The report was approved.

It would appear that the impetus for such a request began with the Southeastern Jurisdiction Association of Native American Ministry (SEJANAM). Later, in the summer of 1985, Simeon F. Cummins, an Assembly trustee and coordinator of SEJANAM wrote to Superintendent Rogers, "Have you had an opportunity to give some thought to organizing the committee for the establishment for a memorial to Chief Junaluska?"[29]   Subsequently, the trustees appointed a committee to study the matter and to recommend some sort of memorial. The committee was made up of Judge Taylor Phillips of Macon, Georgia, Simeon Cummins, and Ms. Juanita Wolf of Cherokee, North Carolina.

As the committee began its work, another possibility for recognition of the Cherokee leader emerged. R. H. Ross, of Winston-Salem, North Carolina, suggested that a bronze bas-relief plaque honoring Junaluska and placed on a rock pedestal would be an appropriate recognition. Ross, himself somewhat a scholar of Cherokee history, even offered to finance the project.[30] Ross's father, Rev. C. R. Ross, had built a house on Atkins Loop in 1913. Ross had spent many summers at the Assembly during his boyhood. At one point, he had worked for the Junaluska station master delivering telegrams to persons at the Assembly. He noted that, in early days, he would walk barefoot to deliver telephone messages to the hotels since the only telephone was in the depot.[31]

Ross had an intense interest in Cherokee Indian history. He had compiled a sizable body of historic material related to the Cherokees and had written a paper entitled "A Brief History of the Cherokee Nation" for the *North American Moravian Journal*. Ross contended strongly for his concept of a bronze marker while SEJANAM envisioned a sculpture of a bust of Junaluska. At one point, it was proposed that there be perhaps two monuments. Likewise, the location of the markers was a major question. Early in the planning, it was suggested that perhaps one of them might be placed in the Heritage Center museum.

Finally, in a letter to Ross, Rogers indicated that the trustees had decided on just one monument and that the Native American Caucus of the SEJ would play a major role in the fundraising and development of the project.[32] He expressed appreciation for Ross's offer and encouraged him to add suggestions to the group. When Ross became aware that the committee was not going to use his design nor his choice of location for the marker, he withdrew his interest for and support of the project.

In a meeting on May 3, 1987, the committee decided on a life-sized bust from the waist up. After studying the work of several well-known sculptors, Paul Van Zandt of Red Springs, North Carolina was commissioned to create the statue. He was to be paid six thousand five hundred dollars plus travel.

Also at the meeting, the group decided to locate the monument near the Stuart Auditorium and that the unveiling would be scheduled for the opening of the 1988 Jurisdictional Conference.

The primary fundraising for the project was left to SEJANAM. A fundraising brochure was produced by the association. In this brochure, the total cost of the project is listed as ten thousand dollars.[33] The funds were raised that enabled the completion of the project and the 1988 Jurisdictional Conference began with the ceremonial unveiling.

From the earliest days of the Assembly, there had been speculation about the feasibility of building a footbridge across the narrow portion of the lake near the west end. This area was known simply as The Narrows. Nothing was ever done about the project for various reasons, including lack of funds and the opposition of some of the residents on the south side of the lake. A model of the area created as a part of a long range planning project by Mississippi State University in 1983 includes just such a bridge. By the eighties, renewed interest in the project was growing.[34]

It took two dedicated persons who had experienced the need for such a structure to fulfill the vision of others. For fourteen years, Paul and Willie Mae Turbeville brought youth from First Methodist Church in

Bradenton, Florida to the Assembly. On most of those visits, they walked around the lake even though it meant walking a mile along Highway 19. They saw the need for a footbridge and offered to build it. The Turbevilles, members of First United Methodist Church, gave one hundred fifty thousand dollars specifically for the construction of the bridge. It was to be eight feet wide and span the one hundred thirty-two feet between the north and south shores of the lake. At one point, it was designed to be high enough to enable the Assembly boat, the *Cherokee,* to pass under it. The bridge was completed the summer of 1988 and the dedication service took place on July 3rd at 2:00 PM.[35]

Later in 1992, a generous gift by Bill and Joetta Rhinehart made possible the completion of the walking path around the lake.[36] They, too, had become aware of the problems involved in trying to share the road with automobiles. Like the footbridge, the walking path had been a project of the Junaluska Associates and was awaiting funding. The bridge and the completed walking path opened a new opportunity for persons to walk the two and a half miles around the lake. Thus, the generosity of the two families opened a new opportunity for recreation and exercise to both the Junaluska community and the entire county.

The gift of the bridge also made possible another construction project for the Assembly. In 1987, the Junaluska Associates had begun a fund for the purpose of building the footbridge. The initial allocation for the fund was fifty thousand dollars. The Turbeville gift freed this fund for another purpose, namely the building of an amphitheater just below the Junaluska Cross. The amphitheater, which would seat two hundred persons was built as an indirect result of the gift by the Turbevilles. By 1989, the amphitheater was completed and in use.

Down at the dam, changes were taking place. For more than sixty years, the turbines that had amazed thousands by generating electricity to light the auditorium for the first service in 1913 sat unused. In 1979, congress had passed a bill requiring utility companies to purchase any electricity generated by local providers. The Board of Trustees decided to take advantage of this new legislation and, once again, generate electricity at the Junaluska Dam. Their decision was partially motivated by the knowledge that, under the provisions of the law, if they did not resume generating electricity at the dam someone else could step in and do it. The board also filed for a preliminary permit from the Federal Energy Regulatory Commission for such a project. Likewise, they applied for a thirty-six thousand dollar loan from the Department of Energy for a feasibility study.

In the fall of 1980, the Board of Trustees hired the Charles T. Main Company of Charlotte, North Carolina to study and design a project which would result in the development of a hydro-electric project at the Junaluska Dam.[37] In the March 1981 meeting of the trustees, Mr. Dick Hunt, an engineer with the company, reported the history of efforts to generate electricity at the dam, including the fact that generators that were installed when the dam was built were still in place. He also reported that the existing powerhouse could be used, although the generators were outdated. The conclusion of his report was that the plan to once again generate electricity was indeed feasible.[38]

Finally, in the spring of 1987, Progressive Hydro Corporation was hired to install turbines and other equipment to, once again, generate electricity. The installation would involve cutting new intakes in the dam to enable water to flow through the new turbines.[39] As a result, the lake was lowered in the fall of 1987 to facilitate the installation of the new equipment.

A later article in the *Waynesville Mountaineer* related to the lowering of the lake generated a great deal of concern for the wildlife that might be threatened by the project. Superintendent Barry Rogers reported that Assembly leaders had asked residents and other interested animal lovers to give stranded ducks and fish a home for the coming winter.[40]

The project was plagued by problems. In 1989, Dr. Reginald Ponder, by then executive secretary of SEJAC, reported that Progressive Hydro was in bankruptcy. He indicated that two turbines were in place and that he anticipated that the bankruptcy court would give the equipment to SEJAC and that North Carolina Power and Light (NCP&L) would operate them and also that the power would be used at the Assembly.[41]

Finally on August 6, 1991, the dedication service for the new hydro-electric plant was held with a ribbon cutting at the dam. Representing the Assembly at the service was Rev. Glenn Martin, associate executive director of Lake Junaluska and Clyde Mahaffey, president of the Lake Junaluska Division. Mr. Chuck Fuller, spokesman for NCP&L, indicated that the plant would produce enough power to serve about sixty-five homes.[42] The switches were thrown and, once again, the Junaluska Dam was producing electricity.

Unfortunately, the joy and satisfaction was not to last very long. There were continuing conflicts with the Federal Energy Regulatory

Commission, mainly issues related to dam safety and emergency prepared-
ness. There were demands made that were simply beyond the ability of the
Assembly finances. In early 1993, what was termed as "catastrophic problems" with the generator controls resulted in the bending of the shaft of
the generator.[43] What had occurred was that a lack of lubrication had
caused the generator to overheat and the heat warped the shaft. To remedy
this would have required the replacement of the generators. This, along
with the continuing problems with federal regulators, led to the decision
to cease operations of the plant and to terminate the contract with
NCP&L. Thus by May 31, 1993, after only two years of operation, the
production of electricity at the dam had ceased and the project ended. It
had been an expensive and frustrating experiment.[44]

In the mid-80s a great deal of attention was focused on the possibility
of having some form of health emphasis at the Assembly. This resulted in
the formation of what was called the WELLTH Ministry. In 1985, the
WELLTH Center opened. The beginning of the WELLTH Ministry was
described in a brochure entitled "Welcome to an Emerging Dream . . .
Junaluska Health and Fitness Center."[45] This was a small fitness center.
The first coordinator was Margie Hesson, RN. They offered weight
equipment, pressure screenings, fitness walking classes, health education
lectures, etc. The center was located initially in a portion of the Liner
Building. Later, the center was moved to the Paul Kern Youth Center
building. At first, the use of the center was limited to only the summer
months when the largest numbers of persons were present on the
campus. However, later it became a year-round operation. A letter written
to all WELLTH Center members in the late summer of 1987 gives winter
hours and urges members to get back into the routine of a regular exercise program that fall. It is signed by Cissy Lowry, RN.[46] Memberships
entitled the individual to all the facilities, including the swimming pool.

During the time the WELLTH Center was operating, water aerobics
were an integral part of its program in the summer. These activities took
place in the swimming pool adjacent to the Kern Youth Center. However,
using the pool brought on its own unique set of problems.

In a report to the trustees in 1992, the problems related to the use of
the pool were stated. The report made reference to two filter tanks that
were leaking and beyond their estimated lifespan. An earlier estimate for
the replacement of the tanks alone was twenty-four thousand six hundred
dollars. The pool did not meet Health Department standards. It had no

skimmers and to add them would be prohibitively expensive. The pump was so old that parts were no longer available. Most significant, to replace it would cost one hundred twenty-five thousand dollars and necessitate removing the concrete decking and replacing it.[47]

By the spring of 1994, things were so bad that the Haywood County Health Department stopped short of closing the facility, but reported that the pool did not meet health standards of that day. Finally, at its annual meeting in November of 1994, the Administrative Council approved the building of a new pool and bathhouse, its cost not to exceed seventy thousand dollars.

By July of 1995, both pool and bathhouse were complete. Unlike its predecessor, the new one made no attempt to create the illusion that its water was lake water, but rather was raised and constructed in such a fashion that it would not be necessary to drain the pool when the lake level was lowered. A dedication service was held on July 21st with more than four hundred persons present.

The 1988 Jurisdictional Conference approved a recommendation that there be a task force established for the purpose of initiating the process by which there would be an ongoing SEJ Wellness program. To facilitate this, a SEJ Committee on Health and Fitness was created. This would be the oversight committee for the ministry. In addition to other responsibilities, this committee would be responsible for studying the need for new and viable wellness programs at Lake Junaluska and across the jurisdiction.[48]

In early November 1991, there was a conference at the Assembly entitled The Church's Challenge in Health held at LJA. The conference was co-sponsored by The Carter Center of Emory University and the SEJ. The purpose was to train participants in implementing a church-based Health Risk Appraisal program in local churches. It was coordinated by Millsaps Dye, the director of council programs of the SEJ and responsible to the jurisdictional WELLTH program.[49]

Unfortunately, the WELLTH Center program did not last long. On September 26, 1994, Elaine Wheeler, director of WELLTH Ministry, wrote to the center members: "Writing this letter gives me great pain. A decision has been made to dissolve the WELLTH Fitness Center. Lake Junaluska is experiencing resource difficulties and some areas and positions have been dissolved."[50]

CHAPTER ELEVEN

The 90s

. . . .

W ith the beginning of the decade of the nineties, the Assembly found itself once again struggling with financial difficulties. For several years, the Assembly had experienced operating deficits which were covered by the sale of property. This situation could not continue without there being grave danger to the institution. In an effort to address this problem and to bring stability into the operation, Reginald Ponder, just named executive director of the new Southeastern Jurisdictional Administrative Council brought in David Snipes, a committed layperson and experienced financial manager as business manager and SEJ treasurer. Snipes immediately moved to address the financial challenges. The situation began to improve.[1]

In 1990, Glenn Martin became associate executive director of the Assembly. His duties included oversight of Assembly facilities and also relations with the property owners. Martin took a hands-on approach to dealing with local matters and quickly established a positive rapport with the local community. He was the liaison between the Assembly and contractors on such projects as the hydro-electric endeavor at the dam and the renovation and upgrading of Stuart Auditorium.

As mentioned earlier, the small cove just west of George R. Stuart's summer home, Winona, was the location of one of the five springs that had supplied water for the early summer residents. Further up the cove where Stuart Circle made its 180 degree turn was a small shady ravine which, in more recent years, had grown up into an unsightly area. Yet there was beauty there. The stream that fed Stuart Spring flowed down through it tumbling over rocks in little excited waterfalls. Because of the abundance of moisture, plants flourished amid the weeds and trash.

In 1989, a committee of the Tuscola Garden Club, having just finished creating a bluebird house trail and needing another project, came up with the idea of using the ravine to build a nature center. Corneille Bryan, wife of Bishop Monk Bryan and a member of the committee, suggested that a good project would be to clean up the area and uncover the beauty of its natural state. Likewise, she suggested they might plant some of the native wildflowers and other plants and turn the area into a botanical garden. Two other members of the committee, Harriet Worley and Dorothy Peacock, joined with her in the vision. They then took their idea to the Garden Club which enthusiastically endorsed the project. Unfortunately, in July of 1989 Mrs. Bryan died. An endowment fund for the garden was established and contributions came from individuals, as well as groups such as The Junaluskans and the Garden Club.[2]

At the November 16th, 1989 meeting of the Junaluska Division, the Grounds and Recreation Committee recommended approval of the concept contingent upon, 1) detailed plans, 2) a method of financing, 3) a maintenance endowment plan, and 4) approval of the foregoing by Jim Bozard (chairman), Clyde Mahaffey, and Reginald Ponder, members of the committee. They further called for the center to be named The Corneille Bryan Nature Center. The proposal was approved.[3] Following this action, Ponder wrote to Dr. Paul Worley who was then co-chairman of the Nature Center Committee: ". . . I am writing to authorize you to proceed with the plans you have submitted for Phase I of the project. . . . We want to work with you to insure that the project will be completed and that adequate maintenance endowment will be provided for its care in perpetuity."[4]

Mrs. Maxilla Evans, a botanist with a love for wildflowers of all kinds and particularly native plants of the area, was named as the planting chairperson and quickly became the driving force for the project. The assistance of experts in the field of wildflowers of the Western North Carolina mountains was supplied by Anne Grosso, a faculty member at Haywood Community College; David Curtis, county agent for Haywood County; Bill Hooks, a retired national park ranger and wildflower expert; and Dan Pattillo, professor of biology at Western Carolina University. Hundreds of hours of volunteer labor were provided by local persons.[5] On July 14, 1990 the Corneille Bryan Nature Center was dedicated. In 2002, the Nature Center Committee changed the name to the Corneille Bryan Native Garden to better communicate the particular character of the area.[6]

The Asbury Trail is a half-mile portion of the walking path around the lake. It stretches from just east of Colonial Hotel to the bridge over the dam. It is one of the oldest portions of the pathway. It is maintained by a committee of the Junaluskans. Reverend Esdras Gruver was chairman of the committee for several years. When Gruver died, several of his friends wished to honor his memory. Three of these, George Whitaker, Bob Brown, and Bill Stanford, decided to build a waterfall along the trail. There was a large outcropping of rock almost buried along the side of a high bank. They removed the earth from around the rock and decided that if they could arrange for water to run over the rock, they would have a beautiful waterfall. Plans were drawn and the proposal was presented to the Southeastern Jurisdictional Council for approval. The council gave them permission to continue. They installed a standpipe in the lake, buried plastic water pipe from the lake to the top of the ridge, and installed a pump. In the summer of 1991, the pump was turned on for the first time and the Gruver Memorial Falls became a reality.[7]

Later in 1994, the Tuscola Garden Club added a butterfly garden to the area just below the west gate to the Asbury Trail and very close to the Gruver Falls. The Shell Oil Company, in association with the National Council of State Garden Clubs, awarded the Tuscola club a Petals Incentive Grant of five hundred dollars.[8] The funds were used to build the butterfly garden. A meditation area was included. Club members would plant annuals each year and water the garden as needed. The plantings also included perennials that are known to be attractive to butterflies.[9]

Hugh Garner was a worried man. Pastor of First Baptist Church in Waynesville, Garner had surprised many persons when he purchased one of the Tri-Vista Villas condominiums. It was unusual for the pastor of one of the local Baptist churches to live at the United Methodist Assembly. At times, when speaking at the monthly meeting of the Junaluskans, Garner would introduce himself by saying, "For those of you who might not know me, I am the token Baptist in the Junaluskans." He was highly respected as a local religious leader and a supporter of the community in which he lived. But at this time, he was in the difficult position of being at odds with the Assembly.

Garner wrote a letter to Lachlan Hyatt expressing his concerns. He began by expressing his regret for having to write such a letter, indicating his love for the area and Lake Junaluska in particular. Earlier, he had been one of the first to purchase one of the new condos. Now there were many problems. In his letter, he noted that the dam for the reflection lake had broken. The paint on the porches was peeling and coming up. Plumbing in several units had failed. Garner wrote, "What should have been a pleasure in purchasing a condominium at Lake Junaluska has, for the present, become a nightmare. . . . I look to the one who sold me the property to make things right"[10]

Garner was not by himself. Down at the new Tri-Vista Villas, there were, indeed, problems. In the late 1980s, the Tri-Vista (homeowners) Association began to complain to the Assembly administration about faulty and shoddy construction in the condos. Woodwork on decks and stairways was rotting. Paint was peeling in places. Gutters were leaking. There were many plumbing problems. Plastic pipe used in the plumbing was leaking due to high water pressure. To make matters worse, the paving of the streets was breaking down. Life in the condos was not the pleasant experience that their owners had anticipated.

President of the condo owner's association Harold Lumbley was trying to cope with the problems, while at the same time dealing with the Assembly leadership. Attempts to work with the Assembly were proving to be frustrating. In addition, there were concerns about management, financial records, and use of service charges. Attempts to inform the jurisdictional leadership of the problems were seemingly ignored.

After years of efforts to resolve the situation through direct discussion with the administration and outside mediation, the association filed a suit in Haywood County entitled:

Tri-Vista Villas Owners Association, a North Carolina non-profit corporation by and through its Board of Directors on behalf of unit owners, Plaintiffs vs. Southeastern Jurisdictional Administrative Council, Inc. and North Carolina Corporation, Inc. and Lachlan L. Hyatt; F. Edward Broadhead; and Charles E. Nesbitt, Individually, Defendants in the General Court of Justice, Superior Court Division, State of North Carolina, County of Haywood, File No. 92 CVS 10[11]

The suit was filed in 1992.

After the suit was filed, retired Bishop Edward Tullis, who himself owned property on the south side of the lake, came to the condominium complex to see for himself what the difficulties were. He was appalled at what he discovered. After reporting back to the administration, further investigation followed and an out-of-court settlement was agreed upon. Finally, the issue had been resolved and repairs were made.[12]

Since its beginning, the epicenter of the Assembly was Stuart Auditorium. Not only was it the first structure built, but it was also where the major gatherings took place. Its design was extremely functional with its main platform the center of attention and the seats radiating in a huge semicircle in front of the pulpit. When first constructed, there was a large choir loft immediately behind the pulpit. The floor was dirt and was covered with sawdust during use. The congregation sat on hard wooden pews. As already noted, over the years, a concrete floor and walls with windows were added along with theater seats. No one had given much thought to the aesthetic appearance of the building; no one that is until the late 1980s. The Buildings and Grounds Committee of the Board of Trustees, after considering the needs of the auditorium, recommended to the board the consideration of a major remodeling. Certainly improvements were in order. Earlier, the choir loft had been removed and replaced by a rehearsal room for the Junaluska Singers. A sound system had been installed and improved on several occasions. A movie projection booth had been added. But there were additional needs for new features and for the upgrading of other areas. This time, the question of appearance was considered.

The architectural firm of Hayes, Seay, Mattern & Mattern, Inc. was hired to design the changes. Their proposal was an ambitious one. Behind the wall in the rear of the platform, a hall would be created and behind it a new enlarged rehearsal area, primarily for the Junaluska Singers. On the outside overlooking the lake would be a new deck. Restrooms would be added on either side of the area. The platform itself would be refinished. In the seating area, new upholstered seats would be installed. All of this would greatly improve the use of the building. This time, the exterior of the structure would get serious attention. A portico supported by fifteen columns would be added to the front. The exterior front wall of the building would get a wainscoting of rock. The appearance of the structure would be dramatically changed.[13]

When the proposal was presented to the SEJAC, the price tag was likewise ambitious. The estimated cost was five hundred thousand dollars, not including the cost of the new seating. Nevertheless, after debate and some changes, the project was approved. On August 30, 1991, the contract was awarded to McCarroll Construction, Inc. Construction began at the end of the summer season.[14]

On April 24, 1992, a formal opening and open house was held to introduce the newly remodeled George R. Stuart Auditorium. Joetta

THE NEW JUNALUSKA CROSS WAS ERECTED IN 1994 AND IS AN EXACT REPLICA OF THE 1922 CROSS

Rhinehart, Assembly public relations director, gave the welcome. This was followed by remarks by Reginald Ponder and a brief history of the structure by Glenn Martin, who had served as project supervisor. A walking tour of the building followed and the auditorium was declared open for the upcoming season.[15]

In May of 1993, Joseph W. Lasley, a long-time member of the Southeastern Jurisdictional Commission on Archives and History and its chairperson from 1993 to 1996, published his *Names and Places: A Lake Junaluska Cyclopedia and the Junaluska That Never Was*. The book quickly became an important historical resource for anyone desiring to know the origin and meaning of the names of buildings, roads, structures, and other features of the Assembly. It was used in training boat and trolley guides, by those who are in positions where they would receive questions from guests, and by visitors who simply want further information. In 1996, the Haywood County 911 Addressing Service issued new guidelines for addresses in the county. Among them was the ruling that no two streets in the county could have the same name and that, in the event of duplication, the earliest named street would keep that name. Likewise, over the years changes naturally occur. Thus the book had to be revised to reflect the changes. The revision is in progress at the time of the publication of this book.

Erected in 1922, the Junaluska Cross had stood for more than sixty years overlooking the lake and sending forth its message that the Assembly was a gathering place for followers of Christ. By the early 1990s, despite frequent repairs and upgrades, it was obvious that it had to be replaced. Thus it was that a headline in the March 28, 1994 issue of the *Waynesville Mountaineer* stated, "New Cross at Missionary Point." It reported than on the previous Friday, a brand new lighted cross had been put in place. The old 1922 cross had been removed earlier in the year so that it could be used as a pattern for the new cross, which would be an exact replica. The new cross was a gift from Mr. and Mrs. Alfred Bohanan of Gastonia, North Carolina.

Following the erection of the new cross another problem arose. No one seemed to know how to dispose of the old cross properly. There were suggestions that the old cross be placed in the Heritage Center museum or that it be erected in another location. But, unfortunately, the cross was much too large to get in the building and other locations were not acceptable. For several years, it lay ignominiously on its side on the patio under the upper porch of the Harrell Center. The problem was finally solved when a petition was presented to the Jurisdictional Conference of 1998 on behalf of the Mount Shepherd Retreat Center, a United Methodist facility located near Asheboro, North Carolina. The petition requested a "permanent loan" of the cross with the understanding that it would be restored and put into service at the center. The conference approved the petition and the cross still stands at the entrance to the center.[16]

In 1994 , Dr. Gordon Goodgame became executive director of the Southeastern Jurisdiction. Goodgame had served on the Transitional Committee during the reorganization of the Jurisdiction in the 1980s. Goodgame immediately moved to deal with several problems facing the Assembly. Among these were several years of deficits in operations. The outlook for 1994 was no better with another deficit for the current year projected. Immediate steps were taken to deal with the problem. Input from bishops and Council on Ministries directors were solicited. A consultant, Victor Dingus, was contracted. More than one hundred staff leaders were involved in imagining and planning. The importance of quality of service was emphasized. A series of leadership training workshops were held on the theme "7 Habits of Principle-Centered Leadership," and were based on Stephen R. Covey's book *The Seven Habits of Highly Effective People.*

During 1994, there were 991 groups participating in activities at the Assembly. Guest nights in lodging facilities increased to 140,953. Among the results of this was a decrease in the operating deficit. Other strategies included outsourcing of operations that had produced deficits. Included in these were such functions as soft drink machines, the cafe in the Harrell Center, the soda shop at the Kern Youth Center, along with the taping ministry at Stuart Auditorium. In most cases, in the past, the above services were manned by whatever staff happened to be available. This different approach added additional income.

As 1995 approached, the cost cutting measures continued and the budget for the coming year was reduced by two hundred fifty thousand dollars. By the end of that year, the improvement in the financial condition enabled the granting of a 3 percent pay raise, a significant contribution of the Maintenance Reserve Fund, and a positive balance of more than sixty thousand dollars. Likewise, income from the sale of property was placed in a quasi-endowment.[17]

By the close of 1997, improvement in the overall financial situation enabled the Assembly to move forward with a renovation of the Kern Youth Center and much needed repairs to the center section and cupola at Lambuth Inn. Likewise, the year resulted in a 6 percent increase in guest nights.[18]

In 1996, a major change in operation at the Assembly took place with the creation of the Department of Residential Services. Almost from the beginning of the Assembly there had been problems in the area of relations between the property owners and the Assembly management. On the one hand, there were those across the Southeastern Jurisdiction who were convinced that jurisdictional funds were used for the maintenance of the residential community. Thus, in a sense, the members of churches across the jurisdiction were supporting the home owners. On the other hand, there was the feeling among property owners that their assessments through the annual service charge were being used for Assembly operations and other non-residential needs. Likewise the maintenance and repair of the residential areas was handled by the Assembly maintenance department and some felt that Assembly needs were given priority over residential needs. There probably was some element of truth in all of the allegations. The creation of the Department of Residential Services addressed this problem head on. First, the funds received through service charges were placed in separate accounts. Initially, these accounts were used for residential needs. If, at the end of the year there were surplus funds, they would roll over into the Assembly general fund. On the other hand, should there be a shortfall the Assembly would make up the difference. Still later, in 2002, the residential services funds were designated as restricted funds which could be used only for residential purposes. At that point, the Assembly became a customer of Residential Services, paying service charges and utilities just as did the property owners. Secondly, a separate residential maintenance department was formed. The creation of the Department of Residential Services was a huge step toward eliminating the misconceptions of both the churches of the jurisdiction and those of the property owners.

The first manager of the Department of Residential Services was Don Harbaugh, who had served as a city manager. A hard worker and a man of good relational skills, Harbaugh was a good choice and was well received. He was followed in 1999 by Robert Mitchell, who served until 2001. In September of 2001, Mitchell "Buddy" Young was named manager.

Over the years, the original big boat, the *Cherokee,* had been replaced twice. The *Cherokee II* was launched in 1951. It was not as long lived as its predecessor and developed many problems. It was replaced by the *Cherokee III* in 1967. The third *Cherokee* was a pontoon boat with an upper deck, which presented a real danger of capsizing when loaded with passengers. Ultimately, the upper deck was removed which reduced the number of passengers by half. By the nineties, it was obvious that it was time for a new *Cherokee.* A considerably larger and more stable boat was dedicated on September 28, 1997. The new *Cherokee IV* was given in honor of John and Sara McWorter by Mr. and Mrs. Alfred Bohanan. This gift followed an earlier gift by the Bohanans which made possible the replacement of the original Junaluska Cross.

By the mid 1990s, most of the original twelve hundred acres of the original land purchased had been developed either as Assembly structures or sold for the development of private homes. The one remaining area was on the south side of the southeast side of the lake. The sale of lots in this area might well bring in some much-needed income for the endowment. In fact, some had estimated that development of this property might well add $3.5 million dollars. This would strengthen the ministry base of the Assembly. Early planning for this was underway. The outcome was the development of the Hickory Hill subdivision. By 1998, phase I of the project was complete and construction of homes was underway.

On the last Monday morning in June of 1998, April Ensley got into the family Chevrolet and headed for Sunset Inn where she worked. She arrived at the Assembly at about 7:30 and as she had done many times before, turned in the east gate and started to cross the dam. This time something went terribly wrong. The car crashed through a guard rail and fell over the back side of the dam landing upside down forty feet below on the ground beside the creek. April was killed instantly. No one observed the accident, but several heard the noise and rushed to the scene. A newspaper account of the accident indicated that it was caused by "apparent brief inattention to the road."[19] North Carolina State trooper B. C. Sanders, who was soon on the scene stated, "I think it's just a situation where she probably took her eyes off the road for just a second."[20]

Only one time before, in the history of the Assembly, had there been an accident of this nature. Decades earlier, a car approaching the bridge from the north had slid on frost and plunged off the back side of the dam. In that instance, the car landed right side up in the water at the base of the dam and the two occupants in the car survived.

As a result of the accident, the bridge was immediately closed to all traffic for an indefinite period of time. The closure of the bridge created a hardship in that it cut access to the campus from the east end of the lake. Likewise, residents living on the north side of the lake now had to use County Road as their primary route to the post office, Long's Chapel United Methodist Church, and businesses in that area. For a time, there was discussion as to whether or not to reopen the bridge. There were safety issues and the accompanying liability matters. Likewise, there was the matter of cost. It was obvious that if the bridge were to reopen it would have to be structurally changed to insure that such an accident could not happen again. The bridge remained closed through the rest of that year and through the next year. Finally, plans were developed for a new and structurally stronger bridge. Likewise the funding for the new bridge was shared by the Administrative Council and private funds supplied primarily by the home owners at the Assembly. Construction began in August of 1999 and on March 2, 2000, the bridge over the dam was reopened to traffic. A reopening service was held which included among its participants Bishop Robert C. Fannin, president of SEJAC, Jim Stevens, chairman of the Haywood County Board of Commissioners, Rhoda Peters, vice president of the Junaluska Division of SEJAC, and others.[21] Once again, traffic could enter from the east, drive around the lake, and residents could conveniently reach the post office.

In 1999, the Rose Walk was completely reworked as the result of a project jointly sponsored by the Junaluska Associates and SEJAC. The Associates contributed two hundred fifty thousand dollars and SEJAC matched the funds. The project included shoring up the north bank of the lake and new construction along the walkway. A long outstanding attraction of the Assembly, the Rose Walk along the north side of the lake was featured on the cover of *America Rose Society* magazine.

By the end of the decade, it was apparent that the Assembly would have to make major adjustments in its summer schedule due to the shortening of summer free time as a result of changing school schedules. Whereas in the past the summer season was considered to be from June 1 to September 1, colleges, universities, and public schools were now beginning their fall schedules by mid-August. This impacted both attendance and students who made up the summer staff.

CHAPTER TWELVE

The Future

• • • • • • • • • • • • • •

With the close of 1999 came the end of the first century of the Junaluska Assembly story. Although the one-hundredth birthday would not come until 2013, (the date of the opening event), a hundred years had passed since that fateful carriage ride at Chautauqua Lake, New York. From a few words spoken from father to daughter had come a great institution. From a peaceful farm valley had arisen a facility that would reach thousands of lives and be the setting for transforming experiences for untold numbers of persons. So much had changed. Not only had the peaceful farm land been transformed into a beautiful lake surrounded by a multitude of buildings, but this all represented a community that was a place of residence for more than seven hundred persons, while at the same time a center of Christian growth. It was the location of the largest lake and the largest auditorium in Haywood County, North Carolina. Hundreds of thousands of persons moved through its campus each year. Events of international scope were held there. It was not only a gathering place for United Methodists, but also was ecumenical in that many other religious bodies used its facilities. In addition, given the size and quality of its campus, it was increasingly used as a meeting place for secular events of a nature reflecting the values of its ownership. Looking back on what had happened over the past century, one might well wonder what the next century had in store. The early years of the new century might, indeed, give clues.

One of the first changes was in leadership. At the 2000 Jurisdictional Conference, Jimmy L. Carr was named as executive director of the Southeastern Jurisdictional Administrative Council. Also named at the Jurisdictional Conference was Joy T. Carr as director of ministries for the jurisdiction. The coming of the Carrs brought an emphasis on inclusiveness and a desire to move the Assembly in the

THE HEADQUARTERS FOR THE FOUNDATION FOR EVANGELISM IS LOCATED AT LAKE JUNALUSKA ASSEMBLY

direction of service to the entire United Methodist Church. Since the turbulent days of the late fifties and early sixties, the Assembly had struggled with a racist reputation, primarily among African American Methodists. Although the barriers to race had long since disappeared on the campus and in the minds of the administration, Junaluska was still seen by many as basically a white facility. In the minds of many black Methodists, they perceived that they simply would not be accepted nor would they be comfortable at Junaluska. That this was not true in the hearts and minds of both leadership and residents made no difference. This was a wide-spread perception. One of Jimmy and Joy Carr's primary goals as they looked toward the future was that this would all change.

Likewise, Junaluska Assembly had, both historically and legally, been an institution of Methodists in the South. With its heritage of being birthed by the laity of the Methodist Episcopal Church, South, its ownership by the Southeastern Jurisdiction, and its use (even after the union of the Methodist bodies) primarily by agencies, conferences, local churches, and, in general, Methodist individuals of the South, it might be rightly labeled as a gathering place for southern United Methodist people. This, of course, was not totally true. Already the World Methodist Council had its international headquarters at the Assembly. Likewise, the national headquarters for the Foundation for Evangelism was located on the campus. Each year, training for new United Methodist district superintendents from all over the church was held on campus as were other groups including regular meetings of the Jurisdictional College of Bishops. Physically, there was nothing quite like it in scope and size making it ideal for large national gatherings. All this not withstanding, beyond the borders of the deep South Junaluska Assembly was not perceived as a conference center for all of Methodism. Jimmy Carr thought it should be. This, too, was a goal to be strived for in Carr's mind. Neither of these goals would be easily attained. The cost would be significant both in terms of finances and also effort. The first decade of the new millennium would see movement in the direction of changing both perceptions.

An intentional effort designed to emphasize the open nature of the community was begun. An official agreement was reached with the county which stated that all persons were welcome as long as they followed rules and regulations. Likewise all "no" signs were removed.

Changes in management were coming. Jim Hanna was named director of development, Clyde McDonald became business manager and treasurer. Likewise Bob Ray was promoted to director of the Conference and Retreat Center. Ray was the first person with a background of hotel management training and experience to hold this position.

Planning began in 2001 for a capital funds campaign which would produce ten million dollars. If successful, this effort would fund numerous capital improvement projects as well as strengthen endowment significantly. Among the projects benefiting from the effort would be a new Welcome Center, an entirely new interior for Shackford Hall, renovation and remodeling of the Jones Dining Hall, enlarging and upgrading of the children's building complex, enlarging Stuart Auditorium and Inspiration Point, and other capital needs. Projects would not commence until funds were in hand to insure their completion. The timetable for projects would be determined by designated funds received. By 2003, more than half of the initial goal had been assured. Construction and plans were underway for the Welcome Center, Shackford Hall, Inspiration Point, along with more than two hundred thousand added to the endowment. Later, in 2005, a new golf course clubhouse was added as an additional project.

The Assembly worked closely with the General Commission on Religion and Race and other groups to increase the number of ethnic persons on the staff. The ratio of ethnic persons on staff quickly moved from a low of 4 percent to more than 20 percent during that summer, and 14 percent year round. An intense effort was made to help visitors of color feel more welcome.

During 2002, Clyde McDonald left the Assembly to take a similar position in the Holston Conference of the United Methodist Church. Stan McCleskey was named as interim treasurer. He was replaced in 2003 by Raul Alegria, who became the first Hispanic person to serve on the core team. Likewise, a director of Hispanic Ministries and a director of Korean-Asian Ministries were hired. Lake Junaluska Assembly was named as Employer of the Year by the North Carolina Rehabilitation Association.

From the earliest days of the Assembly, Come-Up Lodge had been a familiar sight along North Lakeshore Drive. Its location just west of the World Methodist Building and the auditorium made it a popular lodging for those attending conferences. Originally privately owned, it was later Assembly-owned after the aforementioned law suit.[1] On Thursday, November 2, 2000, a large crowd gathered in front of the lodge. They had come to watch it take a trip. The large two-story wooden building was to be moved to the rear of Cokesbury Circle behind the Administration Building. The crowd gathered on that fall day would not be disappointed. The house did actually travel down the driveway of the World Methodist Museum. Although it got stuck twice in route, it did arrive at the site on Cokesbury Circle and was renamed Junaluska Lodge after extensive remodeling.

Come-Up Lodge was moved to make room for a new building which would house the administrative offices of the World Methodist Council. The exterior of the Queen Anne style building would be an exact replica of the "Old Rectory" in Epworth, England, which was the boyhood home of John Wesley and was considered to be one of Methodism's most historic sites. Construction of this unique building was made possible by a gift of one million dollars by Royce and Jane Reynolds of Greensboro, North Carolina. Reynolds was a member of the executive committee of the council. The rectory at Epworth had been purchased and restored by the World Methodist Council in 1954. The interior of the new building would house the modern offices of the council, with one exception. A room on the second floor would resemble the room in the original building which was thought to be haunted by a ghost who was named Old Jeffrey by Emily, first of the Wesley's daughters.[2] This building that played such an important role in John Wesley's childhood days would be faithfully replicated at Lake Junaluska Assembly. To date, there has been no reported sighting of Old Jeffrey!

Architect W. B. Cunningham traveled to the original building at Epworth, England to take measurements and photos that would insure that the new building would be, indeed, a true replica. He then supervised the construction by Clark and Leatherwood, Inc. contractors. The new office building was completed and consecrated on March 23, 2002.

The decision to use the location of Come-Up Lodge as the site for the new council building created the necessity for the Foundation for Evangelism to relocate their headquarters. The Foundation for Evangelism is an affiliate of the General Board of Discipleship of the United Methodist Church. Founded in 1949 by the late evangelist Dr. Harry Denman, who served as the general secretary of the Board of Evangelism of the Methodist Church, the foundation seeks to promote, encourage, and provide resources for responsible evangelism, enabling the United Methodist Church to bring persons into a personal relationship with Jesus Christ and help them grow as His disciples. It further seeks to provide leadership for the church who share a passion for evangelism and to provide venture capital for the development of such leaders.[3]

In 1987, the foundation moved its headquarters to Lake Junaluska Assembly. They located their offices in Come-Up Lodge. When the council decided to build their new building on the site of the lodge, it became necessary for the foundation to provide new offices. Initially, the foundation established temporary offices off campus in the town of Waynesville. After considering other sites as a location for a new headquarters building, the foundation approached the Assembly with the proposal that they build near the main entrance of the Assembly at the corner of North Lakeshore Drive and Weldon Way, provided the Assembly would agree to their purchasing the lot. In 2003, the sale of the lot was approved and in early 2005 construction began on a new facility. The ten-thousand-square-foot building uses half of the space for offices of the foundation staff. The remainder of the building includes a multi-media meeting room with an adjacent catering kitchen, a lobby, and a chapel. In December of 2005, the new building was completed and the foundation moved in.

During the year 2000, the owners of Brookside Lodge decided to sell their facility and the Assembly purchased it. An extensive upgrade began and the lodge then became available for use by larger groups that might desire kitchen facilities.

The May 29, 2000 edition of the local newspaper, *The Mountaineer,* featured an ominous headline entitled, "Sediment Problems Threaten Scenic Lake." In the article, Jimmy Carr, the executive director of SEJAC, related to the county commissioners the story of the continuing problem of silt coming into Lake Junaluska, settling to the bottom and thus filling up the lake. He pointed out that once the lake became filled with sediment, it would be designated as a wetland and could not be dredged. This would be the end of the lake. He requested that the commissioners approve a grant of two hundred thousand dollars for silt removal. The commissioners received the request and indicated that they would study it.[4]

When the report of Carr's request was reported in the local newspapers, a very vocal opposition arose. Letters to the editor were both pro and con. Among the sentiments expressed were, "Let those who live there pay for it" and "Methodists want it both ways." Others felt that, if the request be approved, it would be tax funds spent for private use.[5] Ultimately, the commissioners denied the request. Later, the Board of Commissioners passed resolutions in support of the project. The resolutions proved valuable as other sources of funding were sought. Other groups were very supportive. An editorial in *The Mountaineer* was entitled, "Let's Be Good Neighbors: Help Save Lake Junaluska." It went on to point out the economic and recreational value of the Assembly to the county.[6]

In 2001, attorney Chet Holloman came on staff as a volunteer with the responsibility of working with elected officials to find ways of saving the lake. Two grants from the state of North Carolina of five hundred thousand dollars each, along with gifts from the Pigeon River Fund and individuals, enabled the Assembly to remove 5,500 loads of silt or 130,000 cubic yards. This temporarily eased the crisis, although a long term solution remained in the future.

In the mid 1990s, during a routine inspection of the dam, the state of North Carolina determined that there were possible structural problems. They then called for the Assembly to do a study to determine the structural integrity of the dam and to correct any such problems. Unfortunately, no action was taken at that time. Early in the new century, the state demanded that the study be done and that immediate action follow. This quickly became a crisis issue which threatened the very existence of the lake. Among other problems discovered was the severe deterioration of the buttresses. The cost for repairing this, along with other problems could possibly amount to two million five hundred thousand dollars and could reach as much as three million dollars.[7] Ultimately, before the end of the repairs the cost approached four million dollars.

During the summer season of 2003, the ninetieth anniversary of the Assembly was observed. Historical vignettes related to past events were presented. A column entitled "Looking Back" was included in the issues of the *Assembly Daily* newsletter. As a part of this, the fiftieth anniversary of the Junaluska Singers was observed.

In 2005, Bishop James Swanson was named the chair of the building committee for the Assembly. He, thus, became the first African American to serve in this position. He was assisted by Dr. Clarence Addison, also an African American, who served through the building of the Welcome Center.

After lengthy study, planning, and debate, the residents of the Assembly, both full and part time, and with the support of Buddy Young, approved a constitution and bi-laws which created the Junaluska Assembly Community Council. The council would serve as an advisory group for the Department of Residential Services. Members of the council were to be elected to represent geographical districts of the residential community. This group would add another level of representation for those who were continuing part of the Junaluska community. It would not replace any existing organization. Later elections were held to name the representatives and the organization began monthly open meetings.

Early in 2005, the marketing department of the Assembly had an inquiry from an unidentified group as to whether there might be space available for a conference to be held that summer on the Labor Day weekend. They were told that, in fact, the date they wanted would be available. Later, they requested booking for a conference sponsored by the Reconciling Ministries Network. Upon learning of this, Assembly Director of Marketing Ken Howle made an unusual call to Jimmy Carr. It was certainly not customary for him to notify Carr of every group desiring to hold a conference at the Assembly, but this one, he realized, could be controversial. The Reconciling Ministries Network was a recognized caucus of the United Methodist Church that promoted the acceptance of professing homosexual individuals as clergy members of conferences and as pastors of local churches. Howle rightly felt that the issue was sensitive enough that it could not be treated as a routine request for use of the facilities. After receiving the call, and before making any decision, Carr called the president of the Southeastern Jurisdictional Administrative Council. He explained that they had been told that space was available for the date they wanted and that the Assembly could honor their request if it so desired. The controversial nature of the request was apparent. The two discussed the matter thoroughly. In light of the fact that the group was now aware that the Assembly could accommodate their event, and that the group was recognized by the church as a caucus group, they decided that in view of the stated purpose of the Assembly that they were ". . . called to be a community of hospitality . . ." and in the spirit of openness, they would allow the meeting to be held on the campus. Their decision was later ratified by the Executive Committee of Southeastern Jurisdictional Administrative Council.

By the early summer, publicity for the conference, which was named the Hearts on Fire Conference, was out and the response began. Mark Tooley, executive director of the United Methodist Action—a committee of the Institute on Religion and Democracy (IRD)—called Assembly Director of Public Relations Joetta Rhinehart to express strong opposition to the group meeting on the campus. Later in July, the group mounted an intensive media campaign designed to inform the church and also to intimidate the Assembly into withdrawing the use of its facilities. Various conservative groups and individuals were encouraged to communicate their opposition to the Assembly's hosting the meeting. Reaction to the news releases related to the conference was, at the beginning, divided about half in favor and half opposed. However, as the campaign sponsored by the IRD began to gain momentum, the majority were opposed. As hundreds of letters with the exact same wording but different signatures were received, it became obvious that this was a well-orchestrated effort. This fact, along with the sheer volume of mail caused the local newspaper to cease printing letters to the editor that were received from out of state addresses. In an editorial explaining the decision, editor Vicky Hyatt stated: "There is an apparent letter-writing campaign regarding the upcoming Hearts on Fire Conference. . . . The volume of letters is simply becoming too large for us to handle . . ."[8] Still later, the paper decided to cut off all letters regardless of their origin. Several advertisements opposing the conference appeared in the newspaper.

An advertisement in the August 24th issue of *The Mountaineer* told of a tent meeting in opposition to the conference which would be held across the highway from a local chicken palace. The newspaper reported the event under the headline "At Hatred Reverend Pauses." The article stated:

> As the time for the meeting drew near so did a heavy thunderstorm and the tent was so rain soaked that the meeting was moved to the nearby Calvary Road Baptist Church, thus not making the visual statement as originally planned. Likewise, the purpose of the meeting was changed to show concern for all sinful practices. The Rev. Alan Blanton stated, "These meetings are not just to oppose homosexuality but all sins."[9]

Various groups including United Methodist Church groups, groups from other denominations, individuals, and even the Ku Klux Klan expressed both support and opposition. Several groups indicated their desire to demonstrate during the conference.

As the date for the Hearts on Fire Conference drew near another request for an event was received. The Transforming Congregations, also recognized by the United Methodist Church as a caucus group, asked to have a meeting in the time frame when the Hearts on Fire Conference was in progress. This group was committed to the concept that, should a person desire to be freed of their homosexual desires, they could do so by repentance and through the power of the Holy Spirit. This group desired to hold a breakfast meeting to counter the claims of the Reconciling Ministry group. The group had the same relationship to United Methodism and the General Conference as did the Reconciling group. During their meeting, individuals who had successfully rejected the homosexual lifestyle shared their experiences. The Assembly welcomed them in the same spirit as the Reconciling group given the fact that this, too, was a caucus group recognized by the general church. However, they stipulated that they could have their meeting during the week that the Reconciling group was meeting, but not on the specific days that sessions of the other group were being held. Carr attended each group's opening session and welcomed them warmly.

On Friday, September 2, the Hearts on Fire Conference began. The Assembly had set aside areas on campus for media and also for demonstrations. A modest number of media representatives were present. Less than a dozen Ku Klux Klan persons arrived, only to be limited to an area at the entrance to the Assembly where they were surrounded by North Carolina Troopers, to the point that it was difficult for them to be seen. Off campus down the street were persons demonstrating against the Klan. *The Mountaineer* newspaper reported the opening with the headline: "Methodists Pushing for Acceptance of Gays Start Meeting Quietly."[10]

Conference sessions continued quietly through the weekend. Attendees were approximately one-third parents of gay and lesbian children, one-third persons seeking information of the issues, and one-third persons reflecting differing sexual orientation. Five bishops of The United Methodist Church attended and participated in the program. On Monday, September 5, the conference ended peacefully. At the conclusion of the conference *The Mountaineer*, in an article headlined, "Conference Ends Peacefully," reported, "The threatened protests to the 'Hearts On Fire' conference ended up with the largest group of people on the grounds besides conference attendees being law enforcement officials."[11]

While the conference was now history, the controversy continued. There were threats to cut off funding for the Assembly. Both local churches and some larger bodies threatened to end their financial support. Interestingly, the local newspaper got into the issue with an editorial in *The Mountaineer*, which observed that there was talk of a boycott or a move to withhold funds from the Assembly. The editorial pled for this not to take place. In it, the editor said, "Let the debate continue, but ensure it is done within the proper channels and at the proper level. . . . The Assembly has been a good neighbor and operations at the Lake need to go forth unhindered."[12]

The issue did result in several cancellations by groups who regularly used the facilities of the Assembly for conferences and other events. Interestingly, the vast majority of these groups were non–United Methodist. Likewise, in the ensuing years, most of these returned. In most cases of cancellations, other groups took their places. There were financial losses but these were temporary.

On August 12, 2005, the Southeastern Jurisdictional Council took a significant step in its attempt to recover unpaid residential service charge funds. The council filed suit in Superior Court of Haywood County against three property owners. Through the years, there had been property owners who contended that the Assembly did not have the right to assess the annual service charges nor the right to require payment of back charges before selling property. In most cases, after a period of time the charges were paid. At this point, the decision was made to go to court with the issue. Upon the filing of the suit, the defendants filed a counterclaim of Slander of Title.

Superior Court Judge E. Erwin Spainhour heard the case on May 22, 2006 and ruled in the favor of the Assembly on the original lawsuit and denied the counterclaim on June 6th.

On November 27, 2006, the defendants filed for appeal. The North Carolina Court of Appeal heard the case on May 22, 2007. On January 15, 2008, the Court of Appeal reversed the Superior Court ruling with a split decision for the defendants and affirmed the decision on the counterclaim. Judge Wanda G. Bryant wrote the opinion, Judge James A. Wynn concurred, and Judge Robin Hudson dissented.

SEJAC then appealed the case to the North Carolina Supreme Court. On February 15, 2008, the Supreme Court agreed to hear oral arguments on September 9, 2008. On October 9, 2009, the Supreme Court reversed the Court of Appeals decision with a vote of five to two. Judge Paul Newby wrote the opinion with Judge Robert A. Edmonds writing a concurring opinion. Judge Robin Hudson wrote the dissenting opinion.

The ruling filed by the Supreme Court is highly significant in that, in many ways, in addition to stating the Assembly's right to collect service charges, it legally defines the role and purpose of the Assembly and its right to govern. The Supreme Court in its ruling stated "the Assembly has existed for nearly a century and has spent the entire time purposefully developing its unique, religious community character. To that end, the Council and its predecessors have subjected the Assembly's residential lots to a wide variety of detailed restrictions."[13] The ruling further stated, "the original intent of the parties was to bind all purchasers of property within the Assembly to any rules the Council deemed necessary to preserve the unique religious character and history of the community."[14]

As in the case of the lawsuit regarding the "right of first refusal" clause in the 80s, this case appears to protect the relationship between property owners and the Assembly and define the Assembly as a unique religious community, thus protecting it from such legal challenges in the future.[15] The years beyond 2005 continue to testify to the resiliency of Lake Junaluska Assembly. Attendance at events in the following years held steady and grew. In 2006, ground was broken for the construction of a new and much needed Welcome Center. This building would afford first time visitors their initial impression of the Assembly. It would be a fitting beginning for any conferee with its large spacious lobby and significant appointments. Its theme would convey openness and acceptance of all who entered. Upon entering, the eye would be drawn to twenty-three organ pipes wrapped in fabrics that represent African American, Native American, Latino, and European settlers.

THE JOSEPH AND SHIRLEY BETHEA WELCOME CENTER GREETS VISITORS TO LAKE JUNALUSKA ASSEMBLY. IT HONORS BISHOP AND MRS. BETHEA AND IS THE FIRST MAJOR BUILDING TO BE NAMED FOR AN AFRICAN AMERICAN COUPLE

Fittingly, the building was named the Bethea Welcome Center for Bishop Joseph and Mrs. Shirley Bethea and would be the first major Assembly structure named to honor the memory of an African American couple. On September 28, 2007, the first group entered and registered for an event. Its completion and opening in 2007 sent forth the message that Lake Junaluska was, indeed, a gathering place for all of God's children.

The new century is a new opportunity to continue a rich ministry which began more than one hundred years ago. Looking back, one can see times when the Assembly has both reflected the local church and also challenged the local church. At times, it has seemingly looked to the local church for direction and, at other times, has been on the cutting edge of prophetic witness. One might well assume that this would continue in the decades to come. There is a sense of vitality, expectation, and excitement as the early days of the millennium unfold. The challenge faced by the Assembly is that of taking hold of the new technology and culture of the day while, at the same time, holding fast to the eternal foundation of faith upon which it was based more than one hundred years ago. With God's help, it will embrace the challenge and continue to be an Antechamber of Heaven for generations to come.

A Timeline of Lake Junaluska

• • • • • • • • • • • • • • • • •

1899 • *James Atkins, while visiting at The Chautauqua Lake Sunday School Assembly in New York, comments during a carriage ride with his daughter, that there needs to be a Southern Chautauqua.*

1900 • *An Ecumenical Missionary Conference is held in New York City from April 21 to May 1.*

1901 • *The Methodist Episcopal Church, South holds a General Missionary Conference in New Orleans. This is to be known as the First General Missionary Conference of the Methodist Episcopal Church, South.*

• *James Atkins brings the entire Sunday School Board of the Methodist Episcopal Church, South to his home in Waynesville, North Carolina to consider the possibility of an Assembly in the Southeast.*

1907 • *Fifty-three representative laymen of the Conferences of the Methodist Episcopal Church, South meet in Knoxville, Tennessee to consider forming a Laymen's Missionary Movement.*

1908 • *One thousand laymen meet at Chattanooga, Tennessee and organize the Laymen's Missionary Movement. Among the clergy present as observers is George R. Stuart, who was pastor of Centenary Methodist Church in that city.*

• *James Atkins sends a telegram to George Stuart asking that he encourage the establishing of an Assembly through the Laymen's Missionary Conference.*

• *During the 1908 conference, Stuart invites a group of laymen to have lunch with him. He shares how much Winona Lake Assembly has meant to him and to his family. One might assume that he also shares his desire to see a similar facility in the Southeast.*

- *Stuart introduces a resolution at the Laymen's Missionary Conference calling for the establishment of such an Assembly and also naming a seven member committee to locate and plan it. The resolution is accepted and passed by the Laymen's Missionary Movement.*

- *The committee appointed by the Laymen's Missionary Conference meets at Tate Springs, Tennessee on June 13th. A prospectus is drafted outlining the rationale for the new Assembly ground.*

1909
- *In July, the Executive Committee meets to hear from several persons who are promoting locations for the proposed Assembly. At a later date, they agree on the Richland Valley near Waynesville, North Carolina.*

- *On March 2, 1909 the North Carolina Assembly passes an Act of Incorporation for the Southern Assembly.*

1910
- *A meeting is held in the Waynesville home of James Atkins for the purpose of adopting the Articles of Incorporation of the Southern Assembly and the naming of the Board of Commissioners.*

- *James W. Seaver is hired as chief engineer for the project. On August 1, the commissioners decide to hire Olmsted Brothers, Landscape Architects, to design the grounds.*

1911
- *At a meeting held on January 2, there is a great deal of discussion related to the sale of stock. Likewise, there is a call for a definite understanding with the Southern Railway regarding the building of a depot and also the kind of passenger service they would provide.*

- *On January 11, a meeting of the incorporators is held. At this meeting, James Atkins is named as president and James Cannon Jr. is named as the first superintendent.*

- *During this year, the location of the auditorium and one or more of the hotels is chosen. Also, construction of the dam is begun.*

1912
- *Activity is to be seen in all directions. Roads are being built. Already some private home locations are chosen.*

1913
- *The auditorium is completed. A large bell is given and placed on the ground near the auditorium.*

- On June 25, the Second General Missionary Conference of the Methodist Episcopal Church, South convenes. The Southern railway runs three excursion trains a day between the Southern Assembly and Waynesville. It is necessary for the attendees to return to Waynesville for their meals.

- The Missionary Conference raises more than $150,000 for missions during the conference.

- On the first day of the conference, a grandson is born to James Atkins in his new summer home.

- Private homes are under construction. By the end of the year there will be thirteen homes completed.

- The dam is completed and water is beginning to fill the lake.

1914
- One year later things have changed. Epworth Lodge located on the northwest corner of Stuart Circle and Lakeshore Drive has been completed and opened. Atkins' home is opened for guests.

- The season runs from July 16th to August 26th. There are six conferences.

- There are additional Chautauqua features including concerts, glee club performances, and others.

- J. Dale Stenz is named as business manager of the Assembly. He is later to become superintendent.

1915
- The Junaluska Depot is completed.

- The Public Service Building/Auditorium Hotel is completed and opened for guests.

- The first big boat, initially named the Oonagusta (later changed to the Cherokee) is launched after being christened by Elizabeth Stuart, daughter of George R. Stuart.

- Four conferences are held during the summer session. They include Missionary, Sunday School, Bible, and Epworth League. Chautauqua features continue as well.

- Miss Della K. Stevens and Mr. Edwin S. Sanders are married in Stuart Auditorium, the first wedding at the Assembly.

1917 • *When the season opens on July 16, there are seven hotels. Private cottage construction continues.*

• *There are only three conferences. Epworth League, Sunday School, and Workers Conference.*

• *The Junaluska Woman's Club is organized.*

1918 • *On July 10, the beautiful Junaluska Inn, the Pride of Junaluska, burns to the ground in the middle of the night. The forty guests escape without serious injury.*

• *Following the loss of Junaluska Inn, the Junaluska Hotel Company purchases the College Inn that is still under construction. It is completed and its name is changed to Terrace Hotel.*

• *In spite of World War I raging in Europe, the Assembly observes its summer season.*

1919 • *The season opens July 15th and closes August 2nd after six conferences and several Chautauqua features.*

• *H. Stockham becomes superintendent of the Assembly.*

• *Epworth Lodge is demolished and rebuilt at the north end of Stuart Circle.*

• *The Junaluska Golf Course is completed and opened.*

1920 • *A permanent bridge is built across the top of the dam.*

• *On October 17th, the Public Service Building/Auditorium Hotel burns.*

• *The Junaluska Inn property is purchased by the Board of Missions of the Methodist Episcopal Church, South.*

• *An attempt is made to give the Assembly to the General Conference of the Methodist Episcopal Church, South, but the church refuses it because of its debt.*

1921 • *Construction of Mission Inn is begun on the site of Junaluska Inn.*

1922 • *Mission Inn (center section) is completed and opened to guests.*

- *The Junaluska Cross is erected. A dedication service is held on July 10th.*

- *The Colonial Hotel is built by Mr. & Mrs. T. L. McLees.*

- *Lakeside Lodge is built by Mr. J. B. Ivey.*

- *Twenty-two new cottages are built.*

- *Mabel Wescott, daughter of the skipper of the Oonagusta Captain Wescott, is crowned the first Queen of Junaluska.*

- *Bishop James Atkins and his second wife build a second home west of his first at the Assembly.*

1923 · *The Religious Education Building (later named Shackford Hall) is completed and opened at the west end of the lake.*

- *The Assembly is saddened by the death of Bishop James Atkins.*

1924 · *The financial crisis, which has been slowly enveloping the Assembly grows. The season is cut to only seven weeks.*

- *There are now eleven lodging facilities at the Assembly.*

- *Junaluska Construction Company is dissolved.*

- *The Southern Assembly purchases Terrace Hotel from the Junaluska Hotel Company.*

1925 · *The financial crisis deepens. The sale of the golf course is considered and rejected.*

- *The bookstore is built. It is a log house with a porch and is located across from the Terrace Hotel.*

1926 · *Hugh Sloan is named superintendent.*

- *An attempt is made to give the Assembly to the church and again it is refused.*

- *The Assembly mourns the death of George R. Stuart. John R. Pepper becomes president of the Board of Trustees.*

1927 · *Ralph E. Nollner is elected as Assembly superintendent.*

1928 • *The Assembly opens June 7th and closes August 29th. There are sixteen different conferences during the season along with five youth camps.*

• *Motion pictures are shown in the auditorium for the first time.*

• *There are now thirteen lodging facilities on the campus.*

• *The Duke Summer School and the Duke School of Religion at Lake Junaluska begin this year with academic credit given by the university.*

1929 • *In another attempt to move ownership of the Assembly closer to the church, the stockholders pass a resolution giving the title to the Assembly to trustees appointed from each annual conference east of the Mississippi River.*

• *As a result of the attempted transfer of ownership, the name of the Assembly is changed from The Southern Assembly to Lake Junaluska Methodist Assembly.*

• *The trustees then offer the property to the Board of Missions of the Methodist Episcopal Church, South but the board declines to accept it.*

• *The auditorium is named in memory of Dr. George R. Stuart.*

• *Ralph Nollner reports that presently there are seventeen miles of graveled roads, an auditorium which seats thirty-five hundred, one hundred private cottages, fourteen hotels and boarding houses, and numerous other public buildings.*

1930 • *The General Conference of the Methodist Episcopal Church, South is invited to meet at Lake Junaluska. The conference declines and meets in Dallas.*

• *The General Conference grants forty thousand dollars to Lake Junaluska and forty thousand to Mount Sequoyah Assemblies.*

1931 • *Telephone service becomes available at Lake Junaluska.*

• *Waynesville and Hazlewood are restrained from putting sewage in Richland Creek. The controversy over this matter will continue for years.*

1932 • *The Assembly is forced into bankruptcy. Jerry Liner is named temporary receiver.*

1933 • *James Atkins Jr. is named as permanent receiver.*

1934 • *The General Conference grants fifteen thousand dollars to each of the two assemblies.*

1935 • *During the season, there are four camps for boys and girls. They are Camp Cheonda for girls, Lake Junaluska Music Camp, Camp Seminole for boys, and Camp Junaluska for Girls. Each of these camps operates for periods from two to eight weeks.*

• *The 1935 season runs from June 1 to August 18.*

1936 • *The College of Bishops approves a campaign to free the Assembly from debt and asks that a preacher be selected to direct the movement. Dr. William A. Lambeth, pastor of Wesley Memorial Methodist Church in High Point, North Carolina is selected. He raises one hundred thousand dollars and pays the mortgage held by the Mercantile Trust Company in St. Louis. Only by the granting of several extensions by the bank is the Assembly saved.*

1937 • *A holding committee is appointed to administer the affairs of the Assembly until the General Conference of the Methodist Episcopal Church, South held in 1938.*

1938 • *The last General Conference of the Methodist Episcopal Church, South accepts the Assembly as the property of the church, thus fulfilling the dream of those who began it in 1913. They further stipulate that no mortgage should ever again be placed against it.*

• *A fifteen member Board of Trustees is named by the bishops of the church.*

• *Dr. William A. Lambeth is named as president, superintendent, and treasurer without salary.*

1939 • *With Methodist unification, the Assembly becomes the property of The Methodist Church.*

• *The East Gate stone structure is constructed and opened.*

• *The first trailer camp is established at the Assembly. The program book reports that there is electricity available for the trailers.*

• *For the first time since bankruptcy, property is again available for purchase.*

• *Once again the proposal is made to bridge the "Narrows."*

• *The 1939 season runs from June 9 to September 3.*

1940 • *The first General Conference of The Methodist Church officially accepts the ownership of the Assembly.*

• *The Junaluska Supply Company building burns. It is replaced in three months. The new building will later be called The Liner Building.*

1941 • *Camp Adventure, a co-educational camp, is opened for the first time. This camp replaces Camp Cheonda.*

• *The Gilbert Center, a meeting place for black persons on the grounds, is built and opened.*

1942 • *A partial concrete floor and a number of theatre seats are added to the auditorium.*

1943 • *Visitors to the Assembly are cautioned in the program book to check with their gasoline ration board to determine if they can secure enough ration coupons for their trip. If not, they are advised to use the train or bus.*

1944 • *Mrs. Franklin D. Roosevelt, wife of the president, visits the Assembly, takes a ride on the big boat, and speaks twice.*

• *Edwin Jones and Elmer T. Clark become members of the Board of Trustees. Both will make significant contributions to the development of the Assembly in future years.*

• *All debts of the Assembly, including even the smallest, are now satisfied.*

• *Mrs. James Atkins donates her home to be the residence of the superintendent of the Assembly.*

• *F. S. Love is elected superintendent and Bishop Clare Purcell becomes chairman of the Board of Trustees.*

• *The Cottage Owners Association initiates a program to raise funds to build a memorial chapel.*

• *James Cannon, the first superintendent of the Assembly, dies.*

1945 • *An abbreviated version of the program book is printed due to wartime restrictions.*

• *The 1945 season begins June 4 and runs to September 2.*

- *An Assembly room seating two hundred is built behind the stage of the auditorium. Four classrooms are also built in this area.*

- *The trustees recommend dredging the lake.*

1946
- *Ground in broken for the Memorial Chapel on August 25th and construction begins.*

- *An additional one hundred theater seats are installed in the auditorium.*

- *Much needed repairs, postponed due to the war, are begun. Lambuth and Terrace Hotels are renovated.*

- *The playground is moved from the auditorium to the west end of the lake.*

- *A rock bathhouse is constructed at the swimming area.*

- *The opera Martha is produced and presented in the auditorium in August.*

1947
- *Trustees purchase Wesley Heights from Florida Southern College for seven thousand five hundred dollars. This is the area bounded by South Lakeshore, Harmon, and Harrell Drives.*

- *The membership of the Board of Trustees is changed to include all active bishops of the Southeastern Jurisdiction, plus twenty-five additional persons.*

- *Paving begins on several Assembly roads.*

- *A highway through Assembly property at the west end of the lake is completed providing a by-pass of Waynesville when traveling from Asheville to Cherokee.*

1948
- *The General Conference of the Methodist Church transfers ownership of the Assembly to the Southeastern Jurisdiction, which accepts it and elects the same membership of the Board of Trustees.*

- *The jurisdiction increases the annual apportionment from four thousand dollars to twenty-five thousand and authorizes the Greater Junaluska Campaign to raise six hundred thousand dollars.*

- *The superintendent reports that the polio epidemic has kept attendance down.*

- *Carolina and Littleton Roads are paved.*

- *The west gate is opened thus giving the Assembly a back door.*

- *The Kentucky Conference Center is constructed.*

- *The property on which the Cherokee Inn once stood is purchased by the Assembly.*

- *Edwin Jones is elected chairman of the Board of Trustees, a position he will hold for twenty years.*

- *The last passenger train runs during this year.*

1949
- *The Memorial Chapel is completed, consecrated, and opened on July 4th.*

- *Paving of roads continues with cottage owners bearing most of the cost.*

- *H. G. Allen becomes superintendent of the Assembly.*

- *The first unit of the Junaluska Apartments is completed.*

- *A Schulmerich Carillon is installed at the Stuart Auditorium.*

- *The bridge over the dam is constructed.*

- *Camp Adventure becomes the property of the Assembly.*

1951
- *The Room of Memory at the Memorial Chapel is completed and opened.*

- *The second unit of the Junaluska Apartments is completed.*

- *The Harrison Colonnade is constructed.*

- *The rest of the concrete floor is installed in the auditorium along with work to enclose the building.*

- *An organ is given to the new Memorial Chapel by James Hamilton in memory of his mother.*

- *Lakeshore Drive, North Lakeshore Drive, and South Lakeshore Drive are officially named.*

1952
- *A new stone Administration Building is built.*

- *The Cherokee II boat is completed and put in service.*

- *The third unit of the Junaluska Apartments is completed.*

- *Additional streets are paved.*

- *More than a half million dollars in pledges is raised in the Greater Junaluska Campaign and more than three hundred thousand dollars is received initially.*

- *Billy Graham preaches for the first time at the Assembly. He is to return at least five more times in the future.*

1953   • *James. W. Fowler is named superintendent of the Assembly.*

- *Bishop Paul B. Kern dies. He had been a great supporter of youth ministries at the Assembly. A new youth center will later be built and will carry his name.*

- *Additional roads for future development are being built on the south side of the lake.*

1954   • *The Kennedy-Skinner Children's Building is completed and formally opened on July 5th.*

- *Dr. George Clary is named as program director for the Assembly.*

- *A new swimming pool is completed and opened. The pool is built out into the lake in front of the bath house.*

- *Street lights are installed along South Lakeshore Drive.*

- *Glendale Road and Stuart Circle are paved.*

- *Flagstone walks are installed in front of the auditorium.*

1955   • *The World Methodist Building is completed.*

- *The Board of Trustees refuses to allow Nels Ferre to speak at the Candler Camp Meeting sparking a controversy throughout the jurisdiction.*

1956   • *The Ninth World Methodist Conference is held at the Assembly.*

- *The Paul B. Kern Youth Center is completed and opened.*

- *Glenn Draper becomes music director for the Assembly.*

- *Billy Graham and William E. Sangster are preachers for the Candler Camp Meeting.*

- *The west wing of Lambuth Inn is completed.*

1957 • *The new Mountainview Lodge is completed on the site of the old one which had been in service since the 1920s. Material from the old Mountainview Lodge is used to construct three cottages on Liberty Road which are sold to Methodist ministers.*

1958 • *Jones Dining Hall is built on the site of the old Sunday School Cafeteria.*

- *A similar lodge is built along side of Mountainview. It is named Sunnyside.*

- *D. Trigg James is named program director.*

- *The Board of Trustees adopts a policy of having no hard and fast rules regarding the admission of blacks to the Assembly. An open door policy is adopted with the admonition that there be nothing neither printed nor published concerning such policies.*

- *The old craft shop across from the Memorial Chapel burns in July.*

1959 • *A memorial stone pillar is erected in front of the auditorium for the purpose of displaying memorial plaques.*

1960 • *The Costen J. Harrell Center across from Terrace Hotel is completed.*

- *The Branscomb Arts and Crafts Building is built near the Junaluska Apartments.*

- *William Quillian, who had attended the first conference in 1913 and who became the executive secretary of the Southeastern Jurisdictional Council, dies.*

- *The World Methodist Center building is enlarged.*

- *An integrated group of students attempt to enter the swimming pool and are turned away. This incident is nationally reported and given the term "swim in." Problems related to race relations that have simmered for several years suddenly are given national attention. A great deal of controversy ensues.*

1962 • *Lee Tuttle plants a group of rose bushes across the street in front of the World Methodist Building. This marks the beginning of the Rose Walk.*

• *Queen of Junaluska Martha Shore Russell is crowned by Miss America, Maria Beale Fletcher.*

• *New tennis courts and shuffleboard courts are constructed.*

• *James Fowler reports to the Board of Trustees that a fictitious report has surfaced concerning negroes at the Youth Center. He then states that, in his opinion, the time has come to voluntarily desegregate fully.*

1963 • *Lake Junaluska celebrates fifty years of operation.*

• *A new nursery wing is added to the Kennedy/Skinner Children's Building.*

• *A new Allen Organ is installed in the auditorium.*

• *Lake Junaluska is featured in Together magazine.*

• *Trustees vote to allow Sunday afternoon swimming.*

• *Haywood County shows interest in the golf course for the location of a new county high school. (They are persuaded to go elsewhere.)*

• *Work begins on the new causeway entrance to the Assembly. (Now the main entrance.)*

1964 • *The east wing of Lambuth Inn is completed and opened.*

• *Bishop Clare Purcell, president of the Assembly trustees in the forties, dies.*

• *The John Branscomb designation in moved from the craft building to the Administration Building.*

• *The Board of Trustees removes all restrictions (i.e. racial) from "entertaining registered guests, delegates, and residents under the supervision of the Superintendent and staff." This is not complete desegregation since it applies only to the persons stipulated.*

1965 • *Barry Rogers is named director of Program and Public Relations.*

- *A new home for the superintendent, located on Burghard Circle (now Cokesbury Circle) is completed. The Atkins Memorial House, which was previously the superintendent's residence, is purchased by Mrs. Odille Ousley who then gives it back to the Assembly.*

- *Speakers for Junaluska Sunday are Harry Denman in the morning and Billy Graham in the evening.*

- *F. S. Love, superintendent of the Assembly from 1944 to 1960, dies.*

- *Nanci Weldon, Queen of Lake Junaluska in 1961, dies of cancer. A memorial fund is established in her memory.*

1966 - *A new boat, Cherokee III, is purchased and put into service.*

- *Chet Huntley, NBC national television news commentator, appears at the Assembly.*

- *Carl King, former trustee and executive secretary of the Western North Carolina Conference Board of education, dies. A proposal is made to the trustees that his name be added to the name of the children's building.*

- *Elmer Clark, first executive director of the World Methodist Council and historian of the Assembly, dies. A proposal for a rustic chapel to be placed on the grounds of the World Methodist Building is received by the trustees.*

- *The gate fee charged to all who come onto the Assembly grounds is eliminated.*

- *Speed bumps are installed for the first time.*

1968 - *The Junaluska Associates organization is created.*

- *The General Commission on Archives and History of the United Methodist Church is established and the offices and archives are located at the Assembly in the World Methodist Building.*

- *Interpreter's House begins. Conceived by Carlyle Marney, it offers clergy and lay opportunities for continuing education and service.*

- *Hugh Massey becomes president of the Board of Trustees. Edwin Jones steps down after twenty years of service.*

1969 • *A new sound system is installed in the auditorium. It is designated the Hart Memorial Sound System.*

• *The Junaluska Associates reports three hundred twenty-five members.*

• *The Korean Room at Lambuth Inn is opened with a formal ribbon cutting ceremony.*

• *The Southern Railway depot is moved to a site on South Lakeshore Drive where it is converted into a private residence.*

• *John W. Shackford, former executive secretary of the Methodist Episcopal Church, South Board of Education, dies. The Christian Education Building is renamed Shackford Hall in his memory.*

1970 • *E. H. Nease is named superintendent of the Assembly.*

• *Barry Rogers resigns as program director.*

• *Waylon Cooke is named as director of Operations and Promotion.*

1971 • *Junaluska Associates membership reaches four hundred thirty-five.*

• *Edwin Jones, president of the Board of Trustees for twenty years, dies.*

• *Colonial Hotel is purchased and renovated by the Assembly.*

1973 • *Georgia governor Jimmy Carter speaks during the Jurisdictional Laity Conference.*

• *J. Manning Potts, the executive director of the Assembly from 1967–71, dies.*

• *The Lakeside Lodges are purchased by the Assembly. The upper lodge is demolished.*

• *The Terrace Hotel is demolished to facilitate the construction of a new hotel.*

1974 • *Construction of the new Terrace Hotel begins. It will be built in two phases with the first phase being the guest rooms and the second the lobby, dining room, meeting rooms, etc.*

1975 • *The Administration Building annex is completed, thus adding four new rooms to the building. The new building is then renamed the Branscomb-Allen Administration Building. A dedication service for the annex is held on August 2.*

- *Membership in the Junaluska Associates reaches six hundred.*

1976 • *Harry Denman, long-time supporter of the Assembly and noted United Methodist layman, dies.*

- *Extensive repairs are made to the dam.*

1977 • *Mel B. Harbin becomes superintendent of the Assembly.*

- *Phase I of the new Terrace Hotel is completed. The guest rooms are opened with a temporary lobby in place.*

- *The new main gate is built at the west end of the lake.*

- *The Liner Building is purchased by the Assembly.*

- *The Chief Junaluska Award is presented for the first time. The recipient is Bishop Paul Hardin.*

- *Rose Ann Haire is elected Queen of Junaluska. She is the last person to be elected queen.*

1978 • *Carlyle Marney dies suddenly. Before the end of the year, Interpreter's House will be closed and its ministry ended.*

- *The Intentional Growth Center is founded and opened by its director, Mark Rouch.*

- *The General Commission on Archives and History votes to move from Lake Junaluska to Madison, New Jersey.*

1979 • *Phase II of the Terrace Hotel is completed and put in service.*

1981 • *The John Wesley Gilbert Room at Lambuth Inn is dedicated. Dr. Gilbert was an African American educator who accompanied Bishop Walter Russell Lambuth on a mission tour of Africa, serving as Lambuth's interpreter.*

1982 • *The owners of Come-Up Lodge enter into an agreement to sell the facility. The Assembly exercises its right of first refusal and buys the property. The intended owners then sue both the owner and the Assembly. The case drags on for years with the courts finally ruling in favor of the Assembly and thus sustaining the legality of the "first refusal clause" in deeds.*

- *Lambuth Inn is placed on the National Register of Historic Sites in the United States.*

1983 • *The Southeastern Jurisdictional Commission on Archives and History opens the Heritage Center in the Harrell Center, lower level.*

- *Lambuth Inn renovation begins.*

1984 • *Lake Junaluska Assembly officially moves to a year-round operation.*

- *Renovation of Lambuth Inn is completed.*

- *The Korean Room becomes a part of the International Room and Lambuth Inn.*

1985 • *Barry Rogers is named executive director of the Assembly.*

- *The new Lakeside Lodge is completed.*

- *The Junaluska WELLTH Center opens. This small health and fitness center is initially located in the Liner Building and later in the Paul Kern Youth Center.*

1986 • *A heating system is installed in Stuart Auditorium.*

- *Tri-Vista Condominiums are completed and occupied.*

- *Mountainview and Sunnyside Lodges are renovated.*

- *Francis Hart becomes the director of the Heritage Center.*

1987 • *The Kentucky Conference Lodge is sold to First United Methodist Church of Morganton, North Carolina.*

1988 • *The Southeastern Jurisdictional Conference establishes the Southeastern Jurisdictional Administrative Council, Inc. This action dissolves the Board of Trustees of the Assembly and places the oversight of the Assembly in the hands of the newly formed Junaluska Division of the Administrative Council. Reginald Ponder is named the executive director of the Council.*

- *The Turbeville Footbridge is completed, fulfilling a dream which existed from almost the beginning of the Assembly. The new bridge makes it possible to walk around the lake without getting on Highway 19 at the west end.*

- *The Harrell Center is extensively renovated and enlarged. Among the improvements is a five hundred-seat auditorium.*

- *An amphitheater is built below the Junaluska Cross.*

- *A bronze bust of Junaluska is placed in front of the Stuart Auditorium.*

- *The hydroelectric plant in the dam is restored and goes into service.*

1989   • *The Branscomb-Allen Administrative Building is enlarged to provide space for the offices of the Southeastern Jurisdictional Program Council which is moving from Atlanta to the Assembly.*

- *The Heritage Center is housed in the newly remodeled Harrell Center. It is the repository for the archives of the Southeastern Jurisdiction Commission on Archives and History, and also includes a museum of the Jurisdiction and of Lake Junaluska Assembly.*

1990   • *Glenn Martin is named as associate executive director for the Assembly.*

- *The Corneille Bryan Nature Center is built.*

1991   • *The Asbury Trail waterfall is built. A service is held July 11th, at which the waterfall is dedicated to the memory of Esdras Gruver.*

1992   • *Stuart Auditorium is extensively remodeled, including a new façade with columns.*

- *A walkway around the lake is constructed.*

1993   • *Names and Places: A Lake Junaluska Cyclopedia and The Junaluska That Never Was is written and published by Joseph W. Lasley.*

1994   • *Dr. Gordon Goodgame becomes executive secretary of SEJAC, which includes the responsibilities of superintendent of Junaluska Assembly.*

- *The original Junaluska Cross is taken down and replaced with a new, exact replica cross. The new cross is in place by March.*

- *The bust, "The Joy of Jesus" is put on display in the Heritage Center Museum.*

- *The Tuscola Garden Club builds a butterfly garden at the entrance to the Asbury Trail.*

- *Nine hundred ninety-one groups participate in Assembly activities during the year.*

- *The WELLTH Center closes.*

1995 • *A new swimming pool and a new bath house are opened.*

1996 • *The Department of Residential Services is created.*

1997 • *The Cherokee IV, a newer and larger version of the big boat, is given to the Assembly and goes into service.*

- *The Liner Building, long a landmark at the east end of the lake, is demolished to make way for the Lakemont Condominiums.*

1998 • *In a tragic accident, a car plunges off the bridge over the dam. The single occupant is killed. The bridge over the dam is closed to traffic indefinitely.*

1999 • *The Rose Walk is completely reworked adding a new fence, lighting, and other improvement. The project is financed by The Junaluska Associates and SEJAC.*

- *As a result of earlier high school and college openings, the summer season is shortened by several weeks.*

2000 • *Jimmy Carr is named as executive director for SEJAC.*

- *Joy Carr is named as director of ministries for the Southeastern Jurisdiction.*

- *Sediment accumulation in the lake threatens its existence.*

- *A new bridge over the dam is built. Once again, traffic moves across the bridge.*

- *Come-up Lodge is moved to Cokesbury Circle to make room for the Old Rectory replica at the World Methodist Complex.*

- *Brookside Lodge is purchased by the Assembly.*

2001 • *Planning begins for a multi-million dollar capital funds drive.*

- *State grants provide funding for control of sediment upstream from the lake thus promising aid for lake problems.*

2002 • *New administrative offices for the World Methodist Council are completed and the new Old Rectory is occupied.*

• *Following reports of structural problems at the dam, an extensive project of repair is begun.*

2003 • *The ninetieth anniversary of the Assembly is observed with special presentations during several events including the annual Junaluska Associates weekend.*

• Seasons in a Wildlife Refuge: An Illustrated Guide to the Corneille Bryan Native Garden *written by Janet Lilley and Linda McFarland is published.*

2005 • *The new Foundation for Evangelism·building is completed and occupied.*

• *Initial planning for the new Bethea Welcome Center is begun.*

• *A conference attended by gay and lesbian individuals, their families, and other supportive persons is held. Named the Hearts on Fire Conference, it generates extreme reaction both in favor and against it.*

Assembly Superintendents

• • • • • • • • • • • • • • •

1911–1919	James Cannon Jr.
1919–1924	W. H. Stockham
1924–1926	J. Dale Stentz
1926–1927	Hugh Sloan (six months)
1927–1932	Ralph E. Nollner
1932	Jerry Liner (temporary receiver)
1933–1938	James Atkins (receiver)
1938–1944	William A. Lambeth
1944–1950	F. S. Love
1950–1953	H. G. Allen
1953–1967	James W. Fowler
1967–1971	J. Manning Potts
1971–1976	Edgar Nease
1976–1985	Mel Harbin
1985–1986	Barry Rogers
1986–1993	Reggie Ponder
1994–2000	Gordan Goodgame
2000–	Jimmy Carr

Presidents of the Junaluska Association

• • • • • • • • • • • • • • •

1968–1972	Dr. Wilson O. Weldon
1972–1976	Bishop Frank L. Robertson
1976–1979	Dr. G. Ross Freeman
1979–1980	Dr. Allen D. Montgomery
1980–1984	Mrs. Catherine T. McSwain
1984–1988	Dr. Ben St. Clair
1988–1992	Mrs. Irene W. Carr
1992–1996	Mr. Robert R. Dart
1996–2000	Dr. Charles Turkington
2000–2004	Dr. William F. Appleby
2004–2008	Dr. James T. Pennell
2008–2012	Dr. Ernie Porter

Recipients of the Chief Junaluska Award

• • • • • • • • • • • • • • • •

This award is given by the Junaluska Associates

1977	Paul Hardin Jr.	1993	Clarence Ploch
1992	Ethel King Wade	1994	George & Mary Whitaker
1978	Hugh Massey	1995	Clyde Mahaffey
1979	Daisy Holler Wilson	1996	Bob Brown
1980	Lee. F. Tuttle	1997	Winston & Mary Lou Sewell
1981	Wilson Weldon	1998	Edward L. Tullis
1982	John Carper	1999	Walton & Marion Garrett
1983	Hardy McCalman	2000	Roger & Nancy Geyer
1984	R. Wright Spears	2001	Henry Bynum
1985	Mary Gatewood Kelly	2002	Darwyn Van Gorp
1986	Edith White and	2003	Lounell Draper
	D. W. Brooks	2004	Janice Baldridge
1987	Anne Mundy	2005	Evelyn Laycock
1988	Jim Butzner	2006	Frank Furman
1989	Ben St. Clair	2007	Charles Turkington
1990	Catherine McSwain	2008	William T. (Bill) Lowry
1991	Mary Cunningham	2009	Bill Appleby
1992	Ethel King Wade		Bill & Joetta Rhinehart

Presidents of the Junaluska Woman's Club

· · · · · · · · · · · · · · · ·

1917–18	Mrs. Frank Siler	1979–80	Alma Madison
1919–23	Mrs. Oliver Stubbs	1980–81	Rubye Duncan
1924–25	Julian Farr	1981–82	Mary Frances Stubbs
1926–27	Mrs. F. M. Jackson	1982–83	Peggy Wannamaker
1928–29	Mrs. J. A. Bullock	1983–84	Evelyn Horton
1929–30	Mrs. S. A. Hearn	1984–85	Merle Heckard
1930–31	Virginia Aldridge	1985–86	Margie Seyle
1931–32	Sarah Patten	1987–88	Ginny Patten
1933–34	Nona Quillen	1988–89	Neva Howard
1935–36	Mrs. J. B. Ivey	1989–90	Dorothy Peacock
1937–39	Mrs. F. A. Love	1990–91	Marian Garrett
1940–41	Mrs. E. O. Harbin	1991–92	Connie Herlong
1941–43	Mable Norton	1992–93	Peggy Ormond
1944–45	Mary Alva Clark	1993–94	Mina Appleby
1946–47	Mrs. C. A. Raushenberg	1994–95	Joetta Rinehart
1948–49	Mrs. R. N. Hawkins	1995–96	Jean Adams
1950–51	Mrs. J. Roy Jones	1996–97	Opal Miller
1952–53	Jane McDonald	1997–98	Jo Ann Fox
1954–55	Anne Mundy	1998–99	Anne Lamb
1955–57	Elizabeth Moore	1999–00	Jeannine Van Gorp
1958–59	Ilva Hart	2001–02	Carolyn Joiner
1960–62	Fannie Larkin	2002–03	Lucy Adams
1963–64	Beatrice Dick	2003–04	Iva Purtee
1965–66	Alma Irwin	2004–05	Peggy Winters
1967–68	Dorothy Peacock	2005–06	Jean Johnson
1969–70	Barbara Mitchell	2006–07	Bonnie Barnes
1970–72	Jean Stockton	2007–08	Julia O'Neil
1973–74	Patricia Haire	2008–09	Marie Metcalf
1975–76	Rebecca Aldridge	2009–10	Ilah King
1977–78	Martha Morgan		

Presidents of the Tuscola Garden Club

• • • • • • • • • • • • • • •

1954–56	Mrs. J. A. Bowen
1955–58	Mrs. Paul McElroy
1958–60	Mrs. J. W. Fowler
1960–62	Mrs. Glenn Hipps
1962–64	Mrs. John Thomas
1964–66	Mrs. Cato Dick
1966–68	Miss Sena Sutherland
1968–70	Mrs. Glenn Hipps
1970–72	Mrs. Gerald Schoonover
1972–74	Mrs. Glenn Hipps
1974–76	Mrs. J. J. Saenger
1976–80	Miss Ada Cornwell
1980–82	Mrs. Paul Harwell
1982–84	Mrs. Leon Stubbs
1984–86	Mrs. Carroll Varner
1986–88	Mrs. Allen Wilkinson
1988–90	Mrs. George Whitaker
1990–92	Mrs. William Pfaff
1992–94	Mrs. Francis Cunningham
1994–96	Mrs. Wilfred Altman
1996–98	Mrs. William Lowry
1998–00	Mrs. Winston Sewell
2000–02	Mrs. Jack Dingley
2002–04	Mrs. Robert James
2004–06	Mrs. Jack King
2006–08	Mrs. Hardy Tippett
2008–09	Mrs. Tom Conway
2009–	Mrs. Don Stanton

Queens of Junaluska

• • • • • • • • • • • • • •

1922	Mabel Wescott		1951	Barbara Russell
1923	Frances Lupo		1952	Betty Anne Robinson
1924	Mary Peace		1953	Joyce Carter
1925	Josephine Coman		1954	Betsy Huggin
1926	Ella Ivey		1955	Sylvia Camlin
1927	Aurelia Adams		1956	Deanne Head
1928	Kitty Stubbs		1957	Kitty Van Geuns &
1929	Effie Winslow			Frances Wannamaker
1930	Mary O. Holler		1958	Janet Jordan
1931	Christine Cuillian		1959	Mary Harriet Wiggins
1932	(none)		1960	Betsy Searcy
1933	Maria Aldridge		1961	Nanci Weldon
1934	(none)		1962	Martha Russell
1935	Frances Bivens		1963	Mary Louisa Rice
1936	(none)		1964	Linda Smith
1937	Daisy Holler		1965	Prentice Fridy
1938	Frances Crum		1966	Alice Weldon
1939	Lucille Medford		1967	Kate Avery
1940	Virginia Spence		1968	Marguerite Ross
1941	Caroline Ashley		1969	Alice Holler
1942	Louise Holcomb		1970	Mary Elizabeth Smith
1943	Jane Loyal		1971	Elodie Elizabeth Hale
1944	Lucy Stubbs		1972	Susan Maria Anderson
1945	Kit Crum		1973	Sylvia Ann Harkness
1946	Virginia Rippy		1974	Ashley Crowder
1947	Polly Dyer		1975	Karen Haire
1948	Peggy Gibson		1976	Anna Katherine Coble
1949	Mary Holler		1977	Rose Ann Haire
1950	Frances Cobb			

Notes

• • • • • • • • • • • • •

CHAPTER ONE

1. Shackford, Love Branner Atkins, *The Origin of Lake Junaluska Southern Assembly* (published by Mrs. Shackford, 1965), 3. The Heritage Center, Lake Junaluska Assembly.

2. Ibid., 6f.

3. Pinson, W. W., *George R. Stuart: Life and Work* (Nashville, TN: Cokesbury Press 1927), 36f.

4. Ibid.

5. Pettyjohn, Elizabeth Stuart, "Papa's Dream," (Pamphlet, Archives, The Heritage Center, Lake Junaluska Assembly, 1991), 1.

6. Winton, G. B. ed., *The Junaluska Conference* (Board of Missions of the Methodist Episcopal Church, South, 1913), 10.

7. Cain, G. W., *The Call of God to Men* (The Laymen's Missionary Movement of the Methodist Episcopal Church, South, 1908), 272.

8. Shackford, *The Origin of Lake Junaluska Southern Assembly*, 7.

9. Pinson, George R. *Stuart: Life and Work,* 122f.

10. Coppock, Paul R., "Mid-South Memoirs—Sunday School 'Doctor,'" *The Commercial Appeal,* n.d. The Heritage Center, Lake Junaluska Assembly.

11. Pepper, J. R. Prospectus of a Great Southern Methodist Chautauqua, Central Methodist, July 9, 1908.

12. Ibid.

13. Crum, Dr. Mason *The Story of Lake Junaluska* (Greensboro, NC: Piedmont Press, 1950), 117.

14. Cannon, James Jr., *Bishop Cannon's Own Story* (Durham, NC: Duke University Press, 1955), 101.

15. It is interesting to note that, adjusted for inflation, in 2005 this would be a promise of more than two million dollars.

16. Crum, *The Story of Lake Junaluska,* 118.

17. Had the dam been built at Howell Mill, the lake would have reached what is now Russ Avenue in Waynesville.

18. Shackford, *The Origin of Lake Junaluska Southern Assembly*, 9.

19. Highfill, Connaree "The Wonderful Junaluska Story" (Pamphlet, The Heritage Center, Lake Junaluska Assembly, 1986), 2.

20. Ibid.

21. "Southern Assembly Grounds to Be at Waynesville," *The Western Enterprise,* June 23, 1910, 1.

22. *The Waynesville Courier,* May 5, 1913.

23. Ibid.

24. Ibid.

25. Miller, Glenine T., *Think on These Things* (Richmond, VA: The Dietz Press, 1999), 88.

26. As told to the author by Dr. Erle Peacock, who is the grandson of Eugene Ward.

27. "An Act To Incorporate the Southern Assembly" (The General Assembly of North Carolina, Heritage Center, Lake Junaluska, 1909), 507.

28. *The Southern Assembly v. W. A. Palmer, Sheriff, etc.,* Supreme Court of North Carolina, (1914) The Heritage Center, Lake Junaluska Assembly, 86ff.

29. Original handwritten minutes, S. C. Sattherwait, Secretary, (The Southern Assembly Board of Commissioners, The Heritage Center, Lake Junaluska Assembly, 1910), 1.

30. Ibid.

31. Ibid.

32. Possibly the *Asheville Citizen.* A transcription of it was contained in a letter written to the Assembly Superintendent by Dr. John W. Shackford, 1962, Junaluska News A-3, 90.1.2 Daisy Holler collection, The Heritage Center, Lake Junaluska, NC.

33. Ibid.

34. The mountain is now named Eagle's Nest.

35. Original handwritten minutes, Sattherwait, 3.

36. Railroad Indentures, 1911, The Heritage Center at Lake Junaluska, Fireproof file.

37. Brochure, The Southern Assembly, penciled date 1911, p. 2, The Heritage Center at Lake Junaluska.

38. Ibid.

39. Cannon, James Jr., *Bishop Cannon's Own Story,* vi–viii.

40. At the time this is written, there are eleven of these houses still standing.

41. Russell, Marty, "Private John Allen," *The Tupelo (MS) Daily Journal,* 1995.

42. Winton, G. B., ed., *The Junaluska Conference,* 15ff.

CHAPTER TWO

1. It would be the summer of 1914 before a crude bridge would be built across the top of the dam.

2. Crum, *The Story of Lake Junaluska*, 56f.

3. "Lake Junaluska Soon to be Filled," *The Waynesville Courier*, June 6, 1913, 1.

4. Ibid. 64f.

5. Crum, *The Story of Lake Junaluska*.

6. Winton, *The Junaluska Conference*, 22.

7. Ibid., 27.

8. Ibid., 22.

9. Ibid., 21f.

10. On Monday morning, as a result of a telegram from Birmingham, Alabama, the total rose to $152,000. Adjusted for inflation this would have be equal to $2,904,706.11 in 2005.

11. Winton, *The Junaluska Conference*, 21.

12. Crum, *The Story of Lake Junaluska*, 128.

13. *The Bible and Evangelistic Conference*, (The Heritage Center, Lake Junaluska, June 30–July 15, 1913), 5.

14. Ibid., 11.

15. "Epworth League and Sunday School Conference," *The Waynesville Courier*, August 6, 1913, 1.

16. "Lake Junaluska Assembly, Program Book—1915" (Program Books, 1912–1979, The Heritage Center, Lake Junaluska Assembly).

17. "Lake Junaluska Assembly, Program Book—1914" (Program Books, 1912–1979, The Heritage Center, Lake Junaluska Assembly).

CHAPTER THREE

1. "Lake Junaluska Assembly, Program Book—1914" (Program Books, 1912–1979, The Heritage Center, Lake Junaluska Assembly); "Lake Junaluska Assembly Program Book—1915" (Program Books, 1912–1979, The Heritage Center, Lake Junaluska Assembly); "Lake Junaluska Assembly, Program Book—1916" (Program Books, 1912–1979, The Heritage Center, Lake Junaluska Assembly).

2. Program Book—1914.

3. In the early 1900s, it was believed that mountain air was curative for several diseases, including tuberculosis. The nature of Mrs. Herbert's illness is not known.

4. Taylor Jr., Edward, *The Junaluska Train Station* (Loose, Box Lake Junaluska Recent History, The Heritage Center, Lake Junaluska Assembly), 6.

5. Ibid.

6. Ross, Kathy, "When Train, Bull Collided," *The Waynesville Mountaineer*, May 11, 1992.

7. Program Book—1914.

8. Offerings during the 1917 season were reduced due to the war.

9. Program Book—1916.

10. A Cherokee word that, according to some, means "drowning bear." It is also said to have been the name of Chief Junaluska's wife.

11. J. W. Seaver. Report to the Board of Trustees, 1920 (Folder: "S" Correspondence, 91.15.Camp, The Heritage Center, Lake Junaluska Assembly).

12. Minutes of the Meeting of Commissioners (Box early minutes, fire-proof file The Heritage Center, Lake Junaluska Assembly August 25, 1918).

13. Siler, Mrs. Frank, *The Junaluskan*, Souvenir Edition, The Heritage Center, Lake Junaluska (1923): 8.

14. Crum, *The Story of Lake Junaluska,* 62

15. Guest Register, Junaluska Inn (The Heritage Center, Lake Junaluska), xx.

16. *The Asheville Citizen*, July 10, 1918.

17. Stuart Jr., George R. *Jackie Boy* (Stuart Biography File, The Heritage Center, Lake Junaluska Assembly).

18. Guest Register, Junaluska Inn.

CHAPTER FOUR

1. Dietrich, A. I., "Report of Business Manager" (The Heritage Center, Lack Junaluska Assembly, March 31, 1920).

2. Seaver, J. W., "Report to Superintendent" (Folder, S correspondence, The Heritage Center, Lake Junaluska Assembly, Box 91.15.Camp, 1920).

3. Dietrich, "Report of Business Manager."

4. Letter recorded in minutes of the Board of Commissioners (Earliest minutes The Heritage Center, Lake Junaluska Assembly, September 4, 1918).

5. Handwritten notation in photo album (Archives, The Heritage Center, Lake Junaluska Assembly).

6. Cannon, *Bishop Cannon's Own Story,* 104.

7. Shackford, John W., *The Old House At Lake Junaluska* (The Heritage Center, Lake Junaluska Assembly, 1915).

8. "School Camp Eureka" (Archives, The Heritage Center, Lake Junaluska, 1915).

9. The location is now a residential area known as Foxfire Estates.

10. "Junaluska Camp for Boys" (Archives, The Heritage Center, Lake Junaluska, 1914).

11. Stentz, J. Dale, letter to stockholders (Trustees Minutes, Archives, The Heritage Center, Lake Junaluska, October 24, 1921).

12. Minutes of the General Conference (The Heritage Center, Lake Junaluska Assembly, 1922), 103.

13. Reference to this is made in an article that appeared in the *North Carolina Christian Advocate* on May 17, 1923. While it only reported that railroad men had asked that the cross be kept lighted, this does give some credence to an oft repeated tale which now has several variations. A copy of the article will be found in the Daisy Wilson collection in the Heritage Center at Lake Junaluska Assembly, North Carolina.

14. See page 135ff.

15. Pinson, William W., *George R. Stuart: Life and Work* (Nashville, TN: Cokesbury Press, 1927), 275.

16. Ibid.

17. Ibid.

18. Lasley, Joseph, *Names and Places—A Lake Junaluska Cyclopedia* (published by author, 1993), 19.

19. Nollner, Ralph P. "The Lake Junaluska Methodist Assembly" (The Heritage Center, Lake Junaluska Assembly, 1930), 3.

CHAPTER FIVE

1. Information is written on the back of a photograph of the plane at rest on the lake (File, "Scenes," Photo file, The Heritage Center, Lake Junaluska Assembly).

2. As told to the author by Jim and Francis Hart of Lake Junaluska who witnessed the take off.

3. Taylor, Edward W., *The Lake Junaluska Train Station* (Lake Junaluska Assembly Early History. The Heritage Center, Lake Junaluska Assembly, 1991), 13.

4. *Cannon, Bishop Cannon's Own Story,* 103.

5. Ibid, 101.

6. Original handwritten minutes, Sattherwait.

7. Nollner, "The Lake Junaluska Methodist Assembly."

8. Crum, *The Story of Lake Junaluska*, 146.

9. Clark, Elmer T., *Junaluska Jubilee* (New York, NY: World Outlook Press, 1963), 26.

10. Ibid, 27.

11. Crum, *The Story of Lake Junaluska,* 151f.

12. *The Christian Advocate* (Folder, Save Junaluska, Box LJ/A6.1., n.d.)

13. Clark, *Junaluska Jubilee,* 31f.

14. Wiley, Anne Gertrude, "Lake Junaluska Playground of High-Salaried Officials of the Methodist Episcopal Church, South," *The Commercial Appeal* (Folder, Newspaper Article, The Heritage Center, Lake Junaluska Assembly, Box LJA/A6.1, November 11, 1938).

CHAPTER SIX

1. Reference to this letter is found in the data base entitled "Race Relations" (Archives, The Heritage Center, Lake Junaluska Assembly).

2. Hart, Rev. L. D., postcard to Mrs. H. D. Atkins (Archives, The Heritage Center, Lake Junaluska, Box 75.19.6., October 17, 1939).

3. Lomax Jr., Rev. Louis Emanuel, "Gilbert Center Report" (Folder, Dr. Carl King, The Heritage Center, Lake Junaluska Assembly, Box 17.19.2., 1942), 3.

4. Atkins, Mrs. Hilliard, letter (Folder J. B. Ivey, The Heritage Center, Lake Junaluska Assembly, Box 75.19.5&6., May 1, 1941).

5. Gilbert, John Wesley (1864–1923), http://encyclopedia.jrank.org/articles/pages/4256/Gilbert-John-Wesley-1864-1923.html, last accessed 1/13/10.

6. Ibid.

7. Ibid.

8. "Big Crew Rebuilding Junaluska Supply Co.," *The Waynesville Mountaineer*, April 25, 1940.

9. "Assembly Carries On," *The Waynesville Mountaineer*, June 17, 1943.

10. "Lake Junaluska Assembly, Program Book—1943" (Program Books, 1912–1979, The Heritage Center, Lake Junaluska Assembly).

11. "Mrs. Roosevelt to Be at Junaluska for Two Talks July 25–26," *The Waynesville Mountaineer*, July 13, 1944.

12. "Mrs. Roosevelt Tells 3,500 At Junaluska of Post War Programs," *The Waynesville Mountaineer*, July 27, 1944.

13. Ibid.

14. Ivey, J. B., *Junaluska News*, June 12, 1942.

15. Love, F.S., letter to J. Q. Schisler (Archives, "Board of Education," The Heritage Center, Lake Junaluska Assembly, Box 75.19.1., September 11, 1945).

16. Near the present location of Granny's Chicken Palace.

17. Trustees Minutes (Archives, The Heritage Center, Lake Junaluska Assembly, October 27, 1947).

18. "500 See MGM Actors at Junaluska," *The Waynesville Mountaineer*, October 13, 1955.

19. "Cottage Owners Raise $25,000 for Proposed Chapel," *The Waynesville Mountaineer*, August 19, 1943.

20. Clark, Elmer, letter to F. S. Love (Folder, Elmer Clark, The Heritage Center, Lake Junaluska Assembly, Box 75.91.1., September 18, 1946).

21. Brockwell, Charles W., *The Memorial Chapel: An Interpretation* (Charlotte, NC: Anderson Press, 1983).

22. Clark, Elmer, letter to Edwin Jones (Archives, The Heritage Center, Lake Junaluska, May 23, 1952).

23. Shipp, Robert, *Glenn Draper: His Music Changed Lives* (Franklin, TN: Providence House Publishers, 2003), 43.

24. Brockwell, *The Memorial Chapel: An Interpretation,* 7.

25. Ibid.

26. Draper, Glenn, telegram to J. W. Fowler (Folder, Telegrams Paid, The Heritage Center, Lake Junaluska Assembly, Box 75.19.10., August 1, 1955).

27. "Glenn Draper is New Minister of Music Minister," *Junaluska News,* 1956.

28. "Cafeteria Names in Honor of Edwin Jones" *Junaluska News,* 1959.

29. Clark, *Junaluska Jubilee,* 34.

30. Estes, Lud H. ed, Minutes, *Journal of the Third Southeastern Jurisdictional Conference of the Methodist Church,* p.114

CHAPTER SEVEN

1. "Resolution, The Bishops of the Southeaster Jurisdiction" (Folder, Greater Junaluska Campaign, The Heritage Center, Lake Junaluska Assembly, Box 75.19.7).

2. Allen, H. A., "Superintendent's Report to the Board of Trustees" (File, Board Trustees—Supt, The Heritage Center, Lake Junaluska Assembly, Box 91.30b.51).

3. Carter, Mrs. W. C. and J. B. Ivey, "Lake Junaluska News, 1952" (File, Junaluska News-A2-1951–1955, The Heritage Center, Lake Junaluska Assembly, Box 90.1.2.).

4. "Minutes of the Lake Junaluska Assembly Board of Trustees" (Folder, Board of Trustees Minutes 1950–59, fireproof file, The Heritage Center, Lake Junaluska Assembly, August 16, 1958).

5. "Formal Opening of The Children's Building" (File, Children's Building, The Heritage Center, Lake Junaluska Assembly, Box 90.1.1., July 5, 1953).

6. "Order of Service for the Dedication of the Children's Building" (File, Children's Building, The Heritage Center, Lake Junaluska Assembly, Box 90.1.1., August 8, 1954).

7. Jones, Edwin, letter to J. W. Fowler, (File, Edwin Jones (1), The Heritage Center, Lake Junaluska Assembly, Box 91.31.54., October 21, 1953).

8. "Lambuth Inn Addition Completely Modern," *Junaluska News,* 1956.

9. Allen, H. G. letter to Art O'Neil (File, Life Guards, The Heritage Center , Lake Junaluska Assembly, Box 75.19.6., May 27, 1953).

10. Allen, H. G. letter to Art O'Neil (File, Life Guards, The Heritage Center, Lake, Junaluska Assembly, Box 75.19.6., January 19, 1953).

11. Lasley, Joseph W., "Summary or Finding Aid—Trustees Minutes" (Fireproof file, The Heritage Center, Lake Junaluska Assembly).

12. O'Neil, Arthur, letter to Rev. & Mrs. A. M. O'Neil, dated 6/26/53, loaned to the author by Arthur O 'Neil.

13. Sharpe, Bill, "The New Junaluska," *The State Magazine,* June 28, 1952.

14. "127 Report of the Recreation Department—Summer of 1952" (File, General Administration 3, The Heritage Center, Lake Junaluska Assembly, Box 91.30b., 1951).

15. Allen, H. G. letter to Mrs. T. W. Aldred (File, Correspondence 2, The Heritage Center, Lake Junaluska Assembly, Box 75.19.3, September 19, 1950).

16. Allen, H. G. letter (File, General Correspondence 2, The Heritage Center, Lake Junaluska Assembly, Box 91.30b., 1951).

17. "Churches Have Obligations In World Issues, Nixon Says," *The Mountaineer,* August 5, 1956.

18. Haymaker, W. G., letter to James W. Fowler (File, Billy Graham, The Heritage Center, Lake Junaluska Assembly, Box 91.35.).

19. Copy of citation (Folder, Harry Denman Day, The Heritage Center, Lake Junaluska Assembly, Box 91.36.Fowler).

20. "The Fifth Annual Southeastern Jurisdictional Conference on Evangelism and Candler Camp Meeting August 14–21, 1955" (Box LJ Brochures I, The Heritage Center, Lake Junaluska Assembly).

21. Baldwin, J. A., letter to Edwin Jones (File, Jones, Edwin L. Sr. archives, The Heritage Center, Lake Junaluska, Box 75.19.38., June 13, 1955).

22. McDonald, Jane, letter to Edwin Jones (File, Mc Archives, The Heritage Center, Lake Junaluska, Box 75.19.9, August 17, 1955).

23. "Minutes of the Board of Trustees of Lake Junaluska Assembly" (File, Trustees Minutes 1950–1959, fireproof file, The Heritage Center, Lake Junaluska Assembly, July 10, 1955).

24. "Minutes of the Annual Meeting of the Board of Trustees of Lake Junaluska Assembly" (File, 1950 Board Minutes, fireproof file, The Heritage Center, Lake Junaluska Assembly, July 30, 1955).

25. Franklin, Marvin, letter to Edwin Jones (File, Jones, Edwin L. Sr., The Heritage Center, Lake Junaluska Assembly, Box 75.19.8., September 13, 1955).

26. Ferre, Dr. Nels, letter to Dr. J. W. Fowler (File, Personal and Confidential, The Heritage Center, Lake Junaluska Assembly, Box 91.39.misc., 1955).

27. Clary, George, letter to James Fowler (File, Clary, Dr. Geo, The Heritage Center, Lake Junaluska Assembly, Box 75.19.8., 1955).

28. *Proceedings of the Eight Ecumenical Conference—Oxford 28th August—7th September, 1951* (London: The Epworth Press, 1952), 299.

29. Ibid., 322.

30. Allen, H.G., letter to Elmer Clark (Archive, file, Dr. Elmer T. Clark, The Heritage Center, Lake Junaluska Assembly, Box 91.30b, 1951).

31. Jones, Edwin, letter to H. G. Allen (Archive, file, Jones, Edwin L. Sr., The Heritage Center, Lake Junaluska Assembly, Box 75.19.8., March 12, 1955).

32. Brochure, (File, Archives Building—1955, The Heritage Center, Lake Junaluska Assembly, Box 75.19.8.).

33. News release, *Methodist News Service* (File, Fanning, O. B.—1955, The Heritage Center, Lake Junaluska Assembly, Box 75.19.8., October 1955).

34. "Ninth World Methodist Conference Set at Lake," *Junaluska News,* 1956.

35. Elmer C. Clark, *Junaluska Jubilee,* 37.

36. "Proceedings of the Ninth World Methodist Conference" (The Methodist Publishing House, archives, The Heritage Center, Lake Junaluska, 1956), 85.

37. Ibid.

38. Others present that day were: Mrs. J. A. Bowen, Mrs. Sarah Camlin, Mrs. M. L. Eggen, Mrs. Roy Floyd, Mrs. Dewey Lavender, Mrs. Everett McElroy, Mrs. Paul McElroy, Mrs. A. R. Phillips, Mrs. Mack Setser, Mrs. Kenneth Stahl, and Mrs. E. S. Stark.

39. "Craft Hut Razed By Flames," *Junaluska News,* August 1, 1958.

40. Barrett, Troy, letter to F. S. Love (File B, The Heritage Center, Lake Junaluska Assembly, Box 75.19.7., July 28, 1948).

41. Love, F. S., letter to Troy Barrett (File B, The Heritage Center, Lake Junaluska Assembly, Box 75.19.7., August 4, 1948.

42. See Chapter 5.

43. Jones, Edwin, "Lake Junaluska Assembly, Year 1961" (File, Edwin Jones Sr., The Heritage Center, Lake Junaluska Assembly, Box 91.33. Fowler).

44. Moore, Bishop Arthur J., letter to F. S. Love (The Heritage Center, Lake Junaluska Assembly, February 12, 1949).

45. Harrell, Costen J., letter to J. B. Ricketts and copy to F. S. Love (File, H, The Heritage Center, Lake Junaluska Assembly, Box 75.19.3., April 14, 1950).

46. Fowler, J. W., "Report at the Superintendent of Lake Junaluska Assembly" (Folder, Trustees–August 1962, Archives, The Heritage Center, Lake Junaluska Assembly, Box 91.31.Fowler, August 4, 1962), 1f.

47. Tullis, Edward L., *Our Faith Journey,* n.d. p.32. archives. The Heritage Center, Lake Junaluska Assembly.

48. Ibid

49. Open letter to Board of Trustees (File, General Correspondence, The Heritage Center, Lake Junaluska Assembly, Box 91.29.1951, June 9, 1951).

50. Ibid.

51. "National Conference on Race," *Daily Motive,* August 25, 1960.

52. Yates, Gayle Graham, letter to Edwin Jones (File, Jones, Edwin L. correspondence (integration), The Heritage Center, Lake Junaluska Assembly, Box 91.39misc., June 2, 1962).

53. Jones, Edwin L, letter to Gayle Graham Yates (File, Edwin Jones Sr., The Heritage Center, Lake Junaluska Assembly, Box 91.33.Fowler, July 6, 1962).

54. Miss Moore was the only African American present.

55. Campbell, Ila, secretary, Minutes of the special committee meeting of the Board of Trustees (File, MSM Committee Meeting, The Heritage Center, Lake Junaluska Assembly, Box 91.39.Misc., July 30, 1962).

56. Yates, Gayle Graham email to Bill Lowry (personal archive of author, Lake Junaluska, July 9, 2005).

57. Campbell, Ila, secretary, Minutes of the special committee meeting of the Board of Trustees.

58. Stafford, J. P., letter to Edwin L. Jones (File, S, The Heritage Center, Lake Junaluska Assembly, Box 71.34.Fowler, August 16, 1962).

59. Fowler, J. W., letter to J. P Stafford (File, S, The Heritage Center, Lake Junaluska Assembly, Box 71.34.Fowler, August 21, 1962).

60. Ibid.

61. Board of Trustees Minutes (Fireproof file, The Heritage Center, Lake Junaluska Assembly, August 1, 1964).

62. Nease, Edgar H., letter to Dr. Robert F. Lundy (File, Nease, Edgar H.-Lund Correspondence 1970–71, The Heritage Center, Lake Junaluska Assembly, July 20, 1971).

CHAPTER EIGHT

1. "Buildings and Grounds Committee Report to the Executive Committee" (Folder, Committee Reports, 1958–59, The Heritage Center, Lake Junaluska Assembly, Box 91.32.1959., November 7, 1958).

2. "Minutes of Board of Trustees Meeting" (File, Trustees Minutes 1960–69, fireproof file, The Heritage Center, Lake Junaluska Assembly, August 5, 1961).

3. "Minutes of the Board of Trustees of Lake Junaluska Assembly" (reported by Joseph Lasley, Summary of Minutes 1947–73, fireproof file, The Heritage Center, Lake Junaluska Assembly, August 22, 1959).

4. "New Harrell Center Honors Great Junaluskan," *Junaluska News,* 1961.

5. "Dedication of the Nanci Weldon Memorial Gymnasium" (Folder, Nanci Weldon-Misc., The Heritage Center, Lake Junaluska Assembly, Box 91.36.Fowler, June 4, 1969).

6. "Annual Queen Coronation Now Planned for August 8th," *Junaluska News,* 1952.

7. Fowler Jr., J. W., letter to the Executive Committee of the Board of Trustees, (Folder, Trustees Minutes—Executive Committee, The Heritage Center, Lake Junaluska Assembly, Box 91.36.Fowler, November 29, 1965).

8. "Beautification of Grounds Committee, Board of Trustees" (File, Trustees—August '62, The Heritage Center, Lake Junaluska Assembly, Box 91.34 Fowler, August 4, 1962).

9. "Minutes LJA Trustees Executive Committee" (Folder, Executive Committee Meeting, The Heritage Center, Lake Junaluska Assembly, Box 91.34 Fowler, November 20, 1961).

10. "Minutes of the Ex Com of LJA" (File, L.J. D Trustees Minutes, archives etc., Box 91.6.Potts, February 27, 1969).

11. "Minutes of the Board of Trustees of Lake Junaluska Assembly"(File, Board of Trustees minutes 1960–69, fireproof file, The Heritage Center, Lake Junaluska Assembly, August 3, 1963).

12. "Junaluska News" (File, Junaluska News Archives, The Heritage Center, Lake Junaluska, 1966).

13. Blackwell, Michael C. "Carlyle Marney as Ethicist," *Christian Ethics Today*, 4, no. 017 (August 1998).

14. Metcalf, Clifton, "Southern Baptist Leader Will Direct Interpreter's House," *The Mountaineer*, April 19, 1967.

15. Rouch, Dr. Mark, *The Lake Junaluska Intentional Growth Center: The First 10 Years* (File, IGC General, The Heritage Center, Lake Junaluska Assembly, Box 91.42.Roger, 1987), 3.

16. "The Lake Junaluska Intentional Growth Center" (File, Intentional Growth Center, The Heritage Center, Lake Junaluska Assembly, Box 91.14.Rogers, n. d.).

17. Ibid.

18. "Buildings & Grounds Committee Report, Board of Trustees" (File, Summary of Minutes, fireproof file, The Heritage Center, Lake Junaluska Assembly, October 31, 1963).

19. "Golden Jubilee Observance Will Begin July 28," *Junaluska News,* 1963.

20. Fowler, Dr. H. G. "Executive Directors Report to the Board of Trustees Report to the Board of Trustees" (The Heritage Center, Lake Junaluska Assembly, 1967).

21. "Minutes of the Meeting of the Board of Trustees, Lake Junaluska Methodist Assembly" (File, Trustees Minutes—1960–1969, fireproof file, The Heritage Center, Lake Junaluska Assembly, August 6, 1966).

22. News release (File, R, The Heritage Center, Lake Junaluska Assembly, Box 91.37.Potts, March 9, 1967).

23. "Lake Trustees Name Hugh Massie President" *The Mountaineer*, August 9, 1968.

24. "Junaluska: Its Past, Present, Future (File, L. J. Assoc., The Heritage Center, Lake Junaluska Assembly, Box 91.27., n. d.).

25. Lists of Associates presidents and recipients of the Chief Junaluska Award will be found in the appendix.

26. "Helen Kim, Columbia 250—Celebrates Columbians Ahead of Their Time."

27. George, Evelyn, "The Story of the Korea Room," (File, Korean Room, The Heritage Center, Lake Junaluska Assembly, Box 91.13.Harb, February 19, 1984), 1.

28. "Commission on Archives and History" (File, General Commission on Archives and History-UMC, The Heritage Center, Lake Junaluska Assembly, Box 91.32., 1959).

29. Ness, John H. Jr., "Report of the Secretary—Curator of the Historical Society of the EUB Church to the Commission on Archives and History, The United Methodist Church" (File, General Commission on Archives and History-UMC, The Heritage Center, Lake Junaluska Assembly, August 6, 1968).

30. See page 81.

31. Commission on Archives and History, p.72.

32. "Headquarters—Commission on Archives and History Adopted by Executive Committee of the SEJ Commission on Archives and History" (File, Minutes SEJ Archives and History, The Heritage Center, Lake Junaluska Assembly, Box 91.37.Potts, January 10, 1969).

33. *1976 Journal General Conference Volume II* (The United Methodist Church, The Heritage Center, Lake Junaluska Assembly, 1840).

34. Ibid.

35. Hardin, Paul, letter to Bishop John B. Warman, "Commission on Archives and History" (File, Archives and History, The Heritage Center, Lake Junaluska Assembly, Box 91.23.Nease, July 12, 1977).

36. Spears, Wright, letter to John B. Warman, "Presentation to Commission on Archives and History" (Folder, Lake Junaluska, NC Archives and History, The Heritage Center, Lake Junaluska Assembly, Box 91.5.Hyatt, August 1978).

37. "Presentation to Commission on Archives and History" (Folder, Lake Junaluska, NC Archives and History, The Heritage Center, Lake Junaluska Assembly, Box 91.5.Hyatt, August 1978), 5.

38. Hardin, Paul, letter to Harbin, Spears, and Hardin (File, Archives and History, The Heritage Center, Lake Junaluska Assembly, Box 91.23.Nease, October 19, 1977).

39. Harbin, Melton E., letter to Dr. Paul Hardin (File, Archives and History, The Heritage Center, Lake Junaluska Assembly, Box 91.23.Nease, n.d.).

40. Harbin, Mel, letter to Dr. Larry E. Tise (File, Archives and History, The Heritage Center, Lake Junaluska Assembly, Box 91.23.Nease, October 26, 1977).

41. Brockwell, C. W., letter to Ms. Beverley C. Berry (File, Lake Junaluska, NC Archives and History, The Heritage Center, Lake Junaluska Assembly, Box 91.5.Hyatt., September 25, 1978).

42. Hyatt, Lachlan L., letter to W. Stewart Rogers, AIA (File, Lake Junaluska, NC Archives and History, The Heritage Center, Lake Junaluska Assembly, Box 91.5.Hyatt., October 13, 1978).

43. "I Can't Pull It By Hand," photograph with caption, *The Mountaineer,* c.1969.

CHAPTER NINE

1. "Board of Trustees minutes" (Fireproof file, The Heritage Center, Lake Junaluska Assembly, November 8, 1962).

2. "Minutes, Executive Committee, Board of Trustees" (File, Trustees Minutes—1970–79, fireproof file, The Heritage Center, Lake Junaluska Assembly, November 11, 1971).

3. "New Hope for Tomorrow" (Folder, Special Gifts, The Heritage Center, Lake Junaluska Assembly, Box 91.21b.Nease, 1975).

4. Gatewood, Mary, letter (Folder, Bldg & Grounds Committee "73," The Heritage Center, Lake Junaluska Assembly, Box 91.39.misc., n.d.).

5. Denman, Harry, handwritten note (Folder, Bldg & Grounds Committee "73," The Heritage Center, Lake Junaluska Assembly, Box 91.39.misc., n.d.).

6. Green, Nowelee, handwritten note (Folder, Bldg & Grounds Committee "73," The Heritage Center, Lake Junaluska Assembly, Box 91.39.misc, n.d.).

7. "Terrace Hotel Coming Down," *The Methodist Christian Advocate,* September 23, 1975.

8. "Terrace Hotel Construction Delayed," *Waynesville Mountaineer,* April 28, 1976.

9. Ibid.

10. News Release (File, News Releases, The Heritage Center, Lake Junaluska Assembly, Box 91.20.Nease, February 22, 1974).

11. "Minutes of the Board of Trustees, Lake Junaluska Assembly" (File, Board of Trustees Minutes 1970–1979, fireproof file, The Heritage Center, Lake Junaluska Assembly, February 13, 1976).

12. "Minutes of the Board of Trustees, Lake Junaluska Assembly" (File, Board of Trustees Minutes 1970–1979, fireproof file, The Heritage Center, Lake Junaluska Assembly, October 15, 1976).

13. "Minutes of the Board of Trustees, Lake Junaluska Assembly" (File, Board of Trustees Minutes 1970–1979, fireproof file, archives etc., March 25, 1977).

14. Ibid.

15. McLees, Nellie letter to H. G. Allen (File, Mc, The Heritage Center, Lake Junaluska Assembly, Box 91.51. Allen, May 14, 1951).

16. Nease, Edgar, "Report of Executive Director to BOT" (File, Junaluska Trustees, The Heritage Center, Lake Junaluska Assembly, Box 91.38b.Nease, August 7, 1971).

17. "Junaluska Queen," *Waynesville Mountaineer*, August 10, 1973.

18. A list of all recipients of the Chief Junaluska Award will be found in the appendix.

19. Massie, Hugh, letter to John A. Wall (File, Terrace Hotel, Conference Complex, The Heritage Center, Lake Junaluska Assembly, Box 91.19b.Nease, May 14, 1973).

20. "Minutes, Board of Trustees" (File, Cottage Owners, The Heritage Center, Lake Junaluska Assembly, Box 91.20.Nease, August 3, 1974).

21. "Dedication of West Gate" (File, Buildings & Grounds, The Heritage Center, Lake Junaluska Assembly, Box 91.20.Nease, January 30, 1978).

22. Minutes, Board of Trustees, August 3, 1974.

23. "Service of Dedication, The Allen Annex of the Branscomb Administration Building" (Folder, Allen Annex, The Heritage Center, Lake Junaluska Assembly, Box 91.26.Nease, August 2, 1975).

24. Crum, *The Story of Lake Junaluska*, 54.

25. "Home Owners-Junaluskans Report—Aug. 15, 1979–Dec. 31, 1980" (File, Junaluskans—1981, The Heritage Center, Lake Junaluska Assembly, Box The Junaluskans Organization, December 31, 1980).

26. Miller, John J., "Rational for Organising Property Owners Association" (File, Organizing of LJAPOO, Box LJ Home Owner's Association—LJAPOO—Box 1, The Heritage Center, Lake Junaluska Assembly).

27. Ibid., 87.

28. "Feasibility Study for Proposed Condominium for Junaluska Assembly, Inc.," prepared by Foy and Lee Associates (File, Condominiums, The Heritage Center, Lake Junaluska Assembly, Box 91.11.Harb., March 1, 1979).

29. "Minutes of the Board of Trustees of Lake Junaluska Assembly" (File, Trustees Minutes 1970–79, fireproof file, The Heritage Center, Lake Junaluska Assembly, August, 1979).

30. "Minutes of the Board of Trustees of Lake Junaluska Assembly" (File, Condominiums, The Heritage Center, Lake Junaluska Assembly, Box 91.11.Harb., July 31, 1982).

31. "Minutes of the Board of Trustees" (File, Condominiums, The Heritage Center, Lake Junaluska Assembly, Box 91.11.Harb, July 31, 1982).

32. Ruew, Robert, letter to Lachlan L. Hyatt (File, Junaluska Assembly Housing & Tax Proceedings, The Heritage Center, Lake Junaluska Assembly, Box 91.42.Roger, October 27, 1986).

CHAPTER TEN

1. Emmons, Susan, letter to Mel Harbin (File, Lambuth Inn, The Heritage Center, Lake Junaluska Assembly, Box 91.24.Harb, September 27, 1979).

2. *Journal of the Eleventh Session of the Southeastern Jurisdictional Conference* (The Heritage Center, Lake Junaluska Assembly, July 15–1980), 203.

3. Foy and Lee Architects, "Scope of Project, First Draft" (File, Lambuth Inn, The Heritage Center, Lake Junaluska Assembly, Box 91.11.Harb., April 15, 1982).

4. Ibid.

5. "Gilbert Room Honors Black Methodist," *The Mountaineer,* July 1980.

6. Little, John J., letter to Mel Harbin (File, Lambuth Inn, The Heritage Center, Lake Junaluska Assembly, Box 91.13. Harb., September 29, 1982).

7. "Minutes of the Board of Trustees" (Fireproof file, The Heritage Center, Lake Junaluska Assembly, August 4, 1984).

8. Ibid.

9. "Minutes of the Board of Trustees of Lake Junaluska Assembly" (Folder, Trustees Minutes-1980–87, fireproof file, The Heritage Center, Lake Junaluska Assembly, December 1, 1980).

10. "Minutes of the Board of Trustees of Lake Junaluska Assembly" (Folder, Trustees Minutes-1980–87, fireproof file, The Heritage Center, Lake Junaluska Assembly, March 10, 1981).

11. "Minutes of the Board of Trustees of Lake Junaluska Assembly" (Folder, Trustees Minutes-1980–87, fireproof file, The Heritage Center, Lake Junaluska Assembly, November 8, 1981).

12. The plate, along with a copy of the printed map, is on display in the Heritage Center Museum at the Lake Junaluska Assembly.

13. "The Southeastern United Methodist Heritage Center—A Plan for the Southeastern Jurisdiction Administrative Council on Ministries" (File, Trustees 1981, The Heritage Center, Lake Junaluska Assembly, Box 91.10.Harb., 1981). ·

14. Ibid.

15. Ibid.

16. Fisher, A. Mickey, "Memorandum—to Southeastern Jurisdiction Conference on Architecture and History" (File, The Heritage Center, Lake Junaluska Assembly, Box 91.14.Roger, March 9, 1982).

17. Tullis, Ed, letter to Dr. Kenneth Lile (File, Heritage Center, The Heritage Center, Lake Junaluska Assembly, Box 91.40.Roger, July 2, 1986).

18. Rogers, Barry, letter to Rick Lee of Foy and Lee (File, Adult Center & Harrell Center, The Heritage Center, Lake Junaluska Assembly, Box 91.40.Roger, June 1, 1986).

19. "Minutes of the SEJ Heritage Center Coordinating Committee" (File, Heritage Center, The Heritage Center, Lake Junaluska Assembly, Box 91.40.Roger, December 29, 1986).

20. "Chemical Plant Explosion Turns Hotel into Hospital" *North Carolina Christian Advocate,* May 11, 1982.

21. Wording of original deeds (File, Come Up Lodge, Wright vs. Assembly, archives, The Heritage Center, Lake Junaluska Assembly, Box 91.14.Roger.

22. Brown, Glenn W., letter to John S. Stevens (File, Buildings and Grounds, The Heritage Center, Lake Junaluska Assembly, Box 91.12.Harbin, June 8, 1983).

23. Complaint: Norma Wright vs. Lake Junaluska Assembly, Inc. and Gail Bergstresser and wife, Margaret Bergstresser (File, Buildings and Grounds, archives, The Heritage Center, Lake Junaluska Assembly, Box 91.12.Harbin, March 30, 1983).

24. Order of the General Court of Justice, Superior Court Division, 83-CVS-395, (File, Come Up Lodge, archives, The Heritage Center, Lake Junaluska Assembly, Box 91.42 Roger, March 20, 1986).

25. *Journal of the Twelfth Session of the Southeastern Jurisdictional Conference* (Archives, The Heritage Center, Lake Junaluska Assembly, July 17–21, 1984), 197.

26. "Minutes of the Lake Junaluska Board of Trustees" (Archives, The Heritage Center, Lake Junaluska Assembly, March 1, 1986), 3.

27. *Journal of the Thirteenth Session of the Southeastern Jurisdictional Conference* (Archives, The Heritage Center, Lake Junaluska Assembly, July 12–16, 1988), 161.

28. "Minutes of the Board of Trustees of Lake Junaluska Assembly" (Fireproof file, The Heritage Center, Lake Junaluska Assembly, December 6, 1984), 9.

29. Cummings, Simeon F., letter to Barry S. Rogers (File, Chief Junaluska Marker, The Heritage Center, Lake Junaluska Assembly, Box 91.40.Roger, August 23, 1985).

30. Ross, R. H., letter to Simeon F. Cummings (File, Chief Junaluska Marker, The Heritage Center, Lake Junaluska Assembly, Box 91.40.Roger, April 6, 1986).

31. Ibid.

32. Rogers, Barry, letter to R. H. Ross (File, Chief Junaluska Marker, The Heritage Center, Lake Junaluska Assembly, 91.40.Roger, August 7, 1986).

33. "Fund Raising—Junaluska—A Bronze Monument" (File, Chief Junaluska Marker, The Heritage Center, Lake Junaluska Assembly, 91.40.Roger, n.d.).

34. The model is on display in the Heritage Center Museum in the Harrell Center at Lake Junaluska Assembly.

35. "Turbeville Bridge Makes Walking More Safe," *The Junaluska Associates,* Summer 1988.

36. "Grateful Junaluskan Helps Pave the Way for Pedestrians," *The Mountaineer,* April 29, 1992.

37. "Minutes of the Board of Trustees of Lake Junaluska Assembly" (Fireproof file, The Heritage Center, Lake Junaluska Assembly, October 2, 1980).

38. "Minutes of the Board of Trustees of Lake Junaluska Assembly" (Fireproof file, The Heritage Center, The Heritage Center, Lake Junaluska Assembly, February 10, 1981).

39. "Lake Junaluska Will Sell Electricity Next Summer," *The Mountaineer,* n.d.

40. "Outdoorsman Cares for Carp" *The Mountaineer,* n.d.

41. "Minutes of the Southeastern Jurisdiction Administrative Council" (File, Mahaffey Collection, Lake Junaluska Assembly, November 16, 1989), 1.

42. Junaluska News and Views (File, Mahaffey Collection, The Heritage Center, Lake Junaluska Assembly, August 7, 1991).

43. Nuttall, Douglas J., letter to Dr. Reginald Ponder (File, Hydro Project, Mahaffey Collection, The Heritage Center, Lake Junaluska Assembly, February 23, 1993).

44. Ponder, Dr. Reginald, letter to Mr. Douglas J. Nuttall (File, Hydro Project, Mahaffey Collection, The Heritage Center, Lake Junaluska Assembly, April 28, 1993).

45. "Welcome to an Emerging Dream . . . Junaluska Health and Fitness Center" (Folder, WELLTH Center—Misc., The Heritage Center, Lake Junaluska Assembly, Box WELLTH Center—1980s–90s, March 23, 1986).

46. Lowry RN, Cissy, letter to all Fitness Center members (Folder, WELLTH Center—Misc., The Heritage Center, Lake Junaluska Assembly, Box WELLTH Center—1980s–90s, 1987).

47. "LJA WELLTH Ministries—Pool Problems and Related Costs" (File, Monthly WELLTH Action Report, The Heritage Center, Lake Junaluska Assembly, Box 97.4.2).

48. "Program Recommendations" (File, WELLTH Ministries, The Heritage Center, Lake Junaluska Assembly, Box 97.4.2).

49. "The Churches Challenge in Health" (File, WELLTH Ministries, The Heritage Center, Lake Junaluska Assembly, Box 97.4.2.).

50. Wheeler, letter to members (File, WELLTH Ministries, The Heritage Center, Lake Junaluska Assembly, Box 97.4.2., September 26, 1994).

CHAPTER ELEVEN

1. Goodgame, Gordon, "Thoughts On LJA Ministry as the 20th Century Closed, 1998–2000" (The Heritage Center, Lake Junaluska Assembly, Box LJ Recent History).

2. Lilley, Janet, Linda McFarland, and Dan Pittillo, *Seasons in a Wildflower Refuge: An Illustrated Guide to the Corneille Bryan Native Garden* (Franklin, TN: Providence House Publishers, 2003).

3. "Report of the Grounds and Recreation Committee, Minutes of the Lake Junaluska Division Meeting" (File, Mahaffey Collection The Heritage Center, Lake Junaluska Assembly, November 16–17, 1989).

4. Ponder, Reginald W., letter to Dr. Paul Worley (File, Grounds and Recreation Committee, Mahaffey Collection, The Heritage Center, Lake Junaluska Assembly, January 1, 1990).

5. Lilley, McFarland, and Pittillo, *Seasons in a Wildfire Refuge,* iv.

6. Ibid.

7. "Three Retirees Build Falls and Dedicate It to an Old Friend," *The Mountaineer Newspapers,* May 28, 1992.

8. Certificate of Recognition (Tuscola Garden Club Scrapbook, 1990–99, The Heritage Center, Lake Junaluska Assembly).

9. 2004 Tuscola Garden Club Yearbook, Tuscola Garden Club Scrapbook, 1990–99, The Heritage Center, Lake Junaluska Assembly.

10. Garner, Hugh P., letter to Lachlan L. Hyatt (File, Tri-Vista Suit, The Heritage Center, Lake Junaluska Assembly, Box 01.1.3, January 26, 1988).

11. Copy of Suit (File, Tri-Vista Suit, archives, The Heritage Center, Lake Junaluska Assembly, Box 01.1.3.).

12. The visit of Bishop Tullis and his subsequent support of the condo owners was shared with the author by condo owner David Pierce in a telephone interview on January 24, 2009.

13. "Workers Transforming Auditorium," *The Mountaineer,* April 1, 1992.

14. Contract (Folder, Auditorium Seats & Renovation, The Heritage Center, Lake Junaluska Assembly, Box. 97.1.1.).

15. George R. Stuart Auditorium—1913–1992 (Folder, Auditorium Seats & Renovation, The Heritage Center, Lake Junaluska Assembly, Box. 97.1.1., April 24, 1992).

16. "The Junaluska Cross," www.mtshepherd.org, last accessed 1/13/10.

17. Goodgame, "Thoughts on Lake Junaluska Assembly Ministry as the 20th Century Closed," 1998–2000, 3.

18. Ibid., 4.

19. "Teen Killed in Wreck at Dam," *The Mountaineer,* June 29, 1998.

20. Ibid.

21. "Celebration of the Opening of the Bridge Over the Junaluska Dam" (Box LJ recent history, The Heritage Center, Lake Junaluska Assembly).

CHAPTER TWELVE

1. See page 143ff.

2. "World Methodist Council to Build New Headquarters," *United Methodist News Service,* October 27, 2000.

3. www.foundationforevangelism.org, last accessed 2/26/2010.

4. "Sediment Problems Threaten Scenic Lake," *The Mountaineer,* August 5, 2000.

5. Letters to the Editor, *The Mountaineer,* August 18, 2000.

6. "Let's Be Good Neighbors," *The Mountaineer,* September 27, 2000.

7. Report of Executive Director, Southeastern Jurisdictional Administrative Council meeting, November 2003.

8. Hyatt, Vicky, editorial, *The Mountaineer,* August 19, 2005.

9. "At Hatred Reverend Pauses," *The Mountaineer,* September 2, 2005.

10. "Methodists Pushing for Acceptance of Gays Start Meeting Quietly," *The Mountaineer,* September 3, 2005.

11. *The Mountaineer,* September 5, 2005.

12. Hyatt, Vicky, editorial, *The Waynesville Mountaineer,* August 19, 2005

13. Ruling "In the Supreme Court of North Carolina, no. 62A08." p. 12.

14. Ibid, 13.

15. "Churches Have Obligations In World Issues, Nixon Says," *The Mountaineer,* August 5, 1956.

Index

INDEX

INDEX